Mountain Biking Las Vegas and Southern Nevada

Mountain Biking Las Vegas and Southern Nevada

A Guide to the Area's Greatest Off-Road Bicycle Rides

Paul W. Papa

GUILFORD, CONNECTICUT

An imprint of Globe Pequot

Falcon and FalconGuides are registered trademarks and Make Adventure Your Story is a trademark of Rowman & Littlefield.

Distributed by NATIONAL BOOK NETWORK

Copyright © 2017 by Rowman & Littlefield

Photos by Paul W. Papa unless otherwise noted.

Maps by Melissa Baker © Rowman & Littlefield

British Library Cataloguing-in-Publication Information available

Library of Congress Cataloging-in-Publication Data available

ISBN 978-1-4930-2217-5 (paperback)
ISBN 978-1-4930-2218-2 (e-book)

∞™ The paper used in this publication meets the minimum requirements of American National Standard for Information Sciences—Permanence of Paper for Printed Library Materials, ANSI/NISO Z39.48-1992.

For Brent Thomson—ride in peace my friend.

Rider navigates the large rock on the Landmine Loop

Contents

The Rides

Bootleg Canyon and the Surrounding Area

Honorable Mentions

Cottonwood Valley and the Surrounding Area

Overview

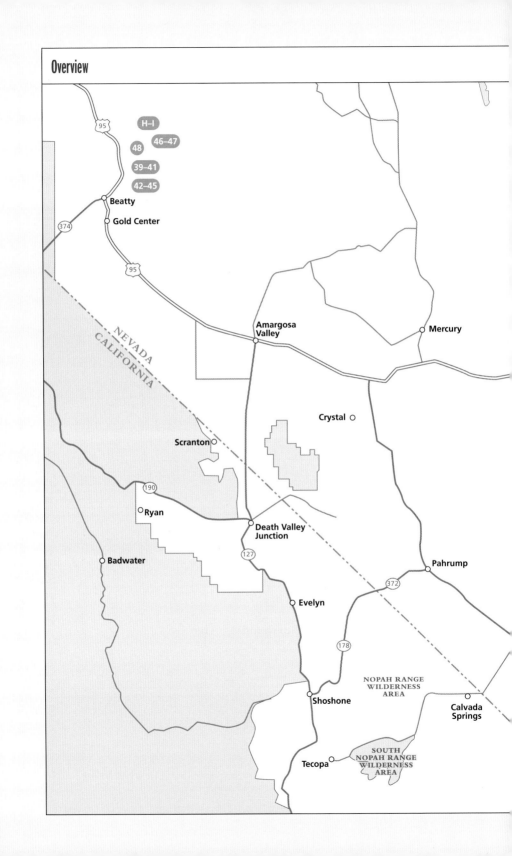

H–I

46–47

48

39–41

42–45

Beatty

Gold Center

NEVADA
CALIFORNIA

Amargosa
Valley

Mercury

Crystal

Scranton

Ryan

Death Valley
Junction

Badwater

Pahrump

Evelyn

NOPAH RANGE
WILDERNESS
AREA

Shoshone

Calvada
Springs

SOUTH
NOPAH RANGE
WILDERNESS
AREA

Tecopa

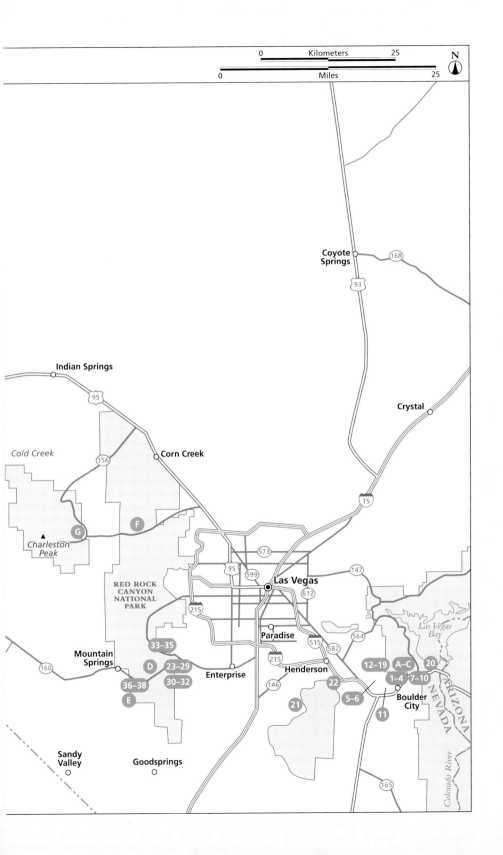

Acknowledgments

Think of bicycles as rideable art that can just about save the world.
—Grant Petersen, bicycle designer

I'd first and foremost like to thank the Southern Nevada Mountain Bike Association (SNMBA), the local chapter of the International Mountain Bike Association (IMBA), and specifically Jonathan "Jonnie Dangerously" Temple for taking me out on rides to learn the trails I was unfamiliar with, answering my numerous questions with patience, and clarifying my issues as needed.

Thanks also goes out to Chris Tuma at McGhie's Bike Outpost for taking the time to walk me through the map of Cottonwood until I got everything straight and to Dave Spicer who gave me a private tour of his ranch, explained how he put the trails together, and let me stay in his body shop overnight. You'll find no greater advocate for the sport of mountain biking than Dave Spicer. I would also like to thank Joshua Travers, the Outdoor Recreation Planner for the Bureau of Land Management, for looking over my proposed list of trails and making sure the ones I chose had the BLM's blessing.

I would especially like to thank the guys at All Mountain Cyclery for hooking me up with the perfect bike, suggesting which improvements to make, and ensuring everything ran correctly as I rode the trails. A special thanks also goes out to Dan Haskin for helping me navigate the trails at Bootleg Canyon. Since he created most of them, he knows them better than anyone. Thanks to Jason Maletsky for taking such an awesome cover shot and to Resty Torres de Lima for being such an outstanding model. I would also like to thank my friend and photographer Jim Laurie for taking many of the photos in the book and all the mountain bikers who posed, jumped, rode, and did it all again when we didn't get the shot the first time. That's you, Resty Torres de Lima, Xavier M. Sanchez-Ompok, Armina Grewell, Aaron Osborne, Randy Barcena, Beth Rudolph, Byronn Hahn, Stan Takashima, and Eugene Prospero. I couldn't have written this guide without the help of people like you! A final thank you goes out to my production editor Lynn Zelem for her obvious desire to make this the best guide book it can be and to David Legere for letting me write it in the first place.

Introduction

Get a bicycle. You will certainly not regret it, if you live.
—Mark Twain, nineteenth-century author and humorist

Mountain biking in Las Vegas, are you kidding? Actually, no. Now I'll admit, when someone mentions Las Vegas, the first thing that comes to mind is not riding a mountain bike. But if you know anything about Southern Nevada in general and Las Vegas in particular, it shouldn't surprise you that some of the best trails in the entire southwest are located in the hills, canyons, and valleys in and around Southern Nevada.

Nevada has forty-seven million acres of public land and the southern part of the state accounts for a good share of that land. Southern Nevada is home to both the largest man-made lake in the United States and the largest national forest in the lower forty-eight. Additionally, there are no less than three national recreation areas, a state park, a conservation area, wetlands, and a dam that was considered a modern marvel when it was constructed in 1935. While tourists spend their days on the Strip, gambling, watching shows, eating in celebrity chef–owned restaurants, or lounging at the pool, locals are busy outside hiking, biking, horseback riding, boating, jet skiing, and bird watching. How many places do you know that offer you an opportunity to see both wild horses and wild burros while riding a mountain bike?

What many people are surprised to discover is that Las Vegas is home to world-class mountain bike trails and is the site of a Silverman Triathlon, an Xterra Championship, and the Nevada State Downhill Championships. In addition, Las Vegas and Henderson have spent millions of dollars building multi-purpose trails around the valley and they have been so successful that the League of American Cyclists has awarded them both the bronze level as a Bicycle Friendly Community. However, in truth, the term "mountain biking" may be a bit of a misnomer when applied to Las Vegas and Southern Nevada. With elevations reaching in the range of 2,000 to 4,000 feet in most of the valley, few of the trails really qualify as "mountain." But while most of the trails in Las Vegas and Southern Nevada vary by only a few hundred feet in elevation, the trails are nonetheless some of the best you'll find anywhere in the southwest.

Las Vegas also has some hidden gems that are only known to locals and those who care to do a bit of exploring. One of these is the Historic Railroad Tunnel Trail where you can ride through the very tunnels once used to transport men, equipment, and supplies to the Hoover Dam construction site more than eighty years ago. Surrounding almost the entire valley is land owned by the Bureau of Land Management (BLM) and it is on this land where some of the best and most scenic bike trails can be found. Some of these trails have even been labeled an "epic" ride by the International Mountain Biking Association (IMBA).

Rider competing in a race at Bootleg Canyon JIM LAURIE PHOTOGRAPHY

Even if I can get people to see past the Strip, I often have difficulty getting them to see past the desert—or more specifically the desert heat. While everyone is familiar with the 100-plus temperatures that invade the valley every summer, few of those same people know the year-round average temperate in Las Vegas is only 69.3 degrees. When most people think of a desert they think of cactus, sand, and, well, not much else. If you see the desert as a place Mother Nature abandoned, look again. The desert has a beauty all its own. A ride through Bootleg Canyon will expose you to some of the most intriguing colors you've ever seen—reds, oranges, yellows, browns, and blues, yes blues. Cottonwood Canyon, the land where the Old Spanish Trail runs through, is replete with some of the most beautiful Joshua trees in all of Nevada. Plus, it is full of all manner of wild animals including burros and horses that, by the way, are not camera shy and just love to watch riders pass on by. The desert is also full of colorful greens, yellows, and reds that all turn a rich golden brown as the sun begins to set.

So, if mountain biking isn't the first thing that comes to mind when you think of Las Vegas and Southern Nevada, you're in for a great surprise. You've already bought this guide. All you have to do now is make sure your tires are inflated, your brakes are working, and your chain is lubed. Then just strap on a helmet and head out into the hills surrounding the valley. Just remember you'll need sunscreen, water, this guide, oh, and a camera so you can take lots and lots of pictures. So grab a frozen burrito, the energy bars of your choice, and let's go ride!

Three Regions

As you might suspect, mountain biking in the Las Vegas Valley requires the rider to travel a bit outside of the actual town. The good news is that for the most part, the trails are in four major areas of the valley: Bootleg Canyon, Sloan Canyon, Cottonwood Valley, and Mount Charleston. Of the four areas, the majority of the trails are in Bootleg Canyon and the Cottonwood Valley and it is for this reason that I have listed them as the main regions. That being said, there are many other trails being developed in other areas of the valley. For example, trails are being established in an area known as the Southwest Ridge and double black diamond trails are on their way to becoming official in an area outside of the Red Rock National Conservation Area, known as the Cowboy Trails. Additionally, Sloan Canyon in the southeast area of the valley is currently home to two trails with more on the way. While many areas are establishing trails that are on track to being officially approved, only those trails that have been deemed "officially legal" at the time of publication have been included in this guide. Stay tuned, however, as a mountain bike community Las Vegas is still growing.

The most famous trails in all of Las Vegas are found in Bootleg Canyon. Located just thirty miles to the southwest of Las Vegas, the small, narrow canyon—made mostly of molten rock uplifted over thousands of years—is home to a series of interconnected trails that are a favorite of mountain bikers from all over the world. Due to the efforts of cycling enthusiast Brent Thomson and brothers Dan and Jeff Haskin, a series of world-class trails—trails that the International Mountain Biking Association deemed an "epic" ride—now run through the canyon. These challenging trails host multiple racing events throughout the year, including the Nevada State Downhill Championships. Bootleg Canyon is also home to Interbike's famous Outdoor Demo, because the trails are perfect for demonstrating the latest bikes with the most advanced technology.

A less technical, but just as fun, grouping of trails is located in the Cottonwood Valley, just to the west of Las Vegas, off State Route 160. Nestled behind the town of Blue Diamond, Nevada, in the Red Rock Canyon National Conservation Area, this series of well-groomed trails has grown greatly in popularity as a place for beginning and intermediate riders. Groups like Ride 2 Recovery make an annual trip to Cottonwood because the trails are easily accessible and the terrain is not as difficult as that found in Bootleg Canyon. Besides the burros and wild horses that frequent the valley, Cottonwood has historical significance as it is one of the few places in America where you can still ride your bike along a portion of history—the Old Spanish Trail.

Trails also exist that are not all grouped together in one defined area. Instead, two may be in one part of the valley while three or four are in another part. Almost all these rides are in national conservation areas, national recreation areas, or national forests, or are part of interstate mountain ranges. Each of these parts of the valley has their own unique trails and while it may take a bit of time to get there, the rides are well worth the trip. I have grouped these by the Las Vegas region to which they are closest.

The last region included in this guide is the Oasis Valley, which is roughly 117 miles to the northwest of Las Vegas and is quickly becoming known for its mountain bike trails. Twelve trails are already open to riders with many more on the way. These trails have been created especially by mountain bikers for mountain bikers and they are a blast!

One of the best things about riding a bike is the freedom it offers. This freedom allows you to travel into areas not accessible by motorized vehicles. When riding a trail, especially a new trail, it can be easy to concentrate on the trail itself and not on your surroundings. Take the time to pay attention to the area through which you are riding. You will find a quiet beauty you may not have expected. But remember, know your limits and only ride as far as you feel comfortable. Also, many of the loops included in this guide can be ridden clockwise or counter-clockwise. Riding a trail essentially backwards provides a different view of that trail and can create new technical challenges. And it can be a great experience. So go out and ride, make the trails your own, and, above all, have fun!

Mountain Biking Guidelines

Mountain Biking Las Vegas and Southern Nevada is meant as a guide to trails and not a how-to book on riding a mountain bike. That being said, there are some safety factors about biking in general and biking in Las Vegas specifically that should be addressed to make your ride safer and more enjoyable.

Single track is a term used to indicate the trail is only wide enough to ride single file and most of the mountain bike trails in this guide are this type of trail. When riding single track there is a certain etiquette that should be followed. In most cases riders climbing have the right of way to riders going downhill—though this is not a steadfast rule. If you are having difficulty climbing a certain portion of the trail and there is a rider waiting to go down the trail, you may want to give way to that rider instead of making him or her wait. If you are the one staying on the trail—that is, you don't get off the trail when you encounter a rider going in the opposite direction—always announce if there are other riders in your party.

When passing trails specifically designated as downhill trails, watch for riders coming down those trails as they will typically not stop. This is because downhill riders are traveling at a high rate of speed and it is more difficult for them to stop than it is for riders crossing downhill trails. Plus, having to stop in the middle of a downhill ride essentially ruins the ride, as it may not be possible to build up enough speed after stopping to take the jumps and navigate the obstacles designed into the trail. Also, because riders don't typically travel up downhill trails, downhill riders aren't used to encountering other riders going in the opposite direction. And because of this, they typically feel free to fly down the trail as fast as they feel comfortable—which is usually pretty fast. When downhill riders start down a trail, they do not expect to encounter other riders and when they do, they expect to have the right of way. To avoid what could be a dangerous collision, it is best to honor that expectation.

Almost all the mountain bike trails in this guide are open to runners, hikers, and horses so it is best, and often safer, for mountain bikers to yield way. You should always get off the trail when you see a runner or hiker and allow them to pass. In my experience runners will heed to this rule while most hikers will get off the trail and yield way to cyclists. Just remember this is a courtesy followed by some hikers, but the rule

Sign marking a trail as off limits

is for the cyclists to get off the trail. If you encounter a horse, announce yourself to the rider from a distance so as not to spook the horse. Get off your bike and stand off the trail on the downhill side. This will make the horse feel more comfortable as carnivores typically attack from an uphill, not downhill, position.

When riding in general, stay on the trail. Don't forge your own trail and do not take a trail if it is marked as not a trail or not a trail for bikes, even if you see bike tracks or actual riders on that trail. When mountain bikers ride on unapproved or unauthorized trails—especially those that are marked as such—it hurts the entire sport and makes it appear as if mountain bikers are a group of people who don't care about or won't follow the rules. So please respect the trails, both official and unofficial.

Another way of respecting the trails is by skidding your tires as little as possible to avoid loosening the dirt. Stay off muddy trails as riding through the mud can create deep grooves and ruts. If you cannot navigate an obstacle on the bike, then do so on foot. Don't create another path around the obstacle. Other riders will follow the path and it can have a detrimental effect on the ecosystem. Remember, the obstacles were planned into the ride and are meant to test the rider and be part of the riding experience. The more you ride, the better you will become and you will eventually master that obstacle. Always follow the mantra "Leave No Trace," which is used to help remind riders to leave the trails the way they were found. Take out whatever you took in. This includes energy bar wrappers, water bottles, and any other form of trash or debris. If you see trash on the trails, even though you didn't put it there yourself, take it out with you.

Preparing for Las Vegas Weather

The Las Vegas Water Authority has a slogan they use to remind people not to waste water. The slogan, "It's a Desert Out There," is especially applicable when riding on the mountain bike trails in and around the Las Vegas Valley and Southern Nevada.

One of the greatest things about mountain biking in Las Vegas is that you can ride here all year long. The only thing that changes is the time of day you choose to ride. While the average temperature in Las Vegas is 69.3 degrees Fahrenheit, temperatures can reach well into the upper 100s with 115 degrees or more being common summer temperatures. It's also important to know that unlike many areas of the United States, the hottest part of the day in Southern Nevada is 5:00 pm, not noon.

When riding in Southern Nevada, water is essential—especially in the summer months. You should never go for a ride without making sure you have an adequate supply of water for the time you will be riding. My advice is to take more water than you think you'll need, especially if you've never ridden in the desert. When biking in the heat, you can easily become dehydrated—a condition that can be life-threatening. It is best, when riding in May through September, to plan your rides early in the morning or late at night. Sunscreen, or sunblock, is another important item to have, regardless of the time of year you ride. The sun is especially hot in the desert—even in the winter—and it takes no time at all to develop a severe sunburn.

Though rain is not a common occurrence in the desert, it does happen and while Southern Nevada only experiences 4.13 inches of rain a year, when that rain does come, it's hard and fast. Flash flooding is a definite possibility in many areas, especially Bootleg Canyon. If you're on the trails in Bootleg Canyon when it starts to rain, it's always safer to get off the trail and follow the wider dirt road back to your car. If signs exist warning of riding in the rain or specifically telling you not to ride that trail in the rain, no matter what part of the valley the trail is located in, those signs should always be heeded. For the most part, if it's raining in Southern Nevada, you shouldn't ride.

Dealing with Critters

One of the best things about riding in the desert is that you encounter all manner of critters. In some areas this can mean desert tortoises, lizards, rabbits, tarantulas, and birds. In other areas it can mean bats, big horn sheep, snakes, burros, and wild horses. While it is great to observe animals in the wild, you should always leave them alone. It's never a good idea to approach a wild animal, as you never know if and when that animal will see you as a threat and attack. Feel free to take a photo or two, just do so at a distance. Avoid the temptation to feed a wild animal, especially wild burros that will happily take food. In some cases, feeding animals can result in a significant fine. While you might think you're helping the animal by feeding it, you're actually teaching it to rely on people instead of nature as a food source. This can cause the animal to become dependent upon that source of food and people are unreliable.

Additionally, handling some animals may actually cause them to die. One of these is the desert tortoise, which is an endangered and protected species in Nevada. Desert tortoises resemble a small brown turtle and if you encounter one on the trail, never touch it or pick it up. Doing so can cause the animal to urinate and when that happens it loses precious water that it may not be able to get back. Losing water can

Desert tortoises are endangered and protected in Nevada.

cause the animal to die. Desert tortoises, as you might expect, move slowly and when confronted with a loud noise—such as your bike tire on the dirt trail—they tend to freeze in place. It is best to dismount and walk around these critters or, better yet, block the trail from other riders with your bike until the tortoise passes safely.

A common desert dweller is the rattlesnake and Southern Nevada is home to three types: speckled, sidewinder, and Mojave. These snakes are most active in the mornings and at dusk when temperatures are between 70 and 90 degrees Fahrenheit. Their most active months are April and October. While I have only seen rattlesnakes a couple of times on the trails in Bootleg Canyon, I never ride any trail without a snakebite kit. Rattlesnakes will warn you of their presence, so the best advice I can give you is to heed the rattle of a rattlesnake. If you hear that rattle, it is best to avoid the area where it came from—especially since you probably won't be able to see the snake. Snakes typically don't attack unless they have to and you can usually avoid them pretty easily once they've given you their warning.

Another critter you might see on the trails is the desert tarantula. Females are typically all brown or tan, while males are brown with black legs. Tarantulas are more commonly seen at night and are, for the most part docile. However, they will aggressively defend themselves if you pick them up—and they're faster than you may realize. Like lizards, they will typically get out of your way when you are riding and it is best to simply avoid them.

Anyone who rides in Cottonwood will tell you that one of the best things about the ride is you are very likely to see wild burros. While these animals will usually avoid you, many people feed them—though it is illegal to do so—and that fact makes them sometimes approach people looking for food. True to their reputation, burros are stubborn and will typically not move out of the way if they are on the trail. This means you will most likely have to go around them. If this is the case, it is best to do so while walking, not riding your bike because riding as you pass could spook them and they like to kick when they're spooked. If the burro is not on the trail, feel free to ride past them. They'll usually just stare at you. As a note, these animals are not camera shy.

Bats are another common critter that can be seen on some of the trails, especially in Bootleg Canyon. Bats typically fly above you, feeding on the insects your bike tires kick up. There are more than 20 species of bats in Southern Nevada. None of them will bother you when you ride and it is actually kind of cool to be followed by a couple of bats. Some of the smaller critters you might encounter on your ride include white-tailed antelope squirrels, coyotes, foxes, and many, many different types of lizards—including Gila Monsters, though they are not common. Most, if not all, of these animals will stay out of your way.

Equipment

While bike helmets aren't required in Southern Nevada, it is simply foolish to ride a mountain bike without one. When buying a helmet, look for one that is approved by the Consumer Product Safety Commission (CPSC) or by private organizations—such as the American Society for Testing and Materials (ASTM) or the Snell Memorial Foundation—which develop safety standards for such things as helmets. Remember that price is not a factor in the amount of protection the helmet offers, meaning as long as the helmet meets the standards set by these organizations, more expensive helmets do not necessarily offer better protection.

I cannot emphasize enough that water is essential when mountain biking in Southern Nevada. It is important to note that in most cases a water bottle will not carry enough water to keep you hydrated. For this reason, you should look to some type of hydration system that can be carried with you—usually on your back. Many of these are large enough to carry extra items such as energy bars, a hand pump, bike tools, and, of course, sunscreen. Eyeglasses should always be worn to protect the eyes from the sun and the drying wind created by biking in the desert.

Some trails, such as those in Bootleg Canyon are extremely rocky and it is always a good idea to have at least one spare tube—even if you are riding tubeless—and the tools needed to change a flat. The desert is also known for its cactus and many of our dirt trails are decorated with these thorny plants. I never ride without at least one spare tube. I also typically choose tubes with some type of anti-flat filler inside. Shin guards are also a useful item when riding in Bootleg Canyon, because of the large sharp rocks in many areas. They don't sell t-shirts that say "I gave blood at Bootleg," for nothing.

Know your equipment. Make sure your bike is always in proper working order. Don't wait until you are on a downhill section of a trail to find out your brakes aren't able to stop the bike or you have a flat and didn't bring a spare and a pump. Most, if not all, of the trails included in this guide are in remote areas of the valley. In many cases cell phone reception may not be possible and it is not always an easy matter to get help. For this reason, it's always a good idea to let someone know what trail you are riding and when you left. If you have any questions whatsoever about the condition of your bike, you should always have it checked over by a professional before you venture onto a trail.

GPS

The distances for miles and directions were calculated from a wrist-mounted GPS I wore while navigating the trails. While mileages should match, if you use your own GPS device, please note that readings can be affected by things such as satellite positions, weather, and natural barriers—all of which can cause errors in readings. Taking side trips off the trails can also affect the mileage. This guide marks the trail in miles and tenths of a mile. As you might suspect, few of the landmarks pointed out on the trails land directly on either a mile or a tenth of a mile. In cases where the landmark didn't fall on these established guide points, I have rounded to the closest tenth of the mile.

Map Legend

Transportation

Interstate/Divided Highway	═══════
U.S. Highway	════
State Highway	────
County/Local Road	────
Featured Bike Route	··············
Bike Route	··············
Dirt Road/Trail	------------
Railroad	┼─┼─┼─┼

Hydrology

Reservoir/Lake	⬭
River/Creek	∼

Land Use

State/Local Park, Open Space	▭
State Line	— ·· — ·· —

Symbols

Interstate	(95)
U.S. Highway	(15)
State Highway	(160)
Trailhead (Start)	**10**
Mileage Marker	17.1◆──
Visitor Center	❷
Point of Interest/Structure	■
Parking	🅿
Tunnel	⊟
Town	○
Mountain/Peak	▲
Direction Arrow	→
Dam	▬

Rider heading down a trail in Bootleg Canyon JIM LAURIE PHOTOGRAPHY

Bootleg Canyon and the Surrounding Area

J ust twenty miles southeast of Las Vegas off US 93 is the town of Boulder City. With little more than 15,000 people, Boulder City is the gateway to the Hoover Dam—the marvel of its time. Built in just five short years, the Hoover Dam is a modern Art Deco masterpiece. The structure is not simply functional, it is truly a work of art, created by craftsmen who took immense pride in their work and who were conscious about building a showcase for the world to see. Constructed in

A stovepipe shooting out of a rock cave is all that is left of a bygone bootlegging era.

the heart of the Great Depression, the dam was an amazing undertaking, one that showed not only America's ingenuity, but also its drive to let nothing stand in the way of progress. The town of Boulder City is a byproduct of the construction of the dam. Its original purpose was to house the dam workers and their families; however, when construction of the dam was completed the town didn't just remain, it thrived.

Just to the west of Boulder City are two sets of rocky hills that reach up from the desert to form a canyon, known as Bootleg Canyon. And it is here where you will find 35 miles of trails located in and around the canyon—trails which have been called an "epic" ride by the IMBA. Bootleg Canyon received its Prohibition-era name when the eighteenth amendment to the constitution forbade the manufacture, sale, and transportation of intoxicating liquors in the United States. Instead of giving into the new law, residents of Las Vegas simply moved to the then unnamed canyon and began the production of bootleg alcohol. They blew holes in the rocks, set up stills, and sold alcohol right out of the canyon until 1933 when the twenty-first amendment overturned the eighteenth amendment, again making the manufacture, sale, and transportation of intoxicating liquors legal. Once the residents of Las Vegas could again buy and sell alcohol out in the open, they abandoned the canyon, leaving behind their tools of the trade. Riding through the canyon it is possible to see smoke-stacks protruding out of rocks, cans, bottles, mattress springs, and even an old car, all rusted and all the remnants of a bygone era when outlaws took over the canyon in defiance of a national law.

The trails at Bootleg Canyon got their start when Brent Thomson and brothers Dan and Jeff Haskin decided the canyon would be a great place for mountain bikers to ride. They started with a trail aptly named "Mother" and twenty-some trails later, they created a system of interconnected trails than span more than 30 miles. The trails are laid out so that just about every one of them is connected to another trail in the canyon. This means it is entirely possible to ride from one trail to the next without having to stop or to drive to a different trailhead. Because of this, there aren't really certain "trails" that are ridden. Instead, there are, for the most part, common rides that incorporate two or more trails into the ride. I have followed this pattern when laying out the rides in this section of the guide. That said I have also included several trails—Girl Scout, West Leg, Caldera, Inner Caldera—that are in and of themselves a ride, as well as combining these trails with others to create a longer ride. The guide is laid out so that every trail in Bootleg Canyon is represented in at least one of the rides. Room is left for you, the reader, to create your own combination of trails to find the ride or rides that you enjoy the most.

Bootleg Canyon is famous for its downhill trails. These trails are located on the east side of the canyon. There are also cross-country trails on this side of the canyon and some of those trails cross these downhill trails. When riding trails like Middle/ Lower Lake View Loop, Middle/Upper Lake View Loop, and Lower/Upper Lake View Loop, it is a good idea to keep an eye upward toward the top of the canyon to make sure no one is hurtling down one of the downhill trails. Downhill riders go a lot faster than the typical trail rider and it is more difficult for them to stop, so it is best to give downhillers the right of way.

Most of the trails in Bootleg Canyon are accessed by the main road at the mouth of the canyon. Here you will find a small parking lot, as well as restrooms. If that lot is full, a larger dirt lot is located below that parking lot and is the place most people park when staying overnight. Another dirt lot is located at the top of the first hill, after the asphalt road has turned into a dirt road. This lot is mainly used to access Caldera and Inner Caldera, but can be used to access other trails and as a spare lot if the other lots are full.

I have also included in this section three other trails, two in the nearby Sloan Canyon and one just outside of Bootleg Canyon near Lake Mead. This last trail, the Historic Railroad Trail, is one of my favorite trails in Las Vegas. It is the only place where you can ride through the very tunnels once used by the Union Pacific Railroad when building the Hoover Dam. This family-friendly, easily-accessed trail, which follows the route used by the railroad, offers great scenic views of Lake Mead and the surrounding area and is one of the best places to see bats. But don't worry; the tracks have long been removed.

Local Bike Shops

All Mountain Cyclery: 1404 Nevada Hwy., Ste. C in Boulder City; (702) 453-2453; allmountaincyclery.com

Aspen Creek Cycling: 1590 W. Horizon Ridge Pkwy. #140, Henderson, NV; (702) 893-2453; aspencreekcycling.com

Bike Shop: 2570 Wigwam Pkwy., Henderson, NV; (702) 897-1618; bikeshop-lv.com

Bike World: 2320 E. Flamingo Road, Las Vegas, NV; (702) 735-7551; bikeworldlv.com

Irwin Cycles: 10080 W. Tropicana Ave. #165, Las Vegas, NV; (702) 625-2453; irwincycles.com

McGhie's Ski, Bike, and Board: 19 S. Stephanie St., Ste. 100, Henderson, NV; (702) 800-3636; mcghies.com

REI: 2220 Village Walk Dr. #150, Henderson, NV; (702) 896-7111

River Mountain Bike Shop: 2310 E. Lake Mead Pkwy., Henderson, NV; (702) 564-3058

1   **Mother**

Many moons ago, before Bootleg Canyon became the modern mountain biking park it is today, Brent Thomson and brothers Dan and Jeff Haskin carved a trail high into the canyon walls. This original trail, which became known as "Mother," is not one for the faint of heart. It follows the ridge of the canyon, way up high, and there is a steep, rocky drop that follows the trail almost the entire way. There are also some extremely technical drops and downhill sections, which combine to make this a fun but challenging ride.

Start: The parking lot below the restrooms at the entrance to Bootleg Canyon
Distance: 2.6 miles
Elevation gain: 198 feet
Riding time: Advanced riders, 45 minutes; intermediate riders, 1 hour
Fitness effort: Physically challenging due to steep climbs and rocky, technical spots
Difficulty: Technically challenging with very rocky spots, much climbing, and some very steep drops

Terrain: Mostly dirt, large rocks, and loose gravel
Map: All Mountain Cyclery, allmountaincyclery .com
Nearest town: Boulder City
Other trail users: Hikers and runners
Dog friendly: Yes
Trail contact: Boulder City; bcnv.org/ Facilities/Facility/Details/Bootleg-Canyon -Park-18

Getting there: Take U.S. Highway 93 toward the Hoover Dam (Boulder City). Bootleg Canyon is easily visible on the left-hand side of the road. It is marked by a large white "BC" which actually stands for Boulder City, not Bootleg Canyon. Turn left on Veteran's Memorial Drive and follow it to Canyon Road. Turn left on Canyon Road and follow it to the parking lot below the restrooms. Park here and then ride your bike up that dirt road to the first telephone pole on the left. You'll see the trailhead by the telephone pole. GPS: N35 59.119'/ W114 51.882'
    Note: If the parking lot is full, you can park in the dirt lot just below the asphalt lot.

The Ride

While many trails in Bootleg Canyon can be ridden up and back or clockwise and counter-clockwise, Mother is really only meant to be ridden one way. Not that you can't ride it up and back, it's just that this trail has what mountain bikers would call some "gnarly" drops—one section of which is known as the Three Sisters—that are extremely difficult to ride back up, once you have descended. However, you can carry your bike (commonly called hike-a-bike) up those trails if you want to ride back.

    Mother begins by heading up the dirt road to the trailhead. The entrance can easily be seen to the left of the road at just about where the telephone pole and the road meet. You'll see the point where the trail cuts out from the road. Take that trail to the left up the short climb. Once at the crest of the short hill, the trail splits into

A particularly tricky portion of the Mother Trail known as the Three Sisters

two. Mother is the trail to the left; the trail to the right is West Leg. Both trails are clearly marked.

When the trail splits a second time at 0.3 mile, take the trail to the right. Going straight will put you on the IMBA trail. Mother is also clearly marked with a small wood sign. From this point you begin a fairly steep, rocky climb. This trail is made more arduous due to the fact that it follows the ridgeline of the canyon wall and there is a very steep drop on the left side of the trail; a drop replete with large, loose rocks. At 0.8 mile, stay straight when the trails meet at the end of the climb. Do not take the trail to the right. It leads to a section called the saddle, which eventually connects with West Leg.

The next portion of the trail is high up on the canyon wall, allowing you views of the lower canyon and the lower trails. This can be a bit difficult for those with height issues as not only are you high on the canyon wall, but the left side of the trail is a steep drop the entire way. Almost a mile into the ride, the trail enters a tricky down-hill section known as the Three Sisters. The dirt single track disappears at this point and is replaced by rock. This section follows all the way down through the Three Sisters until the trail turns back into dirt. At the end of the Three Sisters is a technically difficult drop. When the trail splits, stay straight. The trail to the left leads to the POW Trail and eventually Par None and the IMBA trail. A short 0.3 mile after this section Mother officially ends where a large rock seems to jet out into the trail.

While the trail officially ends at 1.32 miles, the physical trail actually continues on—in fact, it would eventually connect with the Caldera Trail if ridden all the way. Although

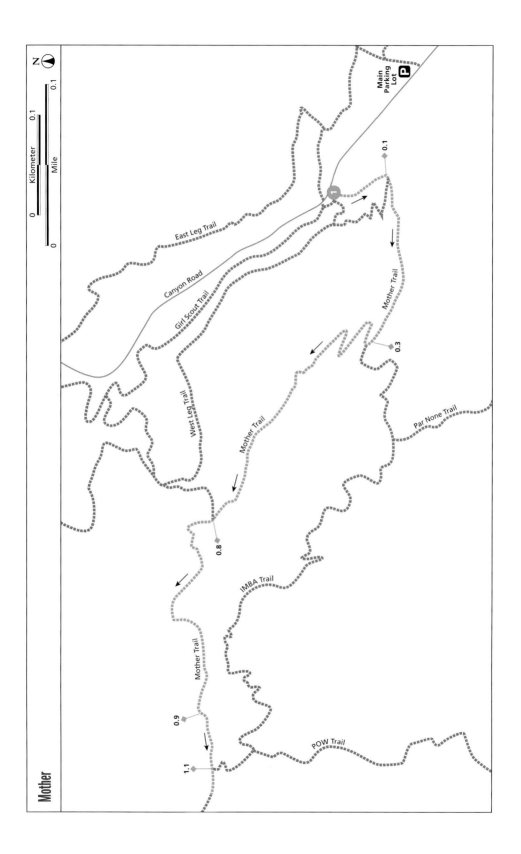

Mother

East Leg Trail

Canyon Road

Girl Scout Trail

West Leg Trail

Mother Trail

IMBA Trail

Mother Trail

POW Trail

Par None Trail

Mother Trail

Main Parking Lot

P

N

Kilometer

0   0.1   0.1

Mile

0   0.1

0.1

0.3

0.8

0.9

1.1

many mountain bike riders routinely use this portion of the trail, it is officially on Bureau of Land Management land and that entity has not given permission for riders to use that portion of the trail. And, for that reason, this guide stops the trail at the official ending point. If you choose to continue riding, you do so at your own risk of being fined.

From here you can either turn and head back up Mother or you can turn right at the point where Mother meets the IMBA/POW connector trail. This trail heads into a series of downhill switchbacks, eventually leading to the POW and IMBA trails. You can then take the IMBA trail on the left and head back to the trailhead or you can take the POW trail to the right into a fun, fast downhill trail that leads to the Par None Trail and eventually the IMBA Trail, which you can take to the Mother trailhead. Both these routes are included elsewhere in this guide.

Miles and Directions

0.0 Start at the trailhead to the left of the telephone pole. Take the trail to the left and climb a small hill.

0.1 When the trail splits keep left, entering Mother. The trail is clearly marked. Follow the trail into a tricky rock obstacle and then straight for a short distance.

0.3 When the trail splits, take the trail to the right. There is a small wood sign marking the trail as Mother. Follow the trail into a steep climb with tight switchbacks.

0.8 When the trails meet stay left. The trail to the right leads to the Saddle and eventually the West Leg Trail. In 0.1 mile the trail splits a second time. Take either trail as they meet back up on the other side of a small hill. The left trail is a more gradual climb.

0.9 Follow the trail into the Three Sisters, a technically difficult downhill section. Take the drop and follow the trail left into a gradual climb.

1.1 Stay straight when the trail splits. The trail to the left leads to POW. Take the short drop and follow the trail straight.

1.3 The trail ends at the rock jetting out into the trail. Turn around and head back or head back on the IMBA trail.

2.6 Arrive at the trailhead.

Ride Information

Local Events and Attractions

Boulder City is full of many antique stores, all within walking distance of each other. Many of these places have even been featured on national television shows. They can all be easily found in *The Country Register*, a free guide to specialty shops and events available from most businesses in downtown Boulder City.

Restaurants

Boulder Pit Stop: Best hamburgers in town; located a short distance from the trail; 802 Buchanan Blvd.; (720) 293-7080; boulderpitstop.com

The Coffee Cup: Featured on *Diners, Drive-ins, and Dives*; 512 Nevada Hwy.; (702) 294-0517; worldfamouscoffeecup.com

2 Girl Scout

This trail is one of the most popular rides in Bootleg Canyon, mainly because it offers some of the most wonderful views of the canyon as well as many of the bootlegging artifacts that give the canyon its name. Girl Scout is a challenging technical trail that is an uphill climb all the way—rewarded by a fun downhill ride back to the trailhead. This is a trail, however, that definitely requires shin guards.

Start: The parking lot below the restrooms at the entrance to Bootleg Canyon
Distance: 3.0 miles
Elevation gain: 294 feet
Riding time: Advanced riders, 30 minutes; intermediate riders, 45 minutes
Fitness effort: Physically challenging due to steep climbs and rocky, technical spots
Difficulty: Technically moderate with very rocky spots, much climbing, and some steep drops

Terrain: Mostly dirt, large rocks, and loose gravel
Map: All Mountain Cyclery, allmountaincyclery.com
Nearest town: Boulder City
Other trail users: Hikers and runners
Dog friendly: Yes
Trail contact: Boulder City; bcnv.org/Facilities/Facility/Details/Bootleg-Canyon-Park-18

Getting there: Take U.S. Highway 93 toward the Hoover Dam (Boulder City). Bootleg Canyon is easily visible on the left-hand side of the road. It is marked by a large white "BC," which actually stands for Boulder City, not Bootleg Canyon. Turn left on Veteran's Memorial Drive and follow it to Canyon Road. Turn left on Canyon Road and follow it to the parking lot below the restrooms. Park here and then ride your bike up that dirt road to the first telephone pole on the left. You'll see the trailhead by the telephone pole. GPS: N35 59.119'/W114 51.882'
Note: If the parking lot is full, you can park in the dirt lot just below the asphalt lot.

The Ride

If you're looking for remnants of a time when bootleg alcohol was stilled in rocky crevices, giving the canyon its name, then this is the ride for you. A little more than half a mile into the ride you can see a cave-like formation with a rusted stove pipe protruding upward through the rock. During Prohibition, it was common for bootleggers to blast holes in rocks large enough to house a still, thus keeping it out of view and away from prying eyes. Metal stovepipes were attached to holes drilled into the tops of these crevices to move smoke away from the still. Many of these man-made crevices succumbed to time and vandals; however, one does remain just off a dirt road that runs the entire length of the canyon and it is best viewed from the Girl Scout trail. The dirt road, which is also visible from the trail, is the same road that was once used by bootleggers to transport their illegal brew to their eagerly waiting clients back in Las Vegas.

A rider making his way down Girl Scout JIM LAURIE PHOTOGRAPHY

The ride begins by riding your bike up the dirt road to the trailhead. The entrance can easily be seen to the left of the road at just about where the telephone pole and the road meet. You'll see the point where the trail cuts out from the road. Take that trail to the right. The beginning of the ride is commonly referred to as the "rock garden" because it is filled with all manner of rock obstacles, some small, some fairly large. Once you make your way out of the rock garden the single-track trail is mostly dirt; however, some large rock obstacles still await you at key positions as you climb up to the top of the canyon.

A large dip is followed by a short climb leading to another dirt road about 1 mile into the ride. Cross the dirt road and head into a short downhill section that leads to another dirt road. After crossing the second dirt road, follow the trail as it heads up and into a difficult rock obstacle. Steady speed and constant pedaling is the key to navigating this obstacle successfully. Once you navigate that obstacle, you'll head into a series of small mogul-like hills, followed by another climb.

At the end of the moguls is another large drop that is followed by a sharp left turn and a very steep climb through a couple of switchbacks with sharp turns up the canyon wall. From here you'll head into a series of switchbacks that follow the curves of the foothills as they make their way in and out of the canyon, while still climbing to the top. The trail ends where the switchbacks end. Here you can see the upper dirt parking lot to your right and a large pole to your left, complete with signs marking the trailheads of several trails, including Caldera, Inner Caldera, and West Leg. Once you've reached this point, simply turn your bike around and prepare yourself for a fun and fast downhill ride back to the trailhead.

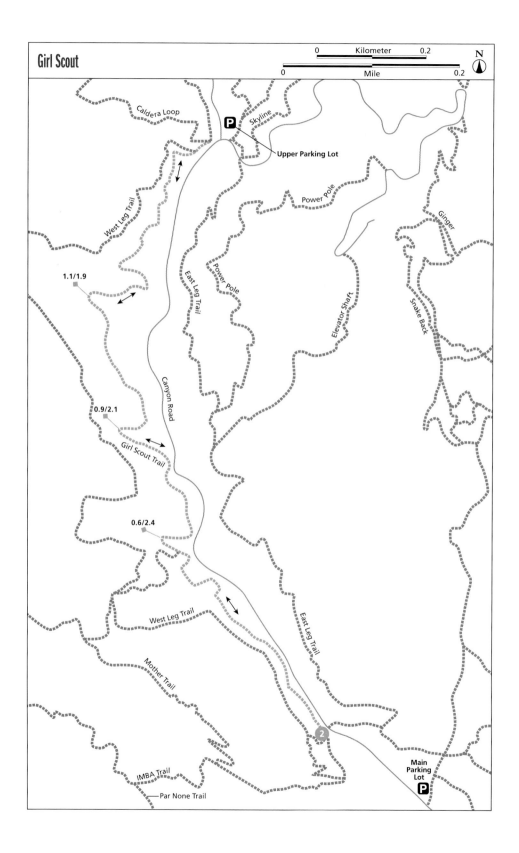

Girl Scout

Caldera Loop

Skyline

P Upper Parking Lot

Power pole

West Leg Trail

Ginger

East Leg Trail

Power Pole

1.1/1.9

Elevator Shaft

Snake Back

Canyon Road

0.9/2.1

Girl Scout Trail

0.6/2.4

West Leg Trail

East Leg Trail

Mother Trail

IMBA Trail

Par None Trail

2

Main
Parking
Lot

P

0   Kilometer   0.2

0   Mile   0.2

N

Miles and Directions

0.0 Start at the trailhead just to the left of the telephone pole. Follow the trail as it climbs up into the canyon. You'll almost immediately enter the rock garden.

0.1 One large rock obstacle followed by another. Stay between the rocks on the second obstacle. You'll reach the last rock obstacle at 0.2 mile.

0.6 Follow the trail between two large rocks. Take the sharp left turn and head into a short, but steep climb. Look off to the right to see the remnants of an old still.

0.9 Take the large dip and continue the small climb. Cross a dirt road at 1.0 mile. Cross a second dirt road and head into a large, difficult rock obstacle.

1.1 Take the large drop followed by a very steep climb and a sharp turn to the right. Follow the trail through a series of tight switchbacks at 1.3 miles.

1.5 The Girl Scout Trail ends. Turn and go back down.

3.0 Arrive at the trailhead.

Ride Information

Local Events and Attractions

Nevada State Downhill Championships: Part of the Bootleg Canyon Winter Gravity Series, this mid-January event includes a Downhill, Dual Slalom, and Super D, and an Open Chain-less DH race; downhillmike.com/bootleg-canyon-home.html.

Mob n Mojave: Part of the Bootleg Canyon Winter Gravity Series, this mid-February event includes a Downhill, Dual Slalom, and Super D race; downhillmike .com/bootleg-canyon-home.html.

Restaurants

Jack's Place: Sidewalk cafe and sports bar; 544 Nevada Way; (702) 293-2200; jacks placebc.com

Milo's Cellar: Sidewalk cafe and wine bar; 538 Nevada Way; (702) 293-9540; milos winebar.com

3 West Leg

West Leg is another popular trail in Bootleg Canyon—one that will test the skills of even the most advanced rider. This trail follows the left side of the canyon from the base of Bootleg to the upper parking lot. West Leg is not only tricky due to the many rock obstacles along the trail, but also because the trail is high on the canyon wall, making it a tricky trail for anyone with height issues. While West Leg can prove a little intimidating, it is a fun challenging ride.

Start: The parking lot below the restrooms at the entrance to Bootleg Canyon
Distance: 4.6 miles
Elevation gain: 345 feet
Riding time: Advanced riders, 45 minutes; intermediate riders, 1 hour
Fitness effort: Physically challenging due to rocky, technical spots
Difficulty: Technically challenging with very rocky spots, much climbing, and some very steep drops

Terrain: Mostly dirt, large rocks, and some loose gravel
Map: All Mountain Cyclery, allmountaincyclery.com
Nearest town: Boulder City
Other trail users: Hikers and runners
Dog friendly: Yes
Trail contact: Boulder City; bcnv.org/Facilities/Facility/Details/Bootleg-Canyon-Park-18

Getting there: Take U.S. Highway 93 toward the Hoover Dam (Boulder City). Bootleg Canyon is easily visible on the left-hand side of the road. It is marked by a large white "BC," which actually stands for Boulder City, not Bootleg Canyon. Turn left on Veteran's Memorial Drive and follow it to Canyon Road. Turn left on Canyon Road and follow it to the parking lot below the restrooms. Park here and then ride your bike up that dirt road to the first telephone pole on the left. You'll see the trailhead by the telephone pole. GPS: N35 59.119'/W114 51.882'
Note: If the parking lot is full, you can park in the dirt lot just below the asphalt lot.

The Ride

West Leg begins by heading up the dirt road to the trailhead. The entrance can easily be seen to the left of the road at just about where the telephone pole and the road meet. You'll see the point where the trail cuts out from the road. Take that trail to the left up the short climb. Once at the crest of the short hill, the trail splits into two. West Leg is the trail to the right; the trail to the left is Mother. Both trails are clearly marked.

From the moment you begin the ride along West Leg, you'll find it's an almost constant climb. A short distance ahead, the trail goes to the left, heading up and over a small hill before taking a sharp turn to the right. Here the trail goes over some rocks and seems to disappear. But you can easily see the trail roughly 10 feet or so ahead.

Two riders coming up West Leg

At 0.2 mile, continue straight. Do not take the illegal downhill trail to the right. At 0.4 mile you'll encounter a quick little drop, followed by several other drops and climbs a short distance ahead. One of these drops has a large rock obstacle on the other side. While the trail is quite narrow at the beginning, it does widen out a bit a little into the trail. However, the trail is single track the entire way. There are many offshoot trails leading down the canyon wall to either the trail below (Girl Scout) or the dirt road. Do not take any of these offshoot trails.

At just about 0.8 mile stay to the left, following the sign to West Leg. Do not take the Girl Scout connector to the right. From here you can go straight into a quick climb or take the trail to the left for a more gradual climb. The trails meet up again in about 15 feet.

About a mile into the trail there is a steep drop, followed by a quick steep climb. If you want a more gradual climb, take the trail to the right on the other side of the drop. At the crest of the hill, follow the trail to the left along the ridge of the canyon and pass a huge rock.

Cross the dry wash and take the gradual climb to the right. Here the trail splits. Going left leads to a drop and quick climb. The trail to the right leads to a more gradual climb. The trails meet up just after another wash, which is followed by a steep climb into a series of switchbacks. Follow the trail into another quick drop and climb, followed by another drop and much steeper climb. The trail splits here, but meets back up just past the crest of the hill. The trail to the left is much steeper than the trail to the right.

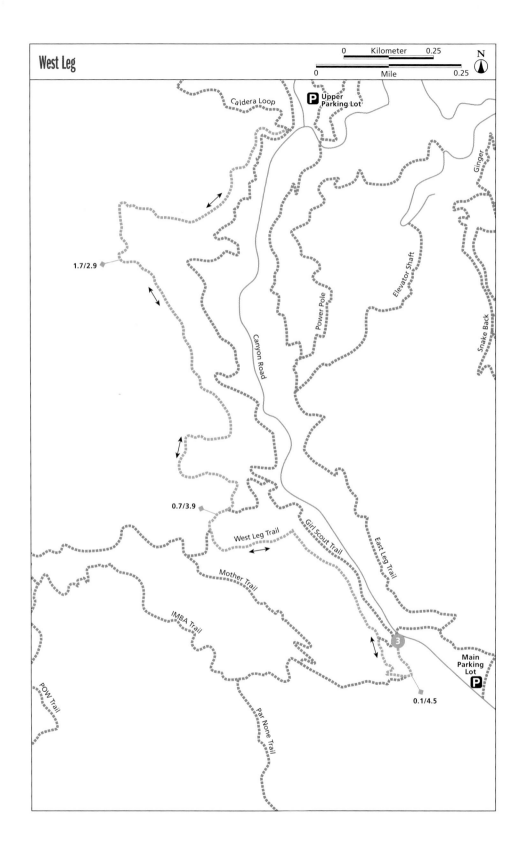

West Leg

Kilometer

Mile

N

Upper Parking Lot

Caldera Loop

Ginger

1.7/2.9

Power Pole

Elevator Shaft

Canyon Road

Snake Back

0.7/3.9

Girl Scout Trail

West Leg Trail

East Leg Trail

Mother Trail

IMBA Trail

3

0.1/4.5

POW Trail

Par None Trail

Main Parking Lot

Near the end of the trail you'll have to navigate a steep drop followed by a technical climb over a large rock. West Leg ends where there is a convergence of trails. Here you can see the upper dirt parking lot to your right and a large pole, complete with signs marking the trailheads of several trails, including Caldera, Inner Caldera, and Girl Scout. From here you simply turn your bike around and prepare yourself for a fun and technical downhill ride back to the trailhead.

Miles and Directions

0.0 Start at the trailhead just to the left of the telephone pole. Take the trail to the left and climb up a small hill.

0.1 When the trail splits, keep right, entering West Leg. The trail is clearly marked. Follow the trail to the left up and over the small hill. Continue straight when the trail seems to disappear. You'll see it about 10 feet ahead.

0.7 Stay straight. Do not take the trail to the left. When the trail splits three ways, stay straight until you connect with the trail ahead, then follow it to the right.

1.7 When the trail splits, take either trail. Left leads to a drop and quick climb. Right leads to a more gradual climb. The trails meet again after the wash.

1.9 The trail splits but meets up again at the crest of the small hill. The left trail is steeper than the right.

2.3 Take the steep drop followed by a tricky climb over a large rock. Then follow the trail to the convergence of trails. Turn around at the sign post.

4.6 Arrive at the trailhead.

Ride Information

Local Events and Attractions

Allan Bible Visitors Center: Here you will find exhibits on Lake Mead, including the animals that make the lake their home. You can also find a full-size relief map of Lake Mead National Recreation Area; nps.gov/lake/planyourvisit/visitorcenters.htm. **Lake Mead Cruises:** A popular attraction on Lake Mead is a cruise on a Mississippi-style paddleboat; lakemeadcruises.com.

Restaurants

Boulder Dam Brewing Company: Local brewery and restaurant started by Seattle native Todd Cook; 453 Nevada Way; (702) 243-2739; boulderdambrewing.com **The Harbor House Café:** Unique floating restaurant and bar; 490 Horsepower Cove; (702) 293-3081; boatinglakemead.com

4 Girl Scout/West Leg/Mother Loop

Like many of the rides in Bootleg Canyon, the Girl Scout/West Leg/Mother Loop is actually made up of three different trails: Girl Scout, West Leg, and Mother—the first trail created in Bootleg Canyon. This is a fun, but technical loop that offers some great views of the canyon, while giving you a chance to test or improve your skills.

Start: The parking lot below the restrooms at the entrance to Bootleg Canyon
Distance: 3.7 miles
Elevation gain: 345 feet
Riding time: Advanced riders, 1 hour; intermediate riders, 1.5 hours
Fitness effort: Physically challenging due to steep climbs and rocky, technical spots
Difficulty: Technically challenging with very rocky spots, much climbing, and some steep drops

Terrain: Mostly dirt, large rocks, and loose gravel
Map: All Mountain Cyclery, allmountaincyclery.com
Nearest town: Boulder City
Other trail users: Hikers and runners
Dog friendly: Yes
Trail contact: Boulder City; bcnv.org/Facilities/Facility/Details/Bootleg-Canyon-Park-18

Getting there: Take U.S. Highway 93 toward the Hoover Dam (Boulder City). Bootleg Canyon is easily visible on the left-hand side of the road. It is marked by a large white "BC," which actually stands for Boulder City, not Bootleg Canyon. Turn left on Veteran's Memorial Drive and follow it to Canyon Road. Turn left on Canyon Road and follow it to the parking lot below the restrooms. Park here and then ride your bike up that dirt road to the first telephone pole on the left. You'll see the trailhead by the telephone pole. GPS: N35 59.119'/W114 51.882'
   Note: If the parking lot is full, you can park in the dirt lot just below the asphalt lot.

The Ride

The ride begins by heading up the dirt road to the trailhead. The entrance can easily be seen to the left of the road at the point where the telephone pole and the road meet. When you see the trail that cuts out from the road, follow it to the right. The beginning of the trail is often called the "rock garden" because it is filled with all manner of rock obstacles, some small, some fairly large. Once you make your way out of the rock garden, the single-track trail is mostly dirt, with some large rock obstacles at key positions.

About 1 mile into the ride, cross the dirt road and head into a short downhill section, which leads to another dirt road. After crossing the second dirt road, follow the trail as it heads up and into a difficult rock obstacle. Continue the climb into a series of mogul-like hills followed by another steep climb, leading into a series of switchbacks and the end of Girl Scout at the convergence of trails. The trail to the left will take you to both the Caldera and West Leg Trails. Take this trail and then take the offshoot to the left a short way up the trail. This offshoot is the West Leg trail and is marked with a small wood sign.

The West Leg Trail, for the most part, parallels Girl Scout back down the canyon, only much higher on the canyon wall. About 2 miles into the ride a park bench, slightly above the trail on the right, provides a great rest spot with wonderful views of the canyon. About a half mile past the park bench is another large drop. A trail just to the left offers a less steep ride down and is a great alternative for less experiences riders. At the bottom of the drop, you can then take the trail to the right for a more gradual climb out. If you choose to take the drop and go straight, be sure to allow yourself enough speed to make the steep climb up the short hill on the other side.

Sign marking the convergence of trails

At 2.9 miles the West Leg trail goes off to the left. Stay on the trail to the right, as it climbs up over a hill and goes down the other side. This is the connector trail to Mother and is commonly called the saddle. The downhill side of the saddle is a long steep decline coated with hundreds of small loose rocks. Toward the bottom of the decline, take the trail to the left. This is Mother.

Follow this trail downward until it meets up with the IMBA trail about 3.4 miles into the ride. Take that trail to the left and follow it back toward the trailhead. At the top of the small hill, the trail splits. Stay straight. The trail to the left is the trailhead to the West Leg trail and the trail to the right is a downhill section that isn't an official trail. Keep straight and follow the trail to the point where the loop began. You can then ride down the dirt road back to the parking lot.

Miles and Directions

0.0   Start at the trail head just to the left of the telephone pole. Follow the trail as it climbs up into the canyon. You'll almost immediately enter the rock garden.

0.6   Follow the trail between two large rocks and turn left. Look off to the right to see the remnants of an old still.

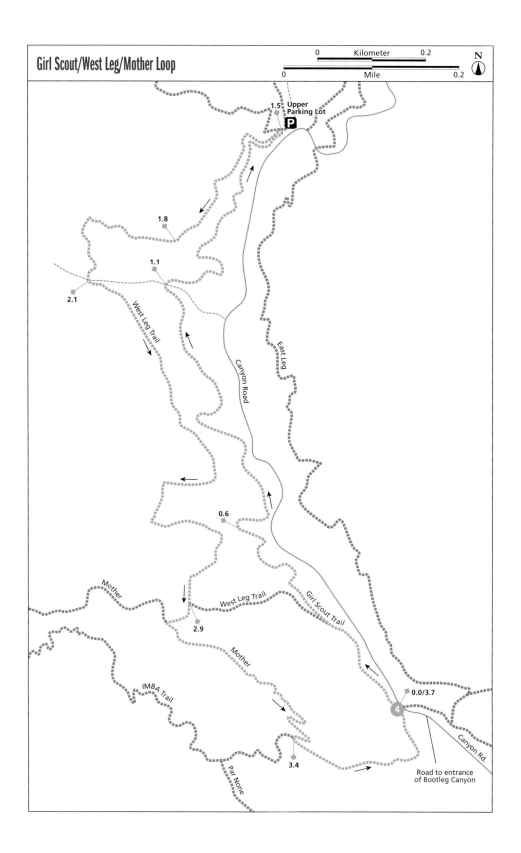

Girl Scout/West Leg/Mother Loop

0.9 Take the large dip and continue the small climb. Cross a dirt road at 1.0 mile. Continue on the short descent, crossing a second dirt road and then a large, difficult rock obstacle.

1.5 The Girl Scout Trail ends. Take the trail to the left and then the offshoot trail on the left a short distance up. Look for a small wood sign to the left of the trail that marks the West Leg Trail.

1.8 Turn right and start a small downhill section. The trail splits at mile 2.0 and you can take either trail.

2.6 Take the big drop or the more gradual drop to the left. At the bottom of the drop take the more gradual climb to the right. Do not take any of the offshoot trails on the left at mile 2.8.

2.9 Follow the trail right onto the saddle and down to Mother. The West Leg trail continues left. This downhill section is very steep with lots of loose rocks.

3.0 Take the sharp left turn and enter a difficult rock area.

3.4 The Mother Trail merges with the IMBA trail. Take the trail to the left.

3.6 Follow the trail though a couple of tricky rock sections. When the trail splits at the top of the hill, follow the trail straight. Do not take the turnoff to the left or the right.

3.7 The trail ends where it began.

Ride Information

Local Events and Attractions

Boulder City is full of many antique stores, all within walking distance of each other. Many of these places have even been featured on national television shows. They can all be easily found in *The Country Register*, a free guide to specialty shops and events available from most businesses in downtown Boulder City.

Restaurants

Boulder Pit Stop: Best hamburgers in town; located a short distance from the trail; 802 Buchanan Blvd.; (720) 293-7080; boulderpitstop.com

Boulder Dam Brewing Company: Local brewery and restaurant started by Seattle native Todd Cook; 453 Nevada Way; (702) 243-2739; boulderdambrewing.com

5 East Leg

Bootleg Canyon is just that, a canyon—one that is divided into two halves by a dirt road. On the west side of the canyon you'll find the more cross-country-style rides: Mother, West Leg, Girl Scout, POW, IMBA, and Par None. To the back of the canyon, on the desert floor where the canyon ends, lie Caldera and Inner Caldera. While there are some cross-country-style rides on the east side of the canyon—namely the Middle, Upper, and Lower Lake View trails—the east side, especially the upper portion of the canyon, is home to the many downhill trails that have helped put Bootleg on the map.

East Leg, as the name suggests, follows the canyon wall on the east side and when Brent Thomson and brothers Dan and Jeff Haskin first built East Leg, they intended it as a beginner's downhill trail and that is exactly what it is. In fact, this trail was commonly used as the starting point for races in the past and there are still a couple of different starting blocks located on the canyon wall above the trail. If you're wondering if downhill riding is for you, this trail is the perfect place to cut your teeth.

Start: To the left of the dirt parking lot located at the top of the dirt road before it climbs the last hill

Distance: 1.7 miles

Elevation gain: 364 feet

Riding time: Advanced riders, 45 minutes; intermediate riders, 1 hour

Fitness effort: Physically challenging, due to some very tricky obstacles and the height of the trail

Difficulty: Technically moderate to challenging, with the technically difficult portion coming at the second half of the ride

Terrain: Mostly dirt, some large rocks, and loose gravel

Map: All Mountain Cyclery, allmountaincyclery .com

Nearest town: Boulder City

Other trail users: Hikers and runners

Dog friendly: Yes, but he or she must be sure footed

Trail contact: Boulder City; bcnv.org/ Facilities/Facility/Details/Bootleg-Canyon -Park-18

Getting there: Take U.S. Highway 93 toward the Hoover Dam (Boulder City). Bootleg Canyon is easily visible on the left-hand side of the road. It is marked by a large white "BC," which actually stands for Boulder City, not Bootleg Canyon. Turn left on Veteran's Memorial Drive and follow it to Canyon Road. Turn Left on Canyon Road and follow it to the parking lot just below the restrooms. Keep driving until the road turns dirt and then follow the dirt road as it winds up the canyon. Drive slow to be courteous and not stir up dust for riders on the trails on either side of the road.

Just to the left of where the dirt road plateaus is a dirt parking lot that is not initially visible. The parking lot is a little lower than the dirt road, making it difficult to see. However, you can find it by driving just a little farther up the road and looking to your left. GPS: N35 59.895'/W114 52.049'

The Ride

Note that while you can ride this trail with the standard mountain bike and mountain bike equipment, you may want to have pads and a full-face helmet, as parts of this trail are very tricky and it does travel fairly high upon the east canyon wall—meaning that if you fall off the trail, the drops are pretty steep and the terrain is unforgiving. If you just want a fun downhill ride that isn't too technical or if East Leg proves not to be your cup of tea, there is an offshoot trail about midway through the ride that allows you to get off East Leg and head down to the main dirt road—avoiding the most technical portions of the trail.

Because East Leg is meant as a beginner's downhill trail, it is not one that is typically ridden back up once it has been ridden down. This means the starting point for the trail will not be the same as the ending point. If you plan on leaving your vehicle at the top parking lot, you will have to ride your bike back up the dirt road once you have completed the ride. As an alternative, you can ride Girl Scout or West Leg back up or you can ride either of those two trails up and East Leg down. One of those combinations of trails—West Leg to East Leg—is included in this guide.

The East Leg trailhead is just to the west of the upper parking lot, on the south side of the dirt road. It can be found to the side of the road at the point where the road just starts another climb. The trail is marked with a small wood sign. Once you enter the trail, it starts a gradual downhill that gets more and more steep as the trail progresses.

When the downhill trail meets up with East Leg, continue on to the right into a rocky hairpin turn followed by a long steep climb. Continue straight when the trails

Riders heading down East Leg Jim Laurie Photography

cross. Going right leads to a downhill trail. An old racing starting gate can be seen on the left a short distance up the canyon wall.

When the trail splits at about 1.1 miles, take the trail to the left if you choose to continue on the trail. The more technical section is about to start. If you want to leave East Leg, take the trail to the right. It heads into a series of switchbacks that eventually leads down to the main canyon dirt road. A short distance ahead, do not take what appears to be an offshoot trail to the right. Continue on the trail as it goes over a difficult rock obstacle, turns to the right and heads into another tricky rock section. Take a sharp left after the second rock obstacle.

Follow the trail as it heads to the right into a rocky section that travels along the edge of a ridge. At about 1.3 miles the trail seems to disappear. Climb up and over the rocks directly ahead of you, then pick up the trail on the other side of the rocks. Head into a very short but technical downhill section that travels over large, sharp rocks. When the more technical section ends, watch for the large rock jetting out into the trail.

Take the rocky hairpin turn to the right followed by a second hairpin turn to the left. Follow the trail into a quick drop and a gradual climb up the other side. From here you can see the restrooms down the hill to the right. At this point you can follow just about any of the trails that lead down to the restrooms.

Miles and Directions

0.0 Start at the trailhead just to the right of the dirt road as it begins to climb the hill. The trailhead is southeast of the upper parking lot.

0.1 Take the steep fast climb then follow the trail right over a rock obstacle and into a series of switchbacks.

0.7 Stay straight when the Power Pole downhill section meets the trail.

0.9 Continue straight when the trails cross.

1.1 Take the trail to the left when the trails split. Alternatively: Follow the trail right, back down to the dirt road, leaving East Leg.

1.2 Do not take the offshoot trail to the right. Go over the difficult rock obstacle and take a sharp left after the second rock obstacle.

1.3 Climb over the rocks when the trail seems to disappear and enter a short, but technical downhill section.

1.4 Watch for the large rock jetting out into the trail. Then follow the trail into a set of rocky hairpin turns.

1.6 At the top of the hill, take the sharp right turn and head back to the restrooms.

1.7 Arrive at the restrooms.

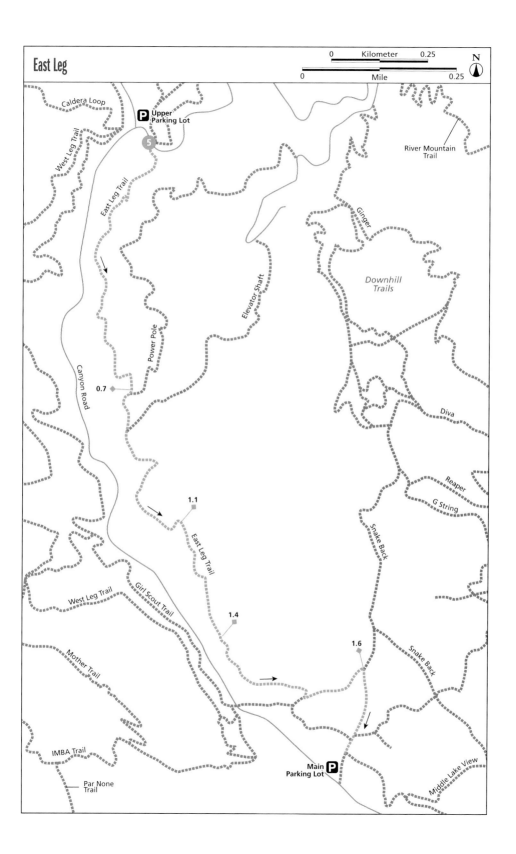

Local Events and Attractions

Nevada State Downhill Championships: Part of the Bootleg Canyon Winter Gravity Series, this mid-January event includes a Downhill, Dual Slalom, Super D, and an Open Chain-less DH race; downhillmike.com/bootleg-canyon-home.html.

Reaper Madness: Part of the Bootleg Canyon Winter Gravity Series, this mid-March event includes a Downhill, Dual Slalom and Super D race; downhillmike .com/bootleg-canyon-home.html.

Restaurants

Boulder Pit Stop: Best hamburgers in town; located a short distance from the trail; 802 Buchanan Blvd.; (720) 293-7080; boulderpitstop.com

Jack's Place: Sidewalk cafe and sports bar; 544 Nevada Way; (702) 293-2200; jacks placebc.com

6 West Leg to East Leg

West Leg is one of the most popular trails in Bootleg Canyon and when combined with a trail intentionally designed to be an introductory downhill course, you have one heck of a fun ride! Note that while you can take the East Leg portion of this ride with the standard mountain bike and mountain bike equipment, you may want to have pads and a full-face helmet.

Start: The parking lot below the restrooms at the entrance to Bootleg Canyon
Distance: 4.0 miles
Elevation gain: 345 feet
Riding time: Advanced riders, 45 minutes; intermediate riders, 1 hour
Fitness effort: Physically challenging due to rocky, technical spots, some very tricky obstacles, and the height of the trail
Difficulty: Technically challenging with very rocky spots, much climbing, and some very steep drops, with a technically difficult downhill portion coming at the second half of the ride

Terrain: Mostly dirt, large rocks, and some loose gravel
Map: All Mountain Cyclery, allmountaincyclery .com
Nearest town: Boulder City
Other trail users: Hikers and runners
Dog friendly: Yes, but he or she must be sure footed
Trail contact: Boulder City; bcnv.org/ Facilities/Facility/Details/Bootleg-Canyon -Park-18

Getting there: Take U.S. Highway 93 toward the Hoover Dam (Boulder City). Bootleg Canyon is easily visible on the left-hand side of the road. It is marked by a large white "BC," which actually stands for Boulder City, not Bootleg Canyon. Turn left on Veteran's Memorial Drive and follow it to Canyon Road. Turn left on Canyon Road and follow it to the parking lot below the restrooms. Park here and then ride your bike up that dirt road to the first telephone pole on the left. You'll see the trailhead by the telephone pole. GPS: N35 59.119'/W114 51.882'
Note: If the parking lot is full, you can park in the dirt lot just below the asphalt lot.

The Ride

West Leg begins by heading up the dirt road to the trailhead. The entrance can easily be seen to the left of the road at just about where the telephone pole and the road meet. You'll see the point where the trail cuts out from the road. Take that trail to the left up the short climb. Once at the crest of the short hill the trail splits into two. West Leg is the trail to the right; the trail to the left is Mother. Both trails are clearly marked.

From the moment you begin the ride along West Leg, you'll find it's an almost constant climb. When the trail goes over some rocks and seems to disappear, you'll find it again about 10 feet ahead. At 0.2 mile, continue straight. Do not take the illegal downhill trail to the right. This section is a narrow single track with a very steep drop

A rider and his dog head up West Leg.

off the right side of the trail. At just about 0.8 mile stay to the left, following the sign to West Leg. Do not take the Girl Scout connector to the right. From here you can go straight into a quick climb or take the trail to the left for a more gradual climb. About a mile into the trail there is a steep drop, followed by a quick steep climb. At the crest of the hill follow the trail to the left along the ridge of the canyon and pass a huge rock.

Cross the dry wash and take the gradual climb to the right. Here the trail splits. Going left leads to a drop and quick climb. The trail to the right leads to a more gradual climb. The trails meet up just after another wash. Near the end of the trail you'll have to navigate a steep drop followed by a technical climb over a large rock. West Leg ends where there is a convergence of trails. Here you can see the upper dirt parking lot to your right and a large pole, complete with signs marking the trailheads of several trails. From here turn right and follow the trail as it heads down to the dirt road.

Follow the dirt road east as it heads farther up the hill. The East Leg trailhead is just to the east of the upper parking lot, on the south side of the dirt road. It can be found to the side of the road at the point where the road just starts another climb. The trail is marked with a small wood sign. Take the steep fast climb then follow the trail as it starts heading downhill.

Stay straight when the downhill trails cross the main trail. When the trail splits at about 1.1 miles, take the trail to the left if you choose to continue on the trail. The more technical section is about to start. A short distance ahead, do not take what appears to be an offshoot trail to the right. It is an illegal downhill section. Continue

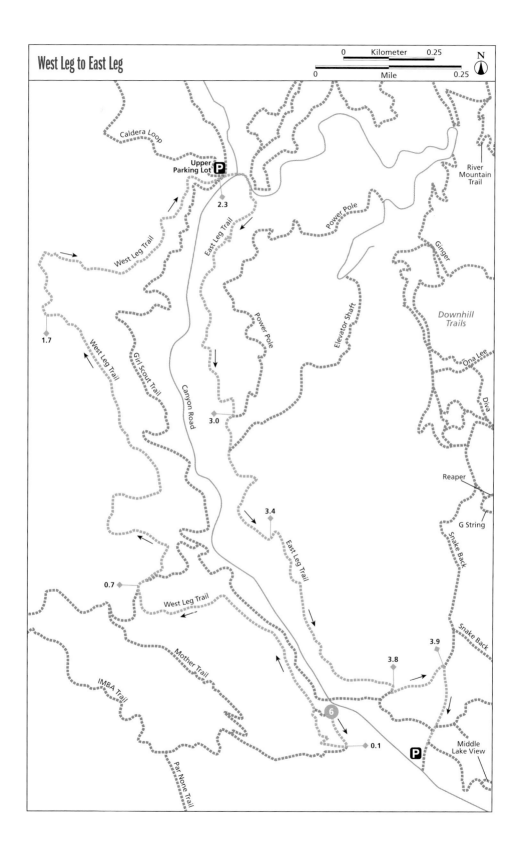

West Leg to East Leg

Caldera Loop

Upper Parking Lot **P**

2.3

West Leg Trail

East Leg Trail

Power Pole

River Mountain Trail

Ginger

Power Pole

Elevator Shaft

Downhill Trails

1.7

West Leg Trail

Girl Scout Trail

Canyon Road

Ona Lee

Diva

3.0

Reaper

G String

3.4

East Leg Trail

Snake Back

0.7

West Leg Trail

Snake Back

3.9

3.8

Mother Trail

IMBA Trail

6

0.1

P

Middle Lake View

Par None Trail

0   Kilometer   0.25

0   Mile   0.25

N

on the trail as it goes over a difficult rock obstacle, turns to the right and heads into another tricky rock section. Take a sharp left after the second rock obstacle.

At about 1.3 miles the trail appears to disappear. Climb up and over the rocks directly ahead of you, then pick up the trail on the other side of the rocks. When the more technical section ends, watch for the large rock jetting out into the trail. When the trail ends at the top of the hill, you'll be able to see the restrooms down the hill to the right. At this point you can follow just about any of the trails that lead down to the restrooms.

Miles and Directions

0.0 Start at the trailhead just to the left of the telephone pole. Take the trail to the left and climb a small hill.

0.1 When the trail splits, keep right, entering West Leg. The trail is clearly marked. Follow the trail left up and over the small hill. Continue straight when the trail seems to disappear. You'll see it about 10 feet ahead.

0.7 When the trail splits three ways, stay straight and connect with the trail ahead, then follow it right.

1.7 When the trail splits, take either trail. Left leads to a drop and quick climb. Right leads to a more gradual climb. The trails meet again after the wash.

1.9 The trail splits but meets up again at the crest of the small hill. The left trail is steeper than the right.

2.2 Take the steep drop followed by a tricky climb over a large rock. Then follow the trail to the convergence of trails. Turn right and follow the trail to the dirt road.

2.3 Follow the dirt road as it climbs up toward the hill. The trailhead to East Leg is to the right of the dirt road and southeast of the upper parking lot.

3.0 Stay straight when the Power Pole downhill trail meets the trail.

3.2 Continue straight when the trail crosses the Elevator Shaft downhill trail.

3.4 Take the trail left when the trails split. Alternatively: Follow the trail right, back down to the dirt road, leaving East Leg.

3.5 Do not take the offshoot trail to the right. Go over the difficult rock obstacle and follow the trail to the right. Take a sharp left after the second rock obstacle.

3.6 Climb over the rocks when the trail seems to disappear and enter a short, but technical downhill section.

3.9 At the top of the hill, take the sharp right turn and head back to the restrooms.

Ride Information

Local Events and Attractions

Blood, Sweat & Beers: This late-February event includes a 5K, 10K, half marathon, 30K, and marathon course. Races run in both the daylight and moonlight or you can compete in both in what is known as the Dirty Double; desertdash.com.

Ironman® 70.3 Silverman Triathlon: An annual race in October where competitors swim, bike, and run. The event starts at Lake Mead and finishes in Henderson; ironman.com.

Restaurants

Boulder Pit Stop: Best hamburgers in town; located a short distance from the trail; 802 Buchanan Blvd.; (720) 293-7080; boulderpitstop.com
Boulder Dam Brewing Company: Local brewery and restaurant started by Seattle native Todd Cook; 453 Nevada Way; (702) 243-2739; boulderdambrewing.com

7 Middle and Lower Lake View Loop

This trail is a fun ride for both beginner and intermediate riders, while still offering some great technical challenges for those with more advanced skills. The trail gets its name because of the great views it provides of the largest manmade lake in the United States—Lake Mead.

Start: Just behind and to the right of the restrooms at the entrance to Bootleg Canyon
Distance: 2.7 miles
Elevation gain: None
Riding time: Advanced riders, 45 minutes; intermediate riders, 1 hour; beginning riders 1.5 hours
Fitness effort: Physically moderate with some challenging areas
Difficulty: Technically moderate with some challenging technical spots, deep drops, and long continuous climbs

Terrain: Mostly dirt, some large rocks, and loose gravel—asphalt trail briefly crossed twice
Map: All Mountain Cyclery, allmountaincyclery .com
Nearest town: Boulder City
Other trail users: Hikers and runners; road bikers when asphalt trail is crossed, downhill riders when downhill trails are crossed.
Dog friendly: Yes
Trail contact: Boulder City; bcnv.org/ Facilities/Facility/Details/Bootleg-Canyon -Park-18

Getting there: Take U.S. Highway 93 toward the Hoover Dam (Boulder City). Bootleg Canyon is easily visible on the left-hand side of the road. It is marked by a large white "BC," which actually stands for Boulder City, not Bootleg Canyon. Turn left on Veteran's Memorial Drive and follow it to Canyon Road. Turn left on Canyon Road and follow it to the parking lot below the restrooms. The trailhead is just behind the restrooms. GPS: N35 58.020'/W114 51.712'
   Note: If the parking lot is full, you can park in the dirt lot just below the asphalt lot.

The Ride

The trail begins between several large rocks located just behind and to the right of the restrooms. The rocks have been placed there specifically to mark the trail. As you head down the hill and come around the bend, there is a large ditch, which is a remnant of the flight line that used to run from the top of the hill. Worried the dangling feet of their passengers would strike bike riders on the trail below, the creators of the flight line dug a ditch for the mountain bikers to ride into. Although the flight line on that particular hill is gone, the ditch remains. If you choose not to ride into the ditch, you can bypass it by taking the trail just to the right.

   Just a bit on the other side of the ditch, the trail splits into the Middle Lake View and the Lower Lake View, both of which are marked by small wood signs. Although the trail was designed to be ridden as presented in this guide, you can also take the loop counterclockwise following the Lower Lake View. Immediately after the sign, the trail takes the first of two deep drops. Once you've successfully navigated the

The view of Lake Mead that gives the Middle and Lower Lake View Loop its name

drops, the trail turns into a series of small hills and dips that are likely the best part of the ride. Here you can build up speed consistent with your particular skills.

The section ends with a fairly steep, but gradual climb that winds its way around the outside of the canyon, offering great views of the canyon walls on the left. Bootleg Canyon is quite scenic, it has some of the most unique colors of rocks in all of Nevada and biking here allows you to experience the beauty of the desert.

Not too far along the trail is another dip. While this drop is not steep, the climb on the other side is and it is also fairly technical. After the dip, follow the trail upward and around a hill to the final dip. This is probably the largest and most difficult of all the dips on the trail. Going downward, the trail splits in two and you can take either route. The key here is to build up momentum for the climb on the other side and to never stop pedaling once you reach that side. The climb consists of soft dirt and loose gravel and requires a certain amount of speed combined with continued pedaling to make it up the other side.

As you make your way down the trail, you'll approach a fork in the road. Here the trail splits into the Upper Lake View Trail and the Lower Lake View Trail. Keep to the right and begin a short, easy downhill section followed by a slight climb that, once completed, offers magnificent views of Lake Mead. Before the climb, the trail crosses the River Mountain Hiking Trail. This trail was created by the Civilian Conservation Corps (CCC) in the 1930s. It is now a hiking trail, not open to bikes and is clearly marked as such. Once you reach the top of the hill, you will have the best

LAKE MEAD

When the Mormons first ventured over the mountains in 1855, they found the grassy meadows that gave the Las Vegas Valley its name. They also found a powerful, meandering river that had traveled for thousands of miles, forming a "grand" American landmark on its way to Mexico. What they didn't find was a lake. In fact, that body of water wouldn't appear in the valley until almost 80 years later.

In the early 1930s the Unites States Department of the Interior built the first major dam to span the mighty Colorado River. Located in the Black Mountains just outside the small town of Boulder City, the Hoover Dam—named after then President Herbert Hoover—formed what would become the largest manmade lake in the United States. The lake, which is part of the Lake Mead National Recreation Area, has more than 550 miles of shoreline, a large portion of which is viewable by mountain bikers who ride the trails on the east side of Bootleg Canyon.

Modern Lake Mead is a popular destination for all types of water sports, fishermen, and people with both party and house boats. Because it is positioned along the north-south migration route, Lake Mead is home to more than 240 different kinds of birds. In addition, many other animals and reptiles call Lake Mead, and the area around Lake Mead, home.

view of Lake Mead from the trail. You can also see Boulder City which spreads out in the valley below.

Follow the trail down the hill into the desert valley below Bootleg Canyon. This portion of the trail is not as technical as the Middle Lake View trail, but it still offers a steady climb out of the desert valley back up to the canyon. Because the Lower Lake View trail is relatively easy to ride, it provides an opportunity to take in the views of the desert fauna and the unique rock colors of reds, purple, and orange which make up the canyon floor and walls.

As the trail progresses, it crosses the River Mountain Loop Trail. This trail is easily recognized because it is asphalt. Crossing the asphalt takes you to a bit of a climb on some dark red clay. Once you complete the first part of the climb, turn to the right and keep climbing. You will cross the River Mountain Loop Trail a second time and head toward a graded area. From here it appears as if the trail may have disappeared. Fear not, if you simply look up the large steep climb on the other side of the grade, you will see the trail again just to the left. Once you've connected back to the main trail, follow it to the trailhead.

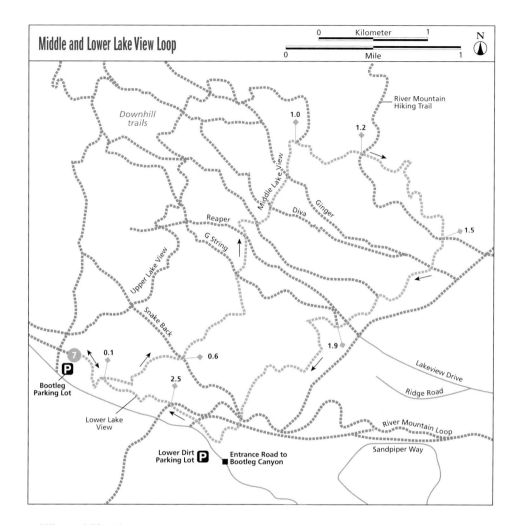

Middle and Lower Lake View Loop

Downhill trails

River Mountain Hiking Trail

1.0

1.2

Middle Lake View

Diva

Ginger

Reaper

1.5

G String

Upper Lake View

Snake Back

1.9

7

0.1

0.6

Lakeview Drive

P

2.5

Ridge Road

Bootleg Parking Lot

Lower Lake View

River Mountain Loop

Lower Dirt Parking Lot **P**

Entrance Road to Bootleg Canyon

Sandpiper Way

Miles and Directions

0.0 Start at the trailhead just behind and to the right of the restrooms. Head down the first incline to the right. When the trail forks, stay left. Going right leads to a jump.

0.1 Stay left when the trail splits into the Middle and Lower Lake View. Both trails are clearly marked.

0.2 Take a sharp left turn. Cross the Snake Back downhill trail. Yield to downhillers.

0.3 Go down the second big dip. Cross the G String downhill trail. In 0.3 mile cross the Reaper downhill trail.

0.7 Go down the big dip, then cross the Diva downhill trail. In 0.1 mile, cross the Ginger downhill trail.

1.0 The trail forks into the Upper and Lower Lake View trails. Stay right and begin a slight descent before another climb.

1.2 Cross the River Mountain Hiking Trail (no bikes allowed). Stay straight and climb the hill.

1.5 Take the trail right. Do not follow the trail marked by the Malaga and Marina Drives sign. Shortly ahead cross the River Mountain Hiking Trail again. In 0.1 mile, cross the downhill trail.

1.8 Cross another downhill trail and do so again in about 6 feet. Take the left turn into the dip then cross the dirt road.

1.9 Take the quick climb up and to the right. Stay right and continue climbing when the trail meets up with a downhill trail. You will be sharing the downhill trail for a few feet.

2.1 Go over a small wooden bridge. In 0.1 mile, go down the big dip.

2.3 Cross another downhill trail. Stay straight and cross the paved River Mountain Loop trail. Go straight and head into a steep climb.

2.5 Cross the River Mountain Loop again. Then cross the grade, heading slightly to the left and climb the steep hill. Pick up the trail at the top of the hill.

2.7 The Middle and Lower Lake View trails meet. Take the trail to the left and follow it back to the restrooms.

Ride Information

Local Events and Attractions

Zipline Bootleg Canyon: If you don't want to see the canyon by trails, you might want to see it by air. This can be done through a series of ziplines positioned on the east side of the canyon; flightlinezbootleg.com.

Art in the Park: In this early-October event, more than 300 artists and crafters display and sell their work; bchcares.org/foundation.

Restaurants

Boulder Dam Brewing Company: Local brewery and restaurant started by Seattle native Todd Cook; 453 Nevada Way; (702) 243-2739; boulderdambrewing.com

Milo's Cellar: Sidewalk cafe and wine bar; 538 Nevada Way; (702) 293-9540; milos winebar.com

8 Middle and Upper Lake View Loop

Like the Middle and Lower Lake View Loop, this trail gets its name because of the great views it provides of Lake Mead, the largest manmade lake in the Unites States. Unlike the Middle and Upper Lake View Loop, this trail is a bit more technically challenging as it heads high up into the canyon walls.

Start: Just behind and to the right of the restrooms at the entrance to Bootleg Canyon
Distance: 2.4 miles
Elevation gain: 216 feet
Riding time: Advanced riders, 45 minutes; intermediate riders, 1 hour; beginning riders 1.5 hours
Fitness effort: Physically moderate with some challenging areas
Difficulty: Technically moderate with some challenging technical spots, deep drops, and long continuous climbs

Terrain: Mostly dirt, some large rocks, and loose gravel—asphalt trail briefly crossed twice
Map: All Mountain Cyclery, allmountaincyclery .com
Nearest town: Boulder City
Other trail users: Hikers and runners; road bikers when asphalt trail is crossed, downhill riders when downhill trails are crossed.
Dog friendly: Yes
Trail contact: Boulder City; bcnv.org/ Facilities/Facility/Details/Bootleg-Canyon -Park-18

Getting there: Take U.S. Highway 93 toward the Hoover Dam (Boulder City). Bootleg Canyon is easily visible on the left-hand side of the road. It is marked by a large white "BC," which actually stands for Boulder City, not Bootleg Canyon. Turn left on Veteran's Memorial Drive and follow it to Canyon Road. Turn left on Canyon Road and follow it to the parking lot below the restrooms. The trailhead is just behind the restrooms. GPS: N35 58.020'/W114 51.712'

Note: If the parking lot is full, you can park in the dirt lot just below the asphalt lot.

The Ride

The trail begins between the large rocks located just behind and to the right of the restrooms. The rocks have been placed there specifically to mark the trail. Once you start down the first hill, stay to the right until you go over the next little hill. After you reach the top of the small hill, keep to the left. Going to the right leads to a fairly difficult jump—one that can cause injury if missed and should only be attempted by riders with advanced skills. As you come around the bend, there is a large ditch, which is a remnant of the flight line that used to run from the top of the hill.

Just a little way on the other side of the ditch the trail splits into the Middle Lake View and the Lower Lake View, both of which are marked by small wood signs. Stay to the left. Immediately after the sign, the trail takes the first of two deep dips. As the trail progresses, there are many places where downhill trails cross the main trail. It's easy to tell which trail is which, so there isn't much reason to worry about getting on the wrong trail. Once you've successfully navigated the two dips, the trail turns into a series of small hills and dips that are likely the best part of the ride.

Not too far along, the trail comes to another dip. While this drop is not steep, the climb on the other side is and it is also fairly technical. After the dip, follow the trail upward and around a hill to the final dip. This is probably the largest and most difficult of all the dips on the trail. The key here is to build up momentum for the climb on the other side and to never stop pedaling once you reach that side.

As you make your way down the trail, you'll approach a fork in the road. Here the trail splits into the Upper Lake View Trail and the Lower Lake View Trail. Take the trail to the left at the small wood sign. Follow the trail into a gradual drop followed by a long gradual climb and a turn to the right. Just as with the Middle Lake View Trail, many downhill trails cross the Upper Lake View Trail at different points in the ride. It is easy to tell which trail is downhill and which is the main trail, so just stay on the main trail. But be sure to watch for riders coming down the downhill trails.

The trail takes several dips and turns as it makes its way up the side of the hill and then heads downward into the valley. You'll go in and out of several washes and areas full of loose rocks. Towards the end of the ride, you'll enter a series of drops and

Quinn Winter takes a jump along the Middle and Upper Lake View Loop.
JIM LAURIE PHOTOGRAPHY

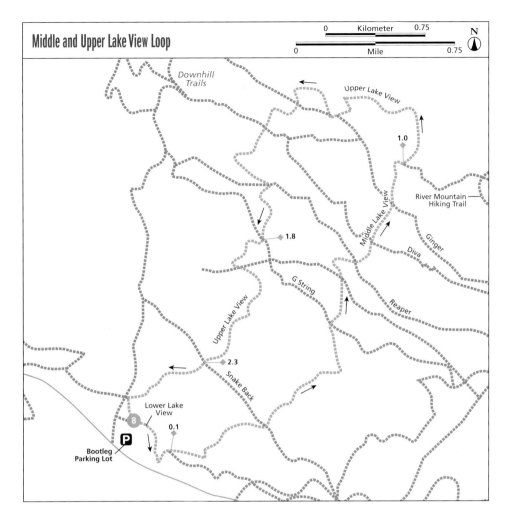

Middle and Upper Lake View Loop

Downhill Trails

Upper Lake View

1.0

River Mountain Hiking Trail

Middle Lake View

Ginger

Diva

1.8

G String

Upper Lake View

Reaper

2.3

Snake Back

Lower Lake View

8

0.1

P

Bootleg Parking Lot

N

0   Kilometer   0.75

0   Mile   0.75

climbs before entering another downhill section along the crest of a hill. At about 2.2 miles into the ride the Upper Lake View Trail crosses another downhill trail. Stay straight and take the gradual drop, followed by a steep climb. When the trail crosses another downhill trail, stay straight. The trailhead is a short distance ahead. Follow the trail to the left, then take the offshoot trail to the right. Go to the left of the jump, or if you wish, take the jump as you head to the restrooms and the trailhead.

Miles and Directions

0.0   Start at the trailhead just behind and to the right of the restrooms. Head down the first incline to the right. When the trail forks, stay to the left. Going right leads to a jump.

0.1   Stay left when the trail splits into the Middle and Lower Lake Views. Both trails are clearly marked.

0.2 Cross the Snake Back downhill trail. Yield to downhillers. In 0.1 mile cross another downhill trail. Repeat in 0.3 and 0.4 mile.

0.8 Take the big dip, then cross the Diva downhill trail.

1.0 Stay left when the trail forks into the Upper and Lower Lake View trails. In 0.3 mile, cross another downhill trail.

1.4 Cross the wash, then follow the trail left before crossing the downhill trail a third time. In about 0.1 mile, cross another downhill trail.

1.8 Cross the downhill trail at the large rock obstacle.

2.2 Take the steep, rocky drop into the wash, then climb out and cross another downhill trail. Cross another downhill trail in 0.1 mile.

2.4 Follow the trail to the left and arrive at the trailhead.

Ride Information

Local Events and Attractions

Zipline Bootleg Canyon: If you don't want to see the canyon by trails, you might want to see it by air. This can be done through a series of ziplines positioned on the east side of the canyon; flightlinezbootleg.com.

Nevada Southern Railway: Visitors sit in a passenger train, riding the rails used to build the Hoover Dam on a free 10-minute ride; nevadasouthern.com.

Restaurants

Boulder Pit Stop: Best hamburgers in town; located a short distance from the trail; 802 Buchanan Blvd.; (720) 293-7080; boulderpitstop.com

Boulder Dam Brewing Company: Local brewery and restaurant started by Seattle native Todd Cook; 453 Nevada Way; (702) 243-2739; boulderdambrewing.com

9 Lower and Upper Lake View Loop

As mentioned elsewhere in this guide, riding a trail in the opposite direction of the "normal" route can often expose you to an entirely different ride. The Lower Lake View Trail is probably one of the best examples of this. The trail was designed to be ridden clockwise, making it an easy, mostly downhill ride, followed by a gradual easy climb across the valley and back up to the trailhead. However, if you ride the trail counterclockwise, the trail turns from an easy trail to a moderate trail, mainly because what was once a downhill trail off the back of a rather high hill, is now a long steep climb up that same hill, switching the easy status to moderate. Now combine that trail with the already difficult Upper Lake View Trail and you have a great, challenging trail.

Start: Just behind and to the right of the restrooms at the entrance to Bootleg Canyon
Distance: 3.4 miles
Elevation gain: 216 feet
Riding time: Advanced riders, 1.5 hours; intermediate riders, 2 hours
Fitness effort: Physically moderate to challenging with some very challenging climbs
Difficulty: Technically moderate with some challenging technical spots and long continuous climbs

Terrain: Mostly dirt, some large rocks, and loose gravel—asphalt trail briefly crossed twice
Map: All Mountain Cyclery, allmountaincyclery.com
Nearest town: Boulder City
Other trail users: Hikers and runners; road bikers when asphalt trail is crossed, downhill riders when downhill trails are crossed.
Dog friendly: Yes
Trail contact: Boulder City; bcnv.org/Facilities/Facility/Details/Bootleg-Canyon-Park-18

Getting there: Take U.S. Highway 93 toward the Hoover Dam (Boulder City). Bootleg Canyon is easily visible on the left-hand side of the road. It is marked by a large white "BC," which actually stands for Boulder City, not Bootleg Canyon. Turn left on Veteran's Memorial Drive and follow it to Canyon Road. Turn left on Canyon Road and follow it to the parking lot below the restrooms. The trailhead is just behind the restrooms. GPS: N35 58.020'/W114 51.712'
Note: If the parking lot is full, you can park in the dirt lot just below the asphalt lot.

The Ride

The trail begins between the large rocks located just behind and to the right of the restrooms. The rocks have been placed there specifically to mark the trail. Once you start down the first hill, stay to the right until you go over the next little hill. After you reach the top of the small hill, keep to the left. Going to the right leads to a fairly difficult jump—one that can cause injury if missed and should only be attempted by riders with advanced skills. As you come around the bend, there is a large ditch, which is a remnant of the flight line that used to run from the top of the hill.

Rider heading along the Lower Lake View Loop Jim Laurie Photography

Just a little way on the other side of the ditch the trail splits into the Middle Lake View and the Lower Lake View, both of which are marked by small wood signs. Take the Lower Lake View Trail to the right as it drops into the wash and up a small hill on the other side. At this point the trail snakes its way down into the valley floor and will eventually follow that floor awhile before climbing back up into the canyon. This portion of the trail is a nice easy ride, mostly downhill, before you get to the long steep climb.

Right where the trail seems to abruptly end, it drops down into a graded area. Looking across the graded area toward the yield sign to the left will bring the trail back into view. Cross the grade and pick up the trail on the other side. Follow the trail before taking the short drop and crossing the paved trail. This is the River Mountain Loop Trail and you will be crossing it again a short distance ahead. After crossing the River Mountain Loop Trail a second time, climb the quick hill on the other side, then stay to the right when the trail splits. The trail on the left is a downhill trail, so be sure to look upward to make sure no downhill riders are coming down the trail. Remember, it is not as easy for them to stop because they are usually traveling very fast. You will cross a series of downhill trails as you travel along both the Lower and Upper Lake View trails. Stay straight every time this occurs.

Follow the trail as it snakes across the valley. When the trail intersects a narrow gravely wash, continue straight. This wash is the River Mountain Hiking Trail and is marked by signs on the right. The hiking trail is open only to hikers, so do not take this trail. You will be crossing the trail again on the other side of the hill.

Shortly after crossing the hiking trail, you'll start the long steep climb up the side of the hill. Follow the trail left at the Malaga Drive and Marina Drive sign. At the top of the hill the trail takes a hairpin turn to the left at the front edge of the hill. Here you get a great view of Lake Mead. The trail heads back toward the canyon before turning right and heading into a short downhill section. At the bottom of the hill, cross the River Mountain Hiking Trail a second time, then begin a climb up into the hills.

At about 2 miles into the ride, the Lower, Middle, and Upper Lake View Trails meet. Take the trail to the right at the small wood sign. Follow the trail into a gradual drop followed by a long gradual climb. You will be climbing up into the canyon walls before eventually heading downward in and out of washes and dips as the trail follows the foothills leading to the trailhead.

At about 3.2 miles into the ride, the Upper Lake View Trail crosses one of the many downhill trails. Stay straight and take the gradual drop, followed by a steep climb. When the trail crosses another downhill trail, stay straight. The trailhead is a short distance ahead. Follow the trail to the left, then take the offshoot trail to the right. Go to the left of the jump, or if you wish, take the jump as you head to the restrooms and the trailhead.

Miles and Directions

0.0 Start at the trailhead just behind and to the right of the restrooms. Head down the first incline to the right. When the trail forks, stay to the left. Going right leads to a jump.

0.1 Stay right when the trail splits into the Middle and Lower Lake Views. Both trails are clearly marked.

0.3 When the trail seems to disappear, take the steep drop and cross the graded area, picking the trail up near the yield sign. Then cross the paved River Mountain Loop Trail.

0.5 Head around the small hill and drop into an area with dark red dirt. Take the sharp left turn and cross the paved River Mountain Loop Trail again.

0.6 Stay right when the trail splits. The trail to the left is the Snake Back downhill trail.

0.8 Cross the small wood bridge and follow the trail into a quick drop and steep climb.

1.2 Follow the trail into a short downhill section. You will be sharing the trail with a downhill trail. At the end of the section take the trail to the left. The downhill trail continues straight.

1.4 Stay straight when the trail intersects with the River Mountain Hiking Trail, then begin a gradual climb.

1.5 Follow the trail left at the Malaga Drive and Marina Drive sign and start the long steep climb.

1.8 Cross the River Mountain Hiking Trail again and begin a gradual climb back toward the canyon.

2.0 Stay right when the Middle, Upper, and Lower Lake View Trails meet.

2.3 Cross the Ginger downhill trail, then head to the right and cross the same downhill trail. In 0.1 mile cross Ginger a third time. In another 0.1 mile, cross the Diva downhill trail.

2.8 Cross the Reaper downhill trail at the large rock obstacle.

3.2 Take the steep, rocky drop into the wash, then climb out and cross the Snake Back downhill trail. In 0.1 mile, cross another downhill trail.

3.4 Follow the trail to the left and arrive at the trailhead.

Ride Information

Local Events and Attractions

Zipline Bootleg Canyon: If you don't want to see the canyon by trails, you might want to see it by air. This can be done through a series of ziplines positioned on the east side of the canyon; flightlinezbootleg.com.

Nevada Southern Railway: Visitors sit in a passenger train, riding the rails used to build the Hoover Dam on a free 10-minute ride; nevadasouthern.com.

Restaurants

Boulder Pit Stop: Best hamburgers in town; located a short distance from the trail; 802 Buchanan Blvd.; (720) 293-7080; boulderpitstop.com

Boulder Dam Brewing Company: Local brewery and restaurant started by Seattle native Todd Cook; 453 Nevada Way; (702) 243-2739; boulderdambrewing.com

10 POW/Par None/IMBA Loop

The POW/Par None/IMBA Loop, commonly called the POW Loop, is actually a combination of three trails that together form a loop through the western outskirts of Bootleg Canyon. Because this ride is not in the canyon area, the terrain is mainly flat with only small hilly areas. Unlike many of the other rides in Bootleg Canyon, this loop does not have difficult rock obstacles or large drops. This makes it a perfect trail for beginning to intermediate riders.

Start: The large rocks just off Veteran's Drive

Distance: 3.7 miles

Elevation gain: None

Riding time: Advanced riders, 45 minutes; intermediate riders, 1 hour; beginning riders, 1.5 hours

Fitness effort: Physically easy to moderate with half the trail being a slow steady climb and half being downhill

Difficulty: Technically easy to moderate with a tricky switchback climb up a steep hill

Terrain: Mostly dirt, some large rocks, and loose gravel—asphalt trail crossed twice

Map: All Mountain Cyclery, allmountaincyclery.com

Nearest town: Boulder City

Other trail users: Hikers and runners, road bikes when the trail crosses the asphalt trail

Dog friendly: Yes

Trail contact: Boulder City; bcnv.org/Facilities/Facility/Details/Bootleg-Canyon-Park-18

Getting there: Take U.S. Highway 93 toward the Hoover Dam (Boulder City). Bootleg Canyon is easily visible on the left-hand side of the road. It is marked by a large white "BC," which actually stands for Boulder City, not Bootleg Canyon. Turn left on Veteran's Memorial Drive and take the first left onto Veteran's Drive. Drive down to the large rock formation which is the trailhead. GPS: N35 58.185'/W114 52.489'

The Ride

The ride starts at an area commonly referred to as "Stonehenge," which is a formation of large rocks that have been arranged in a large circle and stood on their ends, giving them height. There is also a kiosk that houses a map of the trail and advertisements for upcoming events—usually mountain bike races. The map is a little old and can be confusing so it is best to follow the map provided in this guide. The loop is single track the entire way and it is nearly impossible to get lost. The dirt area in front of and just to the right of the rocks is for parking. The River Mountain Loop Trail, which is an asphalt trail, meanders through the hills. This trail, used mainly by road bikers and runners, is crossed briefly on both the climb and the downhill portions of the ride.

Take the trail just to the right of the rock formation to start the POW trail. About halfway up the trail you'll cross the asphalt River Mountain Loop Trail. Watch for people or road bikes on the trail when you cross. At the foot of the hill, you'll travel through a section of lava rocks as you wind around a small hill. Behind that hill the

A biker and her dog head down the POW Trail.

trail splits. Stay to the right and continue straight, beginning the Par None section of the loop. The trail to the left is actually the POW trail and is where the downhill section of the loop meets back with the trail.

Follow the Par None trail as you make your way upward towards the mouth of Bootleg Canyon, but not into the canyon. About 1.1 miles into the ride you'll enter a gravely area that looks like a large wash. It is in this area that desert tortoises are often seen crossing the road. If you encounter one of these animals, do not move or touch it. Doing so can cause the tortoise to urinate, releasing precious water that it may not be able to get back and an animal in a desert without water will die.

About 1.3 miles into the ride there is a steep hill that is navigated through a series of tight switchbacks. On the other side of the hill, the trail comes to a T. This is the end of the Par None as it intersects with the IMBA trail. Both the Par None and IMBA trails are marked with small wood signs. Take the IMBA trail to the left. This portion of the IMBA trail is still a gradual climb for the first part. Once the top of the climb is reached, you'll enter a small downhill section made up of small hills and valleys as it winds its way to the longer downhill section.

BATS AND TARANTULAS

The trails in Bootleg Canyon can be enjoyed both during the day and in the evening hours, although evening rides requires bike- or rider-mounted lights. If you choose to ride during the evening hours, especially at dust, it is not uncommon to see bats flying around high in the air, following you as you ride. There are many species of bats in Bootleg Canyon. Most are small, with bodies typically 3 to 4 inches long. They fly around in what seems to be erratic patterns as they use echolocation to receive signals that paint a picture of their environment. Don't worry about these creatures of the night. They are simply looking for a free meal. Bats are insectivorous, meaning they only eat insects, something they typically do while in flight, right above your head. In fact, bats most likely follow cyclists because the bike stirs up insects and it is an interesting experience being followed by bats as one rides.

Another creature of the night, the desert tarantula, can be seen not in the sky above, but on the trail itself. While they are relatively harmless, it is best to avoid contact with these furry insects. Desert tarantulas are fairly large, 5 inches in most cases. Both males and females are brown; however, males tend to have black legs. While tarantulas will usually leave you alone, they will passionately defend their territory if disturbed. And while they are venomous, their bite is most often compared to that of a bee sting. Just be thankful you're not a male tarantula. After mating, the female sometimes catches and eats the male. Maybe he should have brought chocolates.

When riding on this portion of the trail, pay attention to the scenery. Bootleg Canyon is filled with a kaleidoscope of some of the most beautiful rocks in the entire valley. Here you can see black lava rocks, as well as rocks in colors of purple, pink, yellow, orange, red, brown, and even blue. The colors are simply stunning! It is also not uncommon in this area to see many of the animals that call the canyon their home. It is not uncommon to see big horn sheep, rabbits, ground squirrels, and many, many lizards—which love to run across the road in front of you. It is also not uncommon to see or hear rattlesnakes in this area. While they typically do not go on the trail, they can and it is wise to keep an eye open for these reptiles.

You begin the downhill section by taking the POW trail to the left about 2.2 miles into the ride. The trail is clearly marked with a wood sign. More experienced riders may want to let go and enjoy a fun, fast ride that can take as little as 10 minutes to complete. It is easy to pick up speed here, so be careful. As you get out of the hills back into the valley, you'll go between two large rocks before meeting back up with Par None. You can make another loop by taking the trail to the left and retracing the path you followed to the IMBA trail and eventually the POW trail. If you want to complete the loop, stay to the right and continue down the trail you climbed at the beginning of the ride, eventually ending exactly where you started at the Stonehenge rock formation.

Miles and Directions

0.0 Start at the trailhead just to the right of the rock formation. Follow the trail as it climbs up into the valley.

0.6 Take the Par None Trail to the right when the trail splits.

1.0 Follow the trail into a short downhill section. Stay left when the trail splits in 0.1 mile and keep climbing.

1.3 Follow the trail into a steep climb up a hill. This climb has switchbacks with sharp turns.

1.5 Follow the trail onto a short downhill section on the other side of the hill. When the trail splits, take the IMBA Trail to the left.

2.2 Turn left onto the POW Trail and take the two quick drops into the downhill section. Be careful as you can build up quite a bit of speed.

2.9 Keep right as the trail splits. The trail to the left is the older trail and is more difficult to ride. The trails will connect again in 25 feet. Cross the wash and follow the trail up the side of the hill. This section is rocky and has some tricky parts.

3.1 Follow the POW Trail to the right. The trail to the left is Par None.

3.7 Arrive back at the trailhead.

Ride Information

Local Events and Attractions

Art in the Park: In this early-October event, more than 300 artists and crafters display and sell their work; bchcares.org/foundation.

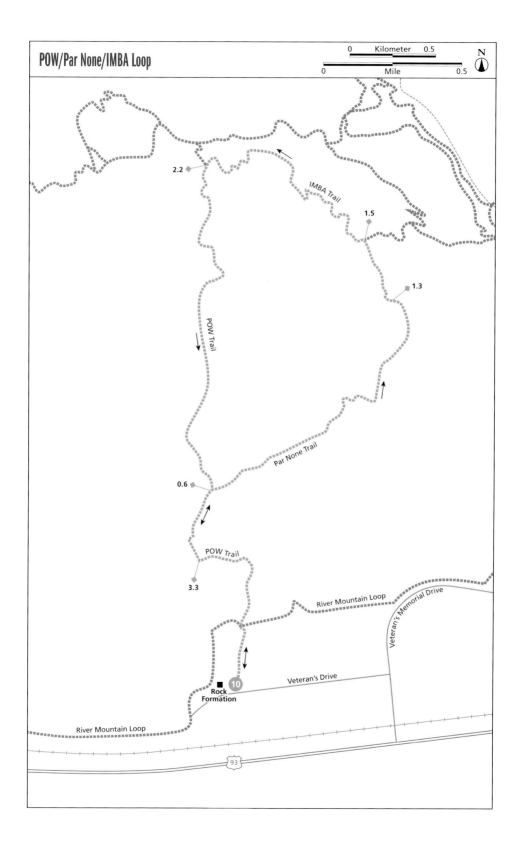

POW/Par None/IMBA Loop

0 Kilometer 0.5

0 Mile 0.5

N

2.2

IMBA Trail

1.5

1.3

POW Trail

Par None Trail

0.6

POW Trail

3.3

River Mountain Loop

Veteran's Memorial Drive

Veteran's Drive

10

Rock
Formation

River Mountain Loop

93

Boulder City-Hoover Dam Museum: Located in the historic Boulder Dam Hotel, this museum tells the story of the dam and the city it created; bcmha.org.

Restaurants

Boulder Pit Stop: Best hamburgers in town; located a short distance from the trail; 802 Buchanan Blvd.; (720) 293-7080; boulderpitstop.com

Grandma Daisy's: Candy and ice cream parlor, featuring candy made on the premises; 530 Nevada Way; (702) 294-6639; grandmadaisys.com

11 IMBA/POW/Par None Loop

The IMBA/POW/Par None Loop is another version of the POW/Par None/ IMBA ride. The main difference is the starting and ending point. This version of the trail also eliminates the long initial climb; however, when you ride the loop this way, there is a little bit of climbing to do after the fun downhill section. Still, this version presents a new way of looking at the trail—one that gives you an entirely new perspective of a fun ride.

Start: The parking lot below the restrooms at the entrance to Bootleg Canyon
Distance: 3.7 miles
Elevation gain: 346 feet
Riding time: Advanced riders, 45 minutes; intermediate riders, 1 hour; beginning riders, 1.5 hours
Fitness effort: Physically easy to moderate with half the trail being a slow steady climb and half being downhill
Difficulty: Technically easy to moderate with a tricky switchback climb up a steep hill

Terrain: Mostly dirt, some large rocks, and loose gravel
Map: All Mountain Cyclery, allmountaincyclery .com
Nearest town: Boulder City
Other trail users: Hikers and runners
Dog friendly: Yes
Trail contact: Boulder City; bcnv.org/ Facilities/Facility/Details/Bootleg-Canyon -Park-18

Getting there: Take U.S. Highway 93 toward the Hoover Dam (Boulder City). Bootleg Canyon is easily visible on the left-hand side of the road. It is marked by a large white "BC," which actually stands for Boulder City, not Bootleg Canyon. Turn left on Veteran's Memorial Drive and follow it to Canyon Road. Turn left on Canyon Road and follow it to the parking lot below the restrooms. Park here and then ride your bike up that dirt road to the first telephone pole on the left. You'll see the trailhead by the telephone pole. GPS: N35 59.119'/W114 51.882'
   Note: If the parking lot is full, you can park in the dirt lot just below the asphalt lot.

The Ride

The IMBA/POW/Par None Loop begins by heading up the dirt road to the trailhead. The entrance can easily be seen to the left of the road at just about where the telephone pole and the road meet. You'll see the point where the trail cuts out from the road. Take that trail to the left up the short climb. Once at the crest of the short hill, the trail splits into two. West Leg is the trail to the right, the trail to the left leads to Mother. Both trails are clearly marked. Take the trail to the left.

A short distance ahead you'll encounter a tricky rock section; after that the trail heads into a nice, easy section that is slightly rocky and complete with small climbs and dips. When the trail splits a second time at 0.3 mile, continue straight, which is the IMBA trail. Mother is the trail on the right and is clearly marked by a small

A biker making his way down the IMBA Trail

wood sign. Head into a short, but fun downhill section complete with mogul-style climbs and dips, followed by a long gradual climb. About a half mile in, the IMBA trail meets the Par None Trail. Stay straight and continue on the IMBA trail. You will be riding up the Par None trail as you complete the loop. Both the Par None and IMBA trails are marked with small wood signs. This portion of the IMBA trail is still a gradual climb for the first part. Once the top of the climb is reached, you'll enter a small downhill section made up of small hills and valleys as it winds its way to the longer downhill section.

Begin the downhill section by taking the POW trail to the left about 1.2 miles into the ride. The trail is clearly marked with a wood sign. After taking the trail to the left, go down two series of drops, with the second more gradual than the first. This portion of the loop has some tricky areas at the beginning, but nothing that can't be navigated by simply slowing down. However, if you're more experienced, you may want to let go and enjoy a fun, fast ride that can take as little as 10 minutes to complete. It is easy to pick up speed here, so be careful. As you get out of the hills back into the valley, you'll go between two large rocks before meeting back up with Par None. When the two trails meet, follow the trail to the left and head onto Par None.

Follow the Par None trail as you make your way upward towards the mouth of Bootleg Canyon, but not into the canyon. About 2.8 miles into the ride, there is a steep hill that is navigated through a series of tight switchbacks. This is probably the more difficult section of the climb. The hill is steep and the switchbacks are sharp. On the other side of the hill, the trail comes to a T. This is the end of the Par None as it

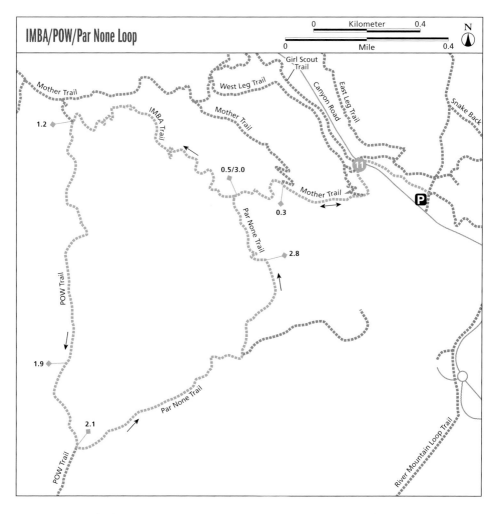

0   Kilometer   0.4

0   Mile   0.4

N

intersects with the IMBA trail. Both the Par None and IMBA trails are marked with small wood signs. Take the IMBA trail to the right and head back to the trailhead.

Miles and Directions

0.0   Start at the trailhead just to the left of the telephone pole. Take the trail left and climb the small hill.

0.1   When the trail splits keep left, entering Mother. The trail is clearly marked. Follow the trail into a tricky rock obstacle and then straight for a short distance.

0.2   Take a short drop and then continue the climb. Stay straight in 0.1 mile when the trail splits. A small wood sign marks the IMBA trail.

0.5   Continue straight when the trails split again. Do not take the Par None trail on the left.

1.2   Turn left onto the POW Trail and take the two quick drops into the downhill section. Be careful as you can build up quite a bit of speed.

2.0 Follow the trail over a small rock section and along the side of the hill, eventually going between two large rocks. In 0.1 mile, take the trail to the left, following the Par None Trail. The trail to the right is POW.

2.8 Follow the trail into a steep climb up a hill. This climb has switchbacks with sharp turns.

3.0 Follow the trail onto a short downhill section on the other side of the hill. When the trail splits, take the IMBA Trail to the right.

3.7 Arrive back at the trailhead.

Ride Information

Local Events and Attractions

Art in the Park: In this early-October event, more than 300 artists and crafters display and sell their work; bchcares.org/foundation.

Boulder City–Hoover Dam Museum: Located in the historic Boulder Dam Hotel, this museum tells the story of the dam and the city it created; bcmha.org.

Restaurants

Boulder Pit Stop: Best hamburgers in town; located a short distance from the trail; 802 Buchanan Blvd.; (720) 293–7080; boulderpitstop.com

Grandma Daisy's: Candy and ice cream parlor, featuring candy made on the premises; 530 Nevada Way; (702) 294–6639; grandmadaisys.com

12 Mother/POW Loop

This ride is a combination of trails that is a great ride for intermediate to advanced riders as it offers technical challenges sandwiched between some fun fast sections. It starts with Mother—the first trail in Bootleg Canyon—which is a black diamond, or technically difficult trail. From here you head into a fun, fast downhill section, were you can go as fast as your skills will let you. At the end of the downhill section, you'll make your way to the Par None Trail, which is a gradual climb, complete with a few drops and a steep, switchback climb up the side of a large hill. From there you'll turn onto the IMBA trail and head back to the trailhead, forming a technically challenging loop.

Start: The parking lot below the restrooms at the entrance to Bootleg Canyon
Distance: 3.7 miles
Elevation gain: 544 feet
Riding time: Advanced riders, 1 hour; intermediate riders, 1.5 hours
Fitness effort: Physically challenging due to steep climbs and rocky, technical spots
Difficulty: Technically challenging with very rocky spots, much climbing, and some very steep drops

Terrain: Mostly dirt, large rocks, and loose gravel
Map: All Mountain Cyclery, allmountaincyclery.com
Nearest town: Boulder City
Other trail users: Hikers and runners
Dog friendly: Yes
Trail contact: Boulder City; bcnv.org/Facilities/Facility/Details/Bootleg-Canyon-Park-18

Getting there: Take U.S. Highway 93 toward the Hoover Dam (Boulder City). Bootleg Canyon is easily visible on the left-hand side of the road. It is marked by a large white "BC," which actually stands for Boulder City, not Bootleg Canyon. Turn left on Veteran's Memorial Drive and follow it to Canyon Road. Turn left on Canyon Road and follow it to the parking lot below the restrooms. Park here and then ride your bike up that dirt road to the first telephone pole on the left. You'll see the trailhead by the telephone pole. GPS: N35 59.119'/ W114 51.882'
   Note: If the parking lot is full, you can park in the dirt lot just below the asphalt lot.

The Ride

Mother begins by heading up the dirt road to the trailhead. The entrance can easily be seen to the left of the road at just about where the telephone pole and the road meet. You'll see the point where the trail cuts out from the road. Take that trail to the left up the short climb. Once at the crest of the short hill, the trail splits into two. Mother is the trail to the left; the trail to the right is West Leg. Both trails are clearly marked.

   When the trail splits a second time at 0.3 mile, take the trail to the right. Going straight will put you on the (IMBA) trail. Mother is also clearly marked here by a

A group of riders heading down the Mother Trail

small wood sign. From this point you begin a fairly steep, rocky climb into several tight switchbacks leading into drops. After the drops, follow the trail as it continues its steep and rocky climb up into the outer walls of the canyon. At 0.8 mile, stay straight when the trails meet at the end of the climb. Do not take the trail to the right. It leads to a section called the saddle, which eventually connects with West Leg.

Almost a mile into the ride, the trail enters a tricky downhill section known as the Three Sisters. The dirt trail disappears at this point and is replaced by rock. This section follows all the way down through the Three Sisters until the trail turns back into dirt. At the end of the Three Sisters is a technically difficult drop. When the trail splits, take the trail to the left and start a downhill switchback section.

When the IMBA and POW trails meet, take the POW trail to the right. The trail is clearly marked with a wood sign. Go down two successive drops, with the second more gradual than the first. You may want to let go and enjoy a fun, fast ride that can take as little as 10 minutes to complete. As you get out of the hills back into the valley, you'll go between two large rocks before meeting up with Par None. When the two trails meet, follow the trail to the left and head onto Par None.

Follow the Par None trail as you make your way upward towards the mouth of Bootleg Canyon. About 2.8 miles into the ride, there is a steep hill that is navigated through a series of tight switchbacks. This is probably the more difficult section of the climb. The hill is steep and the switchbacks are sharp. On the other side of the hill, the trail comes to a T. This is the end of the Par None as it intersects with the IMBA

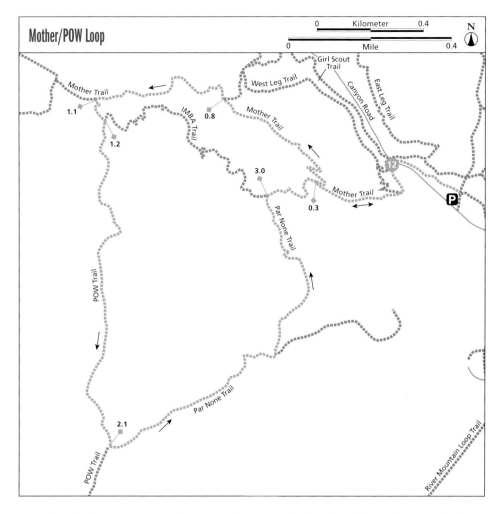

Mother Trail
1.1
1.2
IMBA Trail
West Leg Trail
0.8
Mother Trail
Girl Scout Trail
Canyon Road
East Leg Trail
3.0
Mother Trail
0.3
Par None Trail
POW Trail
Par None Trail
2.1
POW Trail
River Mountain Loop Trail

0   Kilometer   0.4
0   Mile   0.4
N

12
P

trail. Both the Par None and IMBA trails are marked with small wood signs. Take the IMBA trail to the right and head back to the trailhead.

Miles and Directions

0.0   Start at the trailhead just to the left of the telephone pole. Take the trail to the left and follow the trail as it climbs up a small hill.

0.1   When the trail splits, keep left, entering Mother. The trail is clearly marked. Follow the trail into a tricky rock obstacle and then straight for a short distance. In 0.1 mile, take Mother to the right. There is a small wood sign marking the Mother Trail.

0.8   Stay left when the trails meet at the end of the climb. The trail to the right leads to the Saddle and eventually the West Leg Trail. In 0.1 mile the trail splits a second time. Take either trail as they meet back up on the other side of a small hill.

0.9   Follow trail into the Three Sisters, a technically difficult downhill section. Take the drop and then follow the trail left into a gradual climb.

1.1 When the trails split, take the connector trail to the left and head into a series of downhill switchbacks.

1.2 When the IMBA and POW Trails meet, turn right onto the POW Trail and take the two quick drops into the downhill section. Be careful as you can build up quite a bit of speed.

1.9 Keep right as the trail splits. The trails will connect again in 25 feet. Cross the wash and follow the trail up the side of the hill.

2.1 Take the trail to the left, following the Par None Trail. The trail to the right is POW.

2.8 Follow the trail into a steep climb up a hill. This climb has switchbacks with sharp turns.

3.0 Follow the trail onto a short downhill section on the other side of the hill. When the trail splits, take the IMBA Trail to the right.

3.7 Arrive back at the trailhead.

Ride Information

Local Events and Attractions

Boulder City is full of many antique stores, all within walking distance of each other. Many of these places have even been featured on national television shows. They can all be easily found in *The Country Register*, a free guide to specialty shops and events available from most businesses in downtown Boulder City.

Restaurants

Boulder Dam Brewing Company: Local brewery and restaurant started by Seattle native Todd Cook; 453 Nevada Way; (702) 243-2739; boulderdambrewing.com
The Coffee Cup: Featured on *Diners, Drive-ins, and Dives*; 512 Nevada Hwy.; (702) 294-0517; worldfamouscoffeecup.com

13 Figure 8: Option 1

The trails at Bootleg Canyon are laid out in such a way that you can start at one trail and connect with just about every other trail without ever having to get off your bike. This allows you to take shorter trails and turn them into longer trails to extend your ride. However, it can be difficult to know which trails work best to connect and what skill level is needed for each trail. In order to help with this dilemma, I have created several combinations of trails that are commonly ridden by mountain bikers at Bootleg Canyon. The Figure 8 is a combination that is a fun, easy ride. If you are a beginning to intermediate rider, this is a good combination to try when you're ready for a longer ride. The trail combination has no name, but I call it the Figure 8 because it kind of resembles a Figure 8 when mapped out.

Start: Just behind and to the right of the restrooms at the entrance to Bootleg Canyon

Distance: 6.7 miles

Elevation gain: 346

Riding time: Advanced riders, 1.5 hours; intermediate riders, 2 hours; beginning riders, 3 hours

Fitness effort: Physically moderate with some challenging areas

Difficulty: Technically moderate with some difficult technical spots, deep drops, long continuous climbs, and a tricky switchback climb up a steep hill

Terrain: Mostly dirt, some large rocks, and loose gravel—asphalt trail briefly crossed twice

Map: All Mountain Cyclery, allmountaincyclery .com

Nearest town: Boulder City

Other trail users: Hikers and runners; road bikers when asphalt trail is crossed, downhill riders when downhill trails are crossed

Dog friendly: Yes

Trail contact: Boulder City; bcnv.org/ Facilities/Facility/Details/Bootleg-Canyon -Park-18

Getting there: Take U.S. Highway 93 toward the Hoover Dam (Boulder City). Bootleg Canyon is easily visible on the left-hand side of the road. It is marked by a large white "BC," which actually stands for Boulder City, not Bootleg Canyon. Turn left on Veteran's Memorial Drive and follow it to Canyon Road. Turn left on Canyon Road and follow it to the parking lot below the restrooms. The trailhead is just behind the restrooms. GPS: N35 58.020'/W114 51.712'

   Note: If the parking lot is full, you can park in the dirt lot just below the asphalt lot.

The Ride

The trail begins between the large rocks located just behind and to the right of the restrooms. The rocks have been placed there specifically to mark the trail. Once you start down the first hill, stay to the right until you go over the next little hill. After you reach the top of the small hill keep to the left. Going to the right leads to a fairly difficult jump, which you should not attempt unless you have the skills necessary to complete it without getting injured. As you come around the bend,

Rider heading over the connector trail of Figure 8: Option 1 Jim Laurie Photography

there is a large ditch, which is a remnant of the flight line that used to run from the top of the hill.

Just a little way on the other side of the ditch, the trail splits into the Middle Lake View and the Lower Lake View, both of which are marked by small wood signs. Head left. Immediately after the sign, the trail takes the first of its two deep dips. As the trail progresses, there are many places where downhill trails cross the main trail. It's easy to tell which trail is which, so there isn't much reason to worry about getting on the wrong trail.

About a mile into the ride, the trail splits into the Upper Lake View Trail and the Lower Lake View Trail. Keep to the right and begin a short, easy downhill section followed by a slight climb that, once completed, offers magnificent views of Lake Mead. Before the climb, the trail crosses the River Mountain Hiking Trail. After the climb, follow the Lower Lake View Trail down the hill into the desert valley below Bootleg Canyon. Cross the asphalt River Mountain Loop Trail twice, and after the second crossing, pick up the trail again at the top of the hill on the other side of the graded area. Then make your way back up the hill to the trailhead. Head to the left when the Lower and Middle Lake View Trails meet and head around the hill to the restrooms.

Pick up the connector trail on the left side of the restrooms. This trail follows the foothills leading up into the canyon. It will prevent you from having to go up the dirt road to get to the next section of the Figure 8. You can access this connector trail from either the front or back of the restrooms, though the trail starts at the front.

Cross the dirt road and access the second section of the Figure 8 at just about where the telephone pole and the road meet. You'll see the point where the trail cuts out from the road. Take that trail to the left up the short climb. Once at the crest of the short hill, the trail splits into two. West Leg is the trail to the right; the trail to the left leads to Mother. Both trails are clearly marked. Take the trail to the left.

When the trail splits a second time, continue straight, which is the IMBA Trail. Mother is the trail on the right and is clearly marked by a small wood sign. About a half mile in, the IMBA trail meets the Par None Trail. Stay straight and continue on the IMBA trail. You will be riding up the Par None Trail as you complete the loop. Both the Par None and IMBA Trails are marked with small wood signs. This portion of the IMBA Trail is still a gradual climb for the first part. Once the top of the climb is reached, you'll enter a small downhill section made up of small hills and valleys as it winds its way to the main downhill section.

Begin that downhill section by taking the POW Trail to the left about 4.4 miles into the ride. The trail is clearly marked with a wood sign. This portion of the loop has some tricky areas at the beginning, but nothing that can't be navigated by simply slowing down. However, if you're more experienced, you may want to let go and enjoy a fun, fast ride that can take as little as 10 minutes to complete. It is easy to pick up speed here, so be careful. As you get out of the hills back into the valley, you'll go between two large rocks before meeting back up with Par None. When the two trails meet, follow the trail to the left and head onto Par None.

Follow the Par None Trail as you make your way upward towards the mouth of Bootleg Canyon. About 6.0 miles into the ride, there is a steep hill that is navigated through a series of tight switchbacks. This is probably the more difficult section of the climb. The hill is steep and the switchbacks are sharp. On the other side of the hill, the trail comes to a T. This is the end of the Par None as it intersects with the IMBA Trail. This is the intersection you were at previously. Both the Par None and IMBA Trails are marked with small wood signs. Take the IMBA Trail to the right and head back to the dirt road. Once you reach the dirt road, you can either head down the road to the parking lot by the restrooms or use the connector trail to reach the restrooms.

Figure 8: Option 1

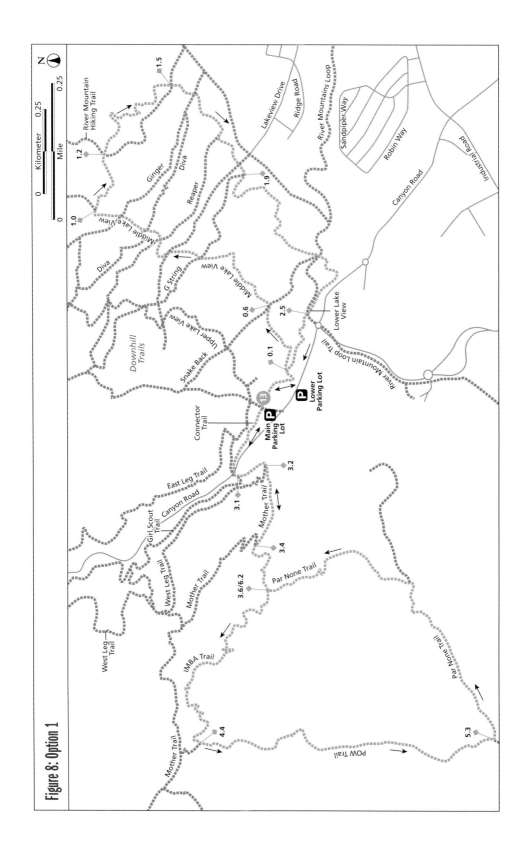

Miles and Directions

0.0 Start at the trailhead just behind and to the right of the restrooms. Follow the trail as it heads down the first incline to the right. When the trail forks, stay left. Going right leads to a jump.

0.1 Stay to the left when the trail splits into the Middle and Lower Lake Views. Both trails are clearly marked.

1.0 The trail forks. Stay right and begin a slight descent before another climb.

1.2 Cross the River Mountain Hiking Trail (no bikes allowed). Stay straight and begin the climb up the hill.

1.5 Take the trail to the right. Do not follow the sign indicating Malaga and Marina Drives. Continue straight and cross the River Mountain Hiking Trail again.

2.3 Cross another downhill trail. Stay straight and then cross the paved River Mountain Loop Trail and take the steep climb to the right.

2.7 Take the trail to the left when the Middle and Lower Lake View Trails meet and follow it back to the restrooms.

2.8 Connect with the trail on the north side of the restrooms.

3.1 Start at the trailhead just left of the telephone pole. Take the trail to the left and climb the small hill.

3.2 Keep to the left when the trail splits, entering Mother.

3.4 Stay straight when the trail splits. A small wood sign marks the trail as IMBA.

3.6 Continue straight when the trails split again. Do not take the Par None Trail on the left.

4.4 Turn left onto the POW Trail and the two quick drops into the downhill section.

5.3 Take the trail to the left, following the Par None Trail. The trail to the right is POW.

6.0 Take the steep climb up a hill. This climb has switchbacks with sharp turns.

6.2 Follow the trail onto a short downhill section on the other side of the hill. When the trail splits, take the IMBA Trail to the right.

6.7 Arrive back at the trailhead.

Ride Information

Local Events and Attractions

Zipline Bootleg Canyon: If you don't want to see the canyon by trails, you might want to see it by air. This can be done through a series of ziplines positioned on the east side of the canyon; flightlinezbootleg.com.

Boulder City–Hoover Dam Museum: Located in the historic Boulder Dam Hotel, this museum tells the story of the dam and the city it created; bcmha.org.

Restaurants

Boulder Pit Stop: Best hamburgers in town; located a short distance from the trail; 802 Buchanan Blvd.; (720) 293-7080; boulderpitstop.com

Boulder Dam Brewing Company: Local brewery and restaurant started by Seattle native Todd Cook; 453 Nevada Way; (702) 243-2739; boulderdambrewing.com

14 Figure 8: Option 2

This trail is a little shorter, but much more challenging than the first Figure 8 trail. If you are an intermediate to advanced rider, this is a good combination to try when you're ready for a longer ride. The trail combination has no official name, but like Figure 8, option 1, I call it the Figure 8 because it kind of resembles a Figure 8 when mapped out.

Start: Just behind and to the right of the restrooms at the entrance to Bootleg Canyon

Distance: 6.4 miles

Elevation gain: 414 feet

Riding time: Advanced riders, 1.5 hours; intermediate riders, 2 hours

Fitness effort: Physically moderate to challenging with some challenging areas

Difficulty: Technically challenging with some difficult spots, deep drops, and long continuous climbs

Terrain: Mostly dirt, some large rocks, and loose gravel

Map: All Mountain Cyclery, allmountaincyclery .com

Nearest town: Boulder City

Other trail users: Hikers and runners; road bikers when asphalt trail is crossed, downhill riders when downhill trails are crossed

Dog friendly: Yes

Trail contact: Boulder City; bcnv.org/ Facilities/Facility/Details/Bootleg-Canyon -Park-18

Getting there: Take U.S. Highway 93 toward the Hoover Dam (Boulder City). Bootleg Canyon is easily visible on the left-hand side of the road. It is marked by a large white "BC," which actually stands for Boulder City, not Bootleg Canyon. Turn left on Veteran's Memorial Drive and follow it to Canyon Road. Turn left on Canyon Road and follow it to the parking lot below the restrooms. The trailhead is behind the restrooms. GPS: N35 58.020'/W114 51.712'

Note: If the parking lot is full, you can park in the dirt lot just below the asphalt lot.

The Ride

The trail begins between the large rocks located just behind and to the right of the restrooms. The rocks have been placed there specifically to mark the trail. Once you start down the first hill, stay to the right until you go over the next little hill. After you reach the top of the small hill, keep to the left. Going to the right leads to a fairly difficult jump. As you come around the bend, there is a large ditch, which is a remnant of the flight line that used to run from the top of the hill.

Just a little way on the other side of the ditch, the trail splits into the Middle Lake View and the Lower Lake View, both of which are marked by small wooden signs. Head left. Immediately after the sign, the trail takes the first of its two deep dips. As the trail progresses, there are many places where downhill trails cross the main trail. It's easy to tell which trail is which, so there isn't much reason to worry about getting on the wrong trail.

A rider heading down the IMBA portion of Figure 8: Option 2

About a mile into the trail, you'll approach a fork in the road. Here the trail splits into the Upper Lake View Trail and the Lower Lake View Trail. Take the trail to the left at the small wood sign. Follow the trail into a gradual drop followed by a long gradual climb. You will be climbing up into the canyon walls before eventually heading downward in and out of washes and dips as the trail follows the foothills leading to the trailhead. Like the Middle Lake View Trail, the Upper Lake View Trail crosses several downhill trails as it progresses through the valley. Stay straight at each intersection.

At about 2.2 miles the trail crosses a downhill trail. Stay straight and take the gradual drop, followed by a steep climb. When the trail crosses another downhill trail, stay straight. The trailhead is a short distance ahead. Follow the trail to the left, then take the offshoot trail to the right. Go to the left of the jump, or if you wish, take the jump as you head to the restrooms.

Pick up the connector trail on the left side of the restrooms. This trail follows the foothills leading up into the canyon. It will prevent you from having to go up the dirt road to get to the next section of the Figure 8. You can access this connector trail from either the front or back of the restrooms; however, the trailhead is toward the front.

Cross the dirt road and access the second section of the Figure 8 at just about where the telephone pole and the road meet. You'll see the point where the trail cuts out from the road. Take that trail to the left up the short climb. Once at the crest of the short hill, the trail splits into two. West Leg is the trail to the right; the trail to the left leads to Mother. Both trails are clearly marked. Take the trail to the left.

When the trail splits a second time, take the Mother Trail to the right. Going straight will put you on the IMBA Trail. Stay straight when the trails meet at the end of the climb. Do not take the trail to the right. It leads to a section called the saddle, which eventually connects with West Leg.

Almost a mile into Mother, the trail enters a tricky downhill section known as the Three Sisters. The dirt trail disappears at this point and is replaced by rock. This section follows all the way down through the Three Sisters until the trail turns back into dirt. At the end of the Three Sisters is a technically difficult drop. After you complete the drop, follow the trail to the left into a gradual climb through lots of loose rocks. When the trail splits, take the trail to the left and start a downhill switchback section.

When the IMBA and POW Trails meet, take the POW Trail to the right and enter a fun, fast downhill section. As you get out of the hills back into the valley, you'll go between two large rocks before meeting back up with Par None. When the two trails meet, follow the trail to the left and head onto Par None.

Follow the Par None Trail as you make your way upward towards the mouth of Bootleg Canyon. Ride up the steep hill that is navigated through a series of tight switchbacks. This is probably the more difficult section of the climb. The hill is steep and the switchbacks are sharp. On the other side of the hill, the trail comes to a T. This is the end of the Par None as it intersects with the IMBA Trail. Both the Par None and IMBA Trails are marked with small wood signs. Take the IMBA Trail to the right and head back to the dirt road. Once you reach the dirt road, you can either head down the road to the parking lot by the restrooms or use the connector trail to reach the restrooms.

Miles and Directions

0.0 Start at the trailhead just behind and to the right of the restrooms. Follow the trail as it heads down the first incline to the right. When the trail forks, stay left. Going right leads to a jump.

0.1 Stay to the left when the trail splits into the Middle and Lower Lake Views. Both trails are clearly marked.

1.0 Stay to the left when the trail forks into the Upper and Lower Lake View Trails.

2.4 Follow the trail left and arrive at the restrooms, then connect with the trail on the north side of the restrooms.

2.7 Start at the trailhead to the left of the telephone pole. Take the trail to the left and follow the trail as it climbs up a small hill.

2.8 When the trail splits keep left, entering Mother. The trail is clearly marked. Follow the trail into a tricky rock obstacle and then straight for a short distance.

2.9 Go right when the trail splits. A small wood sign marks the trail as Mother.

3.5 Stay left when the trails meet at the end of the climb. The trail to the right leads to the Saddle and eventually the West Leg Trail.

3.6 Follow trail into the Three Sisters, a technically difficult downhill section. Take the drop and then follow the trail left into a gradual climb.

Figure 8: Option 2

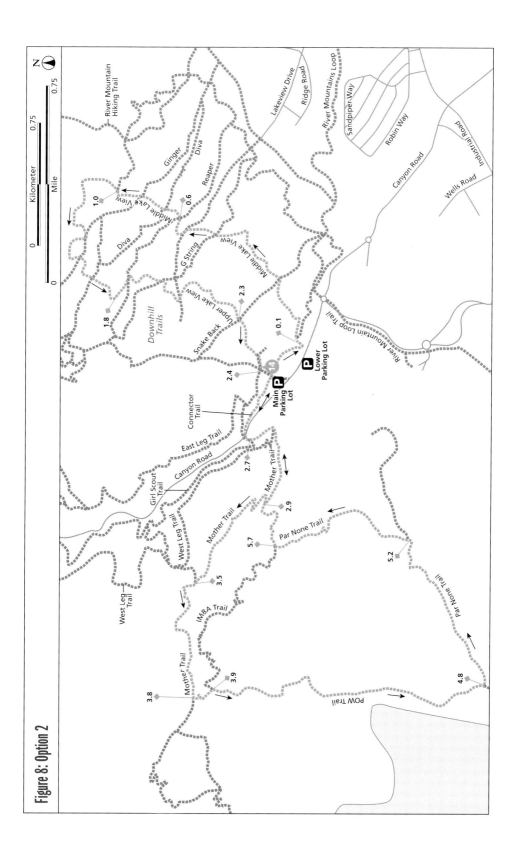

3.8 When the trails split, take the connector trail to the left and head into a series of downhill switchbacks.

3.9 When the IMBA and POW Trails meet, turn right onto the POW Trail and take the two quick drops into the downhill section.

4.8 Take the trail to the left, following the Par None Trail. The trail to the right is POW.

5.5 Follow the trail into a steep climb up a hill. This climb has switchbacks with sharp turns.

5.7 Follow the trail onto a short downhill section on the other side of the hill. When the trail splits, take the IMBA Trail to the right.

6.4 Arrive back at the trailhead.

Ride Information

Local Events and Attractions

Zipline Bootleg Canyon: If you don't want to see the canyon by trails, you might want to see it by air. This can be done through a series of ziplines positioned on the east side of the canyon; flightlinezbootleg.com.

Nevada Southern Railway: Visitors sit in a passenger train, riding the rails used to build the Hoover Dam on a free 10-minute ride; nevadasouthern.com.

Restaurants

Boulder Pit Stop: Best hamburgers in town; located a short distance from the trail; 802 Buchanan Blvd.; (720) 293-7080; boulderpitstop.com

Boulder Dam Brewing Company: Local brewery and restaurant started by Seattle native Todd Cook; 453 Nevada Way; (702) 243-2739; boulderdambrewing.com

15 Girl Scout/West Leg/Mother/IMBA Loop

This combination of trails presents a very technically challenging ride that is more suited to intermediate and advanced riders. It combines two of the most popular trails in Bootleg Canyon with the canyon's original trail, adding a nice easy gradual downhill, followed by a quick, but easy climb back to the trailhead. This long ride will challenge the legs of even the best of riders, as a great majority of the ride is a climb. However, you are rewarded at the end of the trail with a nice gradual downhill that you can ride as fast as your skill level will allow.

Start: The parking lot below the restrooms at the entrance to Bootleg Canyon
Distance: 5.2 miles
Elevation gain: 345 feet
Riding time: Advanced riders, 2 hours; intermediate riders, 2.5 hours
Fitness effort: Physically challenging due to steep climbs and rocky, technical spots
Difficulty: Technically challenging with very rocky spots, much climbing, and some steep drops

Terrain: Mostly dirt, large rocks, and loose gravel
Map: All Mountain Cyclery, allmountaincyclery.com
Nearest town: Boulder City
Other trail users: Hikers and runners
Dog friendly: Yes
Trail contact: Boulder City; bcnv.org/Facilities/Facility/Details/Bootleg-Canyon-Park-18

Getting there: Take U.S. Highway 93 toward the Hoover Dam (Boulder City). Bootleg Canyon is easily visible on the left-hand side of the road. It is marked by a large white "BC," which actually stands for Boulder City, not Bootleg Canyon. Turn left on Veteran's Memorial Drive and follow it to Canyon Road. Turn left on Canyon Road and follow it to the parking lot below the restrooms. Park here and then ride your bike up that dirt road to the first telephone pole on the left. You'll see the trailhead by the telephone pole. GPS: N35 59.119'/W114 51.882'
   Note: If the parking lot is full, you can park in the dirt lot just below the asphalt lot.

The Ride

The ride begins by riding up the dirt road to the trailhead. The entrance can easily be seen to the left of the road at the point where the telephone pole and the road meet. When you see the trail that cuts out from the road, follow it to the right. The beginning of the trail is often called the "rock garden" because it is filled with all manner of rock obstacles, some small, some fairly large. Once you make your way out of the rock garden, the single-track trail is mostly dirt, with some large rock obstacles at key positions. This trail climbs the canyon, getting higher and higher on the canyon wall as the trail progresses. You'll cross a couple of dirt road and washes, go over some tricky rock obstacles, and end Girl Scout at the tight switchbacks that lead to the end of the trail.

Once you've navigated the switchbacks, you'll arrive at a convergence of trails marked by a large wood signpost. Going straight will take you to the Inner Caldera Loop. The trail to the left will take you to both the Caldera and West Leg Trails. Take this trail and then take the offshoot to the left a short way up the trail. This offshoot is the West Leg Trail and is marked with a small wood sign.

The West Leg Trail, for the most part, parallels Girl Scout back down the canyon, only much higher on the canyon wall. This trail is mostly downhill with a couple of steep drops and several tricky rock sections. At 2.9 miles the West Leg Trail goes off to the left. Stay on the trail to the right, as it climbs up over a hill and goes down the other side. This is the connector trail to Mother and is commonly called the saddle.

The other side of the saddle is a long steep decline coated with hundreds of small loose rocks. Toward the bottom of the decline, take the trail to the right. This is Mother, a black diamond trail that makes its way to the outskirts of the canyon, high on the canyon wall. The drops on the left side of the trail are steep and very rocky. The trail follows the ridgeline of the canyon, before eventually heading down into the valley.

Almost a mile into the ride the trail enters a tricky downhill section known as the Three Sisters. The dirt trail disappears at this point and is replaced by rock. This section follows all the way down through the Three Sisters until the trail turns back

A rider heading along the Mother portion of the ride

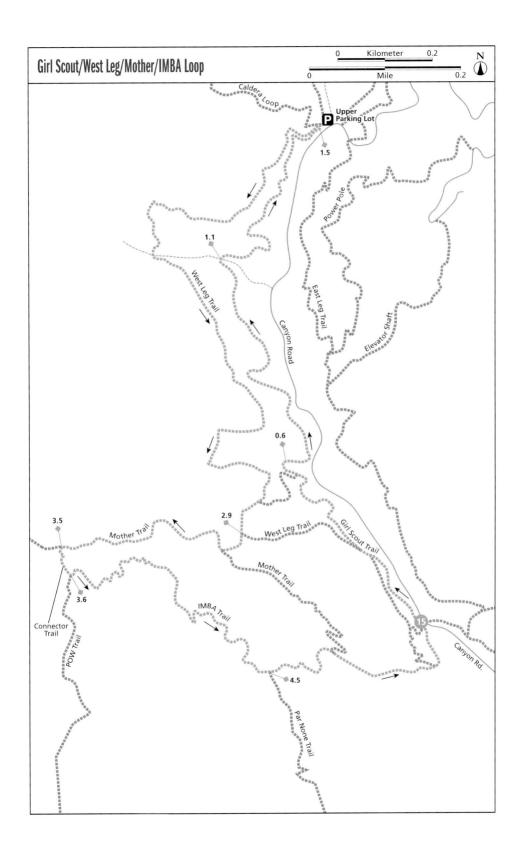

Girl Scout/West Leg/Mother/IMBA Loop

Upper Parking Lot

Caldera Loop

1.5

Power Pole

1.1

West Leg Trail

Canyon Road

East Leg Trail

Elevator Shaft

0.6

3.5

2.9

Mother Trail

West Leg Trail

Girl Scout Trail

3.6

Mother Trail

Connector Trail

POW Trail

IMBA Trail

15

4.5

Canyon Rd.

Par None Trail

0   Kilometer   0.2

0   Mile   0.2

N

into dirt. At the end of the Three Sisters is a technically difficult drop. After you complete the drop, follow the trail to the left into a gradual climb through lots of loose rocks. When the trail splits, take the IMBA/POW connector trail on the left. When the trails split a second time, take the IMBA Trail to the left and follow the trail as it dips in and out of the valley, making its way toward the trailhead with a fun, gradual descent. When the trail meets at the Par None Trail, continue straight and head back to the trailhead. Then take the dirt road back to the parking lot below the restrooms.

Miles and Directions

0.0 Start at the trailhead to the left of the telephone pole. Follow the trail as it climbs up into the canyon. You'll almost immediately enter the rock garden.

0.6 Follow the trail between two large rocks and take the sharp left turn. Look off to the right to see the remnants of an old still.

1.1 Take the large drop followed by a very steep climb and a sharp right turn. Follow the trail through a series of tight switchbacks at 1.3 miles.

1.5 The Girl Scout Trail ends. Take the trail to the left and then the offshoot trail on the left a short distance ahead. A small wood sign to the left marks the West Leg Trail. Take the gradual drop followed by a steep drop.

2.9 Follow trail to the right, entering a steep downhill section. The West Leg Trail continues to the left. The trail to the right puts you over the Saddle and onto Mother. This downhill section is very steep with lots of loose rocks.

3.3 Follow the trail into the Three Sisters, a technically difficult downhill section. Take the drop and follow the trail left into a gradual climb.

3.5 When the trails split, take the connector trail to the left and head into a series of downhill switchbacks.

3.6 When the IMBA and POW Trails meet, take the IMBA Trail to the left.

4.5 Stay straight when the trail meets the Par None Trail on the right and head back to the trailhead.

5.2 Arrive at the trailhead and take the dirt road down to the restrooms.

Ride Information

Local Events and Attractions

Boulder City is full of many antique stores, all within walking distance of each other. Many of these places have even been featured on national television shows. They can all be easily found in *The Country Register*, a free guide to specialty shops and events available from most businesses in downtown Boulder City.

Restaurants

Boulder Pit Stop: Best hamburgers in town; located a short distance from the trail; 802 Buchanan Blvd.; (720) 293-7080; boulderpitstop.com

The Coffee Cup: Featured on *Diners, Drive-ins, and Dives*; 512 Nevada Hwy.; (702) 294-0517; worldfamouscoffeecup.com

16 Caldera Loop

The Caldera Loop, more commonly called Caldera, is one of the few loops in Bootleg Canyon which is not a combination of several trails. It is also not technically in the canyon, but instead covers ground just to the north of the actual canyon. The ride offers great views of the Las Vegas Valley, including the buildings on the famous strip as well as some of the greatest desert views in all of Bootleg Canyon.

Start: To the left of the dirt parking lot located at the top of the dirt road before it climbs the last hill

Distance: 4.3 miles

Riding time: Advanced riders, 1.5 hours; intermediate riders, 2 hours; beginning riders, 2.5 hours

Fitness effort: Physically moderate, but only because of the distance of the ride

Difficulty: Technically easy to moderate, with the moderate portion coming more at the start of the ride

Terrain: Mostly dirt, some large rocks, and loose gravel

Map: All Mountain Cyclery, allmountaincyclery.com

Nearest town: Boulder City

Other trail users: Hikers and runners

Dog friendly: Yes

Trail contact: Boulder City; bcnv.org/Facilities/Facility/Details/Bootleg-Canyon-Park-18

Getting there: Take U.S. Highway 93 toward the Hoover Dam (Boulder City). Bootleg Canyon is easily visible on the left-hand side of the road. It is marked by a large white "BC," which actually stands for Boulder City, not Bootleg Canyon. Turn left on Veteran's Memorial Drive and follow it to Canyon Road. Turn Left on Canyon Road and follow it to the parking lot just below the restrooms. Keep driving until the road turns to dirt and follow it as it winds up the canyon. Drive slow to be courteous and not stir up dust for riders on the trails on either side of the road.

Just to the left of where the dirt road plateaus is a dirt parking lot that is not initially visible. The parking lot is a little lower than the dirt road, making it difficult to see. However, you can find it by driving just a little farther up the road and looking to your left. GPS: N35 59.895'/W114 52.049'

The Ride

The Caldera Loop is mostly smooth single track with some rocky areas and some areas filled with loose dirt and small loose rocks. The trailhead is actually a congruence of three trails: Girl Scout, Caldera, and the Inner Caldera Loop. Going straight up the hill will lead to Caldera. Going to the left leads to Girl Scout and to the right leads to the Inner Caldera Loop. Shortly into the ride, you'll see the West Leg Trail breaking off to the left, above Girl Scout. All these trails are clearly marked with small wood signs.

The trail starts by climbing up the canyon wall past the trailheads mentioned above. At the crest of the hill, the trail takes a sharp turn to the right. The trail can

A rider makes his way past remnants of bootlegging on the Caldera Loop

be a little tricky to spot here, so make sure you don't go over the crest of the hill. If you do go over the crest, you'll quickly realize you've gone the wrong way. It's not dangerous, but it's also not a trail. Because the Caldera Loop is on the outskirts of the canyon, it's very easy to follow. There are few other trails in the area and each requires you to turn off the main trail, so as long as you stay on the main trail, you won't get lost. The terrain is relatively flat with the exception of the first half mile. There are only a couple of drops and some small climbs, but almost all of them are very gradual. The trail could be ridden by a rider with beginner skills; however, the trail is long and once you start down the trail, you're kind of committed because there are no turnoffs.

As the trail begins, it follows the side of several hills, making its way to the flatter desert. The trail can be ridden clockwise or counterclockwise, but the originators of the trail meant for it to be ridden clockwise. Riding it this way makes the first part of the trail, which is a downhill section, much easier. However, take note that riding this trail either way provides a different experience with each direction.

At 1.4 miles into the ride, another trail meets up with Caldera. Stay to the right and do not take this offshoot trail, it is an illegal trail. Shortly after this, another trail shoots off to the right. This trail is a connector between the Caldera Loop and the Inner Caldera Loop and should not be taken. After this connector trail, there are no other offshoot trails until Caldera meets up with the Boy Scout Trail at 3.6 miles into the ride. The trail is mostly dirt; however, there are a few places where you have to cross a rock-filled wash and there is a little climbing involved. At the end of the trail you'll be able to see some old manmade caves that were once used to hide the alcohol

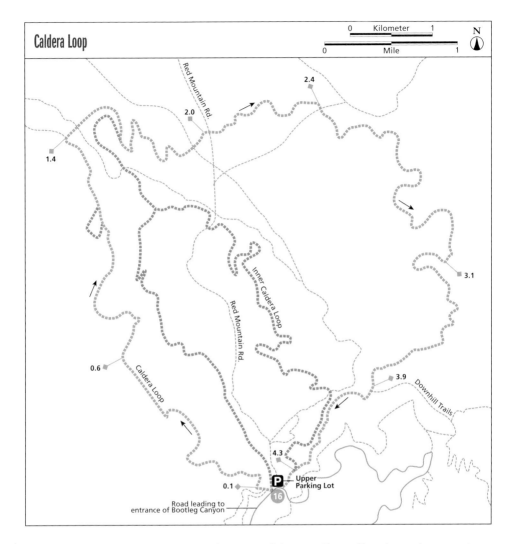

Caldera Loop

0   Kilometer   1

0   Mile   1

N

bootleggers made in the canyon during Prohibition. The trail ends on the opposite side of the parking lot where it began.

Miles and Directions

0.0 Start at the trailhead just to the left of the upper parking lot and head straight up the hill. Do not take the trail to the right or the left and do not take the West Leg Trail that breaks off to the left a short distance up the hill. Turn right just before the crest of the hill.

0.1 Navigate two large rock obstacles at the top of the hill. In 0.1 mile, the trail turns into well-groomed single track.

0.6 Follow the trail into a steep downhill section. This section of the trail offers wonderful views of the Las Vegas Valley.

1.1 Stay straight on the trail. Do not take the offshoot trail to the left.

1.4 Bear to the right. Do not take the offshoot trail to the left.

1.6 Stay straight as two trails merge into one. In 0.2 mile, the trail turns to the left.

2.0 Start an easy, fun level section, going across the dirt road, and heading into a smooth rock area.

2.6 Enter an area of rocky shale. Follow the trail until it turns back into dirt single track.

3.1 Follow the trail as it turns left and heads out of the canyon before eventually going back in. In 0.1 mile, pass through a section of sharp lava rocks.

3.9 Stay straight when Caldera merges briefly with the Boy Scout Trail.

4.3 Caldera merges briefly with the Inner Caldera Trail. Stay to the right when the trail splits and take the right into the parking lot.

Ride Information

Local Events and Attractions

Art in the Park: In this early-October event, more than 300 artists and crafters display and sell their work; bchcares.org/foundation.

Nevada Southern Railway: Visitors sit in a passenger train, riding the rails used to build the Hoover Dam on a free 10-minute ride; nevadasouthern.com.

Restaurants

Jack's Place: Sidewalk cafe and sports bar; 544 Nevada Way; (702) 293-2200; jacks placebc.com

Milo's Cellar: Sidewalk cafe and wine bar; 538 Nevada Way; (702) 293-9540; milos winebar.com

17 Inner Caldera Loop

Like the Caldera Loop, the Inner Caldera Loop is one of the few loops in Bootleg Canyon that is not a combination of several trails. Although it covers much of the same area as does the Caldera Loop, the Inner Caldera Loop is a distinctly different ride. The Inner Caldera Loop, commonly called Inner Calder, is entirely single track, although it does cross several dirt roads used for motor vehicle travel and for this reason the trail can be a little difficult to see at times. However, even in areas where the trail is a bit hard to spot, it can easily be picked up again by simply looking ahead or, as they say, down the road.

Start: To the left of the dirt parking lot located at the top of the dirt road before it climbs the last hill
Distance: 2.5 miles
Elevation gain: None
Riding time: Advanced riders, 1 hour; intermediate riders, 1.5 hours; beginning riders, 2 hours
Fitness effort: Physically easy to moderate
Difficulty: Technically easy to moderate, with a technically difficult portion at the start of the ride

Terrain: Mostly dirt, some large rocks, and loose gravel
Map: All Mountain Cyclery, allmountaincyclery.com
Nearest town: Boulder City
Other trail users: Hikers and runners
Dog friendly: Yes
Trail contact: Boulder City; bcnv.org/Facilities/Facility/Details/Bootleg-Canyon-Park-18

Getting there: Take U.S. Highway 93 toward the Hoover Dam (Boulder City). Bootleg Canyon is easily visible on the left-hand side of the road. It is marked by a large white "BC," which actually stands for Boulder City, not Bootleg Canyon. Turn left on Veteran's Memorial Drive and follow it to Canyon Road. Turn Left on Canyon Road and follow it to the parking lot just below the restrooms. Keep driving until the road turns to dirt and follow it as it winds up the canyon. Drive slow to be courteous and not stir up dust for riders on the trails on either side of the road.

Just to the left of where the dirt road plateaus is a dirt road that is not initially visible. The parking lot is a little lower than the dirt road, making it difficult to see. However, you can find it by driving just a little farther up the road and looking to your left. GPS: N35 59.895'/W114 52.049'

The Ride

The trailhead is actually a congruence of three trails: Girl Scout, Caldera, and Inner Caldera. Going straight up the hill leads to Caldera and going to the left leads to Girl Scout. The Inner Caldera Loop can be accessed by taking the trail to the right. All these trails are clearly marked by wood signs on a large wood pole.

A large and technically difficult drop at the beginning of the trail can make this trail tricky and it is best to walk this obstacle unless your mountain biking skills are

Riders beginning the Inner Caldera Loop with Las Vegas in the background
JIM LAURIE PHOTOGRAPHY

at least intermediate. Note that although the drop can be walked, even doing that requires a bit of skill. Still, this obstacle shouldn't sway you from the trail, because once the first part of the trail is successfully navigated, the rest of the ride is relatively easy.

The trail eventually winds its way down from the outer canyon walls into the valley through a series of switchbacks and short downhill sections. Here the ride offers great views of the Las Vegas Valley and the beautiful Southern Nevada desert. Take time to notice the hundreds of lizards scurrying along the trail and don't forget to look out into the hills to spot various forms of wildlife. About a mile into the trail, a large rock formation can be seen to the right. Many crevices have developed in this rock over the years, and these crevices are often home to many types of wildlife. Like many of the trails in Bootleg Canyon, this trail can be ridden at night, so long as you have the proper lighting on your bike. Doing so allows you to see wildlife, such as bats and tarantulas. As always, when wildlife is spotted, it should be viewed from a distance and left alone. Shortly after the rock formation, you'll encounter a large rock obstacle. Here the rocks are covered with multi-colored lichen. The trail makes its way down into the valley floor before starting its climb back up into the canyon and eventually to the parking lot at the trailhead. The trail ends on the opposite side of the parking lot where it began. Before that it connects with Caldera and Boy Scout before passing a long-ago abandoned bootlegging cave.

While the trail is meant to be ridden clockwise, it can also be ridden counterclockwise. Riding the trail in a different direction presents different obstacles—an

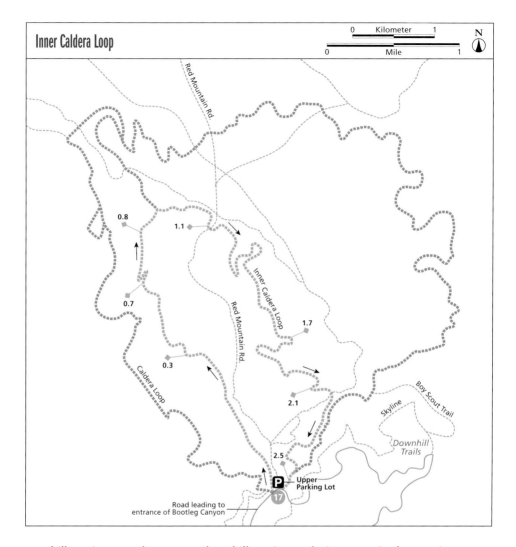

uphill section now becomes a downhill section and vice versa. It also requires you to look at the obstacles in a different way, from a different viewpoint, as it may take a different approach to ride the obstacle going one way than it took going another. Doing this can turn a well-worn ride into a new and exciting experience and is often well worth the effort.

Miles and Directions

0.0 Start at the trailhead just to the left of the upper parking lot. Take the trail to the right. Do not head straight up the hill or take the trail to the left.

0.1 Follow the trail through a large dropoff and a steep climb on the other side. In 0.1 mile, take the gradual drop, noting the tricky rock obstacle at the bottom of the drop and the quick but steep climb on the other side.

0.9 When the trail splits, take the trail to the right. The trail to the left is a connector to the Caldera Trail. In 0.1 mile the trail splits, but meets back up again. Going straight requires navigating some tricky rock obstacles. Going to the left avoids those obstacles.

1.7 Follow the trail over a series of small hills over fairly level ground. Then take a quick little climb, followed by a small drop. Follow the trail right after the drop.

2.1 Follow the trail as it turns right then cuts back left. Take the big drop a short distance ahead then cross the dirt road.

2.4 Go over a series of large, flat rocks, then take the trail to the left. The rock formation—which looks like large clumps of mud—is unique to this area.

2.5 Inner Caldera Trail meets the Caldera Trail. When the trail splits again, take the trail to the right to arrive at the parking lot.

Ride Information

Local Events and Attractions

Boulder City–Hoover Dam Museum: Located in the historic Boulder Dam Hotel, this museum tells the story of the dam and the city it created; bcmha.org.

Art in the Park: In this early-October event, more than 300 artists and crafters display and sell their work; bchcares.org/foundation.

Restaurants

Boulder Dam Brewing Company: Local brewery and restaurant started by Seattle native Todd Cook; 453 Nevada Way; (702) 243-2739; boulderdambrewing.com

Jack's Place: Sidewalk cafe and sports bar; 544 Nevada Way; (702) 293-2200; jacks placebc.com

18 Girl Scout/Inner Caldera to East Leg Loop

This ride is a fun loop that starts and ends at the parking lot just below the restrooms. It combines a very popular trail with another meant as a beginner's downhill trail, adding a nice easy fun ride in between. The trail is perfect for intermediate to advanced riders because it has some very technical spots that make the loop a challenging and fun ride.

Start: The parking lot below the restrooms at the entrance to Bootleg Canyon

Distance: 5.9 miles

Elevation gain: 345 feet

Riding time: Advanced riders, 2 hours; intermediate riders, 2.5 hours

Fitness effort: Physically challenging due to steep climbs and rocky, technical spots

Difficulty: Technically moderate with very rocky spots, much climbing, and some steep drops; there is also a technically difficult spot at the beginning of Inner Caldera

Terrain: Mostly dirt, large rocks, and loose gravel

Map: All Mountain Cyclery, allmountaincyclery.com

Nearest town: Boulder City

Other trail users: Hikers and runners

Dog friendly: Yes

Trail contact: Boulder City; bcnv.org/Facilities/Facility/Details/Bootleg-Canyon-Park-18

Getting there: Take U.S. Highway 93 toward the Hoover Dam (Boulder City). Bootleg Canyon is easily visible on the left-hand side of the road. It is marked by a large white "BC," which actually stands for Boulder City, not Bootleg Canyon. Turn left on Veteran's Memorial Drive and follow it to Canyon Road. Turn left on Canyon Road and follow it to the parking lot below the restrooms. Park here and then ride your bike up that dirt road to the first telephone pole on the left. You'll see the trailhead by the telephone pole. GPS: N35 59.119'/W114 51.882'

Note: If the parking lot is full, you can park in the dirt lot just below the asphalt lot.

The Ride

The ride begins by heading up the dirt road to the trailhead. The entrance can easily be seen to the left of the road at the point where the telephone pole and the road meet. When you see the trail that cuts out from the road, follow it to the right. The beginning of the trail is often called the "rock garden" because it is filled with all manner of rock obstacles, some small, some fairly large. Once you make your way out of the rock garden, the single-track trail is mostly dirt, with some large rock obstacles at key positions.

About 1 mile into the ride, cross the dirt road and head into a short downhill section that leads to another dirt road. After crossing the second dirt road, follow the trail as it heads up and into a difficult rock obstacle. Continue the climb into a series of mogul-like hills followed by another steep climb, leading into a series of switchbacks

Riders heading up Girl Scout on their way to the Inner Caldera Loop
JIM LAURIE PHOTOGRAPHY

and the end of Girl Scout at the convergence of trails. The trail to the left will take you to both the Caldera and West Leg Trails, while the trail straight ahead will take you to Inner Caldera.

A large and technically difficult drop at the beginning of the trail can make this trail tricky and it is best to walk this obstacle unless your mountain biking skills are at least intermediate. Shortly after the first drop you'll encounter a more gradual drop with a tricky rock obstacle at the bottom. The trail eventually winds its way down from the outer canyon walls into the valley through a series of switchbacks and short downhill sections. Here the ride offers great views of the Las Vegas Valley and the beautiful Southern Nevada desert. About a mile into the trail, a large rock formation can be seen to the right. Here the rocks are covered with multi-colored lichen. The trail makes its way down into the valley floor before starting its climb back up into the canyon and eventually to the parking lot at the trailhead.

Follow the trail straight, heading toward the dirt road. The East Leg trailhead is just to the east of the upper parking lot, on the south side of the dirt road. It can be found to the side of the road at the point where the road just starts another climb. The trail is marked with a small wood sign. Take the steep fast climb, then follow the trail as it turns to the right and heads into a tricky rock obstacle followed by a series of switchbacks.

When the downhill trail meets up with East Leg, continue on to the right into a rocky hairpin turn followed by a long steep climb. Continue straight when the trails cross. Going right leads to a downhill trail. An old racing starting gate can be seen on the left a short distance up the canyon wall. When the trail splits at about 5.3 miles, take the trail to the left. The more technical section is about to start. Start a bit of a climb complete with a couple tricky rock obstacles. A short distance ahead, do not take what appears to be an offshoot trail to the right. Continue on the trail as it goes over a difficult rock obstacle, turn to the right and head into another tricky rock section. Take a sharp left after the second rock obstacle.

At about 5.5 miles the trail appears to disappear. Climb up and over the rocks directly ahead of you, then pick up the trail on the other side. When the more technical section ends, watch for the large rock jetting out into the trail. Follow the trail as it makes its way up the hill. From here you can see the restrooms down the hill to the right. At this point you can follow just about any of the trails that lead down to the restrooms.

Miles and Directions

0.0 Start at the trailhead to the left of the telephone pole. Follow the trail as it climbs up into the canyon. You'll almost immediately enter the rock garden.

0.6 Follow the trail between two large rocks, then take the sharp left turn. Look off to the right to see the remnants of an old still.

1.0 Cross a dirt road and continue the short descent, crossing a second dirt road and then a large, difficult rock obstacle.

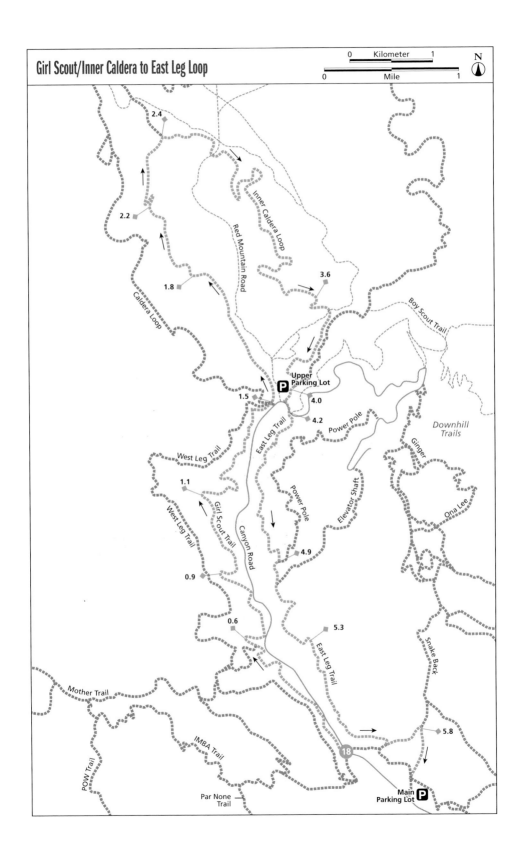

Girl Scout/Inner Caldera to East Leg Loop

2.4

2.2

1.8

Inner Caldera Loop

Red Mountain Road

Caldera Loop

3.6

Boy Scout Trail

Upper Parking Lot

1.5

4.0

4.2

Power Pole

Downhill Trails

Ginger

West Leg Trail

East Leg Trail

1.1

Girl Scout Trail

Power Pole

Elevator Shaft

Ona Lee

West Leg Trail

Canyon Road

4.9

0.9

0.6

5.3

East Leg Trail

Snake Back

Mother Trail

IMBA Trail

18

5.8

Main Parking Lot

POW Trail

Par None Trail

0   Kilometer   1

0   Mile   1

N

1.1 Take the large drop followed by a very steep climb and a sharp right turn. Follow the trails through a series of tight switchbacks at 1.3 miles.

1.5 Continue straight and start at the trailhead for Inner Caldera. Do not take the trail to the left. Follow the trail through a large drop and a steep climb on the other side.

2.4 When the trail splits, take the trail to the right. The trail to the left is a connector to the Caldera Trail. In 0.1 mile the trail splits again, but meets back up. Going straight requires navigating some tricky rock obstacles. Going to the left avoids those obstacles.

4.0 Inner Caldera Trail meets the Caldera Trail. When the trail splits again, continue straight and cross the dirt road.

4.2 Start at the trailhead to East Leg just to the right of the dirt road as it begins to climb the hill. The trailhead is southeast of the upper parking lot.

4.8 Follow the trail right into a rocky section, followed by a sharp left.

4.9 Stay straight when the Power Pole downhill trail intersects East Leg.

5.1 Cross the Elevator Shaft downhill trail.

5.3 Take the trail to the left when the trails split.

5.4 Do not take the offshoot trail to the right. Go over the difficult rock obstacle and follow the trail right. Take a sharp left after the second rock obstacle.

5.8 At the top of the hill, take the sharp right turn and head back to the restrooms.

5.9 Arrive at the restrooms.

Ride Information

Local Events and Attractions

Art in the Park: In this early-October event, more than 300 artists and crafters display and sell their work; bchcares.org/foundation.

Boulder City–Hoover Dam Museum: Located in the historic Boulder Dam Hotel, this museum tells the story of the dam and the city it created; bcmha.org.

Restaurants

Grandma Daisy's: Candy and ice cream parlor, featuring candy made on the premises; 530 Nevada Way; (702) 294-6639; grandmadaisys.com

The Coffee Cup: Featured on *Diners, Drive-ins, and Dives*; 512 Nevada Hwy.; (702) 294-0517; worldfamouscoffeecup.com

19 Girl Scout/Caldera to West Leg Loop

The Girl Scout/Caldera to West Leg Loop is a bit longer, but less technical than the Girl Scout/Inner Caldera to East Leg Loop. However, it still offers a very enjoyable and challenging ride. In fact, this loop combines two of the most popular trails in Bootleg Canyon and adds an enjoyable middle stretch to create one of the longest rides in the entire canyon.

Start: The parking lot below the restrooms at the entrance to Bootleg Canyon
Distance: 8.2 miles
Elevation gain: 345 feet
Riding time: Advanced riders, 2 hours; intermediate riders, 2.5 hours; beginning riders, 3.5 hours
Fitness effort: Physically moderate to challenging due to steep climbs and rocky, technical spots
Difficulty: Technically moderate with very rocky spots, much climbing, and some steep drops

Terrain: Mostly dirt, large rocks, and loose gravel
Map: All Mountain Cyclery, allmountaincyclery .com
Nearest town: Boulder City
Other trail users: Hikers and runners
Dog friendly: Yes
Trail contact: Boulder City; bcnv.org/ Facilities/Facility/Details/Bootleg-Canyon -Park-18

Getting there: Take U.S. Highway 93 toward the Hoover Dam (Boulder City). Bootleg Canyon is easily visible on the left-hand side of the road. It is marked by a large white "BC," which actually stands for Boulder City, not Bootleg Canyon. Turn left on Veteran's Memorial Drive and follow it to Canyon Road. Turn left on Canyon Road and follow it to the parking lot below the restrooms. Park here and then ride your bike up that dirt road to the first telephone pole on the left. You'll see the trailhead by the telephone pole. GPS: N35 59.119'/W114 51.882'
Note: If the parking lot is full, you can park in the dirt lot just below the asphalt lot.

The Ride

The ride begins by heading up the dirt road to the trailhead. The entrance can easily be seen to the left of the road at the point where the telephone pole and the road meet. When you see the trail that cuts out from the road, follow it to the right. The beginning of the trail is often called the "rock garden" because it is filled with all manner of rock obstacles, some small, some fairly large. Once you make your way out of the rock garden the single-track trail is mostly dirt, with some large rock obstacles at key positions.

About 1 mile into the ride, cross the dirt road and head into a short downhill section that leads to another dirt road. After crossing the second dirt road, follow the trail as it heads up and into a difficult rock obstacle. Continue the climb into a series of mogul-like hills followed by another steep climb, leading into a series of switchbacks

Riders heading up Calder from Girl Scout Jim Laurie Photography

and the end of Girl Scout at the convergence of trails. The trail to the left will take you to both the Caldera and West Leg Trails, while the trail straight ahead will take you to Inner Caldera.

Turn left and head straight up the hill. At the crest of the hill, the trail takes a sharp turn to the right. The trail can be a little tricky to spot here so make sure you don't go over the crest of the hill. If you do go over the crest, you'll quickly realize you've gone the wrong way. It's not dangerous, but it's also not a trail. Because the Caldera Loop is on the outskirts of the canyon, it's very easy to follow. There are few other trails in the area and each requires you to turn off the main trail, so as long as you stay on the main trail, you won't get lost. The terrain is relatively flat with the exception of the first half mile. There are only a couple of drops and some small climbs, but almost all of them are very gradual.

At 2.9 miles into the ride, another trail meets up with Caldera. Stay to the right and do not take this offshoot trail; it is an illegal trail. Shortly after this another trail shoots off to the right. This trail is a connector between the Caldera Loop and the Inner Caldera Loop and should not be taken. After this connector trail, there are no other offshoot trails until Caldera meets up with the Boy Scout Trail at 5.4 miles into the ride. The trail is mostly dirt; however, there are a few places where you have to cross a rock-filled wash and there is a little climbing involved. At the end of the trail you'll be able to see some old manmade caves that were once used to hide the alcohol bootleggers made in the canyon during Prohibition. The trail ends on the opposite side of the parking lot where it began. Cross the parking lot and head back to the point where Girl Scout ended and Caldera began. Ride up the hill past the trailhead to Girl Scout. The next trail on the left is West Leg and it is clearly marked.

The West Leg Trail, for the most part, parallels Girl Scout back down the canyon, only much higher on the canyon wall. Not long after you get onto the West Leg Trail, you'll encounter a small but steep drop. After you climb up the hill on the other side of the drop you'll encounter a series of tight switchbacks.

At 7.5 miles the West Leg Trail goes off to the left. Do not take the trail to the right, it climbs over a hill called the saddle and eventually leads to Mother. If you look down and to the left at the foothills of the canyon, you can see the area of the Girl Scout Trail known as the rock garden. Continue straight and head past a large rock obstacle and then into a short climb, complete with large, sharp rocks. Head to the left then climb a short ridge and head down the other side. This section is a narrow single track with a very steep drop off the side of the trail. Continue straight, entering a downhill section. Do not take the illegal downhill trail to the left. When the trail seems to disappear over the rocks, continue straight. You'll see the trail about 10 feet ahead. Take a sharp turn to the left and head up and over a small hill. Then follow the trail as it winds back down toward the dirt road on the right. Take the dirt road back to the parking lot below the restrooms.

Miles and Directions

0.0 Start at the trailhead to the left of the telephone pole. Follow the trail as it climbs up into the canyon. You'll almost immediately enter the rock garden.

0.6 Follow the trail between two large rocks, then take the sharp left turn. Look off to the right to see the remnants of an old still.

1.0 Cross a road. Continue on with a short descent, crossing a second dirt road and then a large, difficult rock obstacle.

1.5 Turn left and head straight up the hill. Do not take the West Leg Trail that breaks off to the left a short distance ahead. Turn right just before the crest of the hill.

2.1 Follow the trail into a steep downhill section. This section of the trail offers wonderful views of the Las Vegas Valley.

2.6 Stay straight on the trail. Do not take the offshoot trail to the left.

2.9 Bear to the right. Do not take the offshoot trail to the left.

3.1 Stay straight as two trails merge into one. In 0.2 mile, turn left.

4.7 Follow the trail through a section of sharp lava rocks into a short, steep climb.

5.4 Stay straight when Caldera merges briefly with the Boy Scout Trail.

5.9 Caldera merges briefly with the Inner Caldera Trail. Stay right when the trail splits a short distance ahead and turn right into the parking lot.

6.0 Cross the parking lot and access the convergence of trails. Head up the hill, taking the second trail on the left. A small wood sign marks the West Leg Trail.

6.3 When the trails split at the crest of the hill, follow the trail into a steep drop then turn right. The trail splits but meets up again.

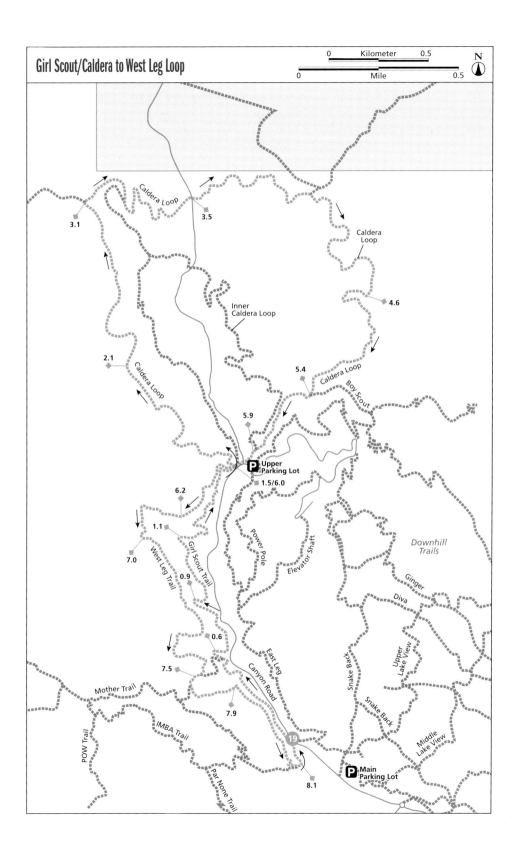

6.5 When the trail splits, take either trail. Right leads to a quick drop and climb. Left leads to a more gradual drop. The trails meet again after the wash.

7.5 When the trail splits three ways, stay straight until you connect with the trail ahead, then go left. Do not take the trail to the right.

8.1 Continue straight when the trail seems to disappear. You'll see it about 10 feet ahead. Take the sharp left turn after coming out of the rocky area. When the trail splits, keep left and head down toward the small hill as the trail makes its way to the dirt road.

8.2 Leave the trail and access the dirt road on the right. Then take the dirt road back to the parking lot below the restrooms.

Ride Information

Local Events and Attractions

Art in the Park: In this early-October event, more than 300 artists and crafters display and sell their work; bchcares.org/foundation.

Boulder City–Hoover Dam Museum: Located in the historic Boulder Dam Hotel, this museum tells the story of the dam and the city it created; bcmha.org.

Restaurants

Boulder Dam Brewing Company: Local brewery and restaurant started by Seattle native Todd Cook; 453 Nevada Way; (702) 243-2739; boulderdambrewing.com

The Coffee Cup: Featured on *Diners, Drive-ins, and Dives*; 512 Nevada Hwy.; (702) 294-0517; worldfamouscoffeecup.com

20 Historic Railroad Tunnel Trail

Las Vegas is a town that regularly implodes its history in favor of the new, bright, and shiny. However, every once in a while a bit of that history is spared from the wrecking ball. Such is the case with the Historic Railroad Tunnel Trail. This trail, which has been around since 1931, is one of the few places in Las Vegas where you can not only see history, you can ride through it. The Historic Railroad Tunnel Trail was once used to get many of the materials needed to build the Hoover Dam to the dam site. While the railroad tracks have long been removed, the overly large tunnels hewn into the iron-rich rocks still exist.

The trail got its start when a conglomeration of six major western firms—called the Six Companies Inc.—got together to build almost 30 miles of railroad in five months. Once the tracks were laid, trains ran to and from the dam site 24 hours a day, carrying machinery, gravel, and supplies to the dam site. Though not difficult to ride, this is a great trail to see many animals native to Nevada. Here you may see owls, big horn sheep, coyotes, and bats. In fact, Mexican Free-tail Bats roost in many of the tunnels. If you ride in the evening, you can often see the bats fluttering around as they leave their daytime roost and head into the night in search of insects. This trail also follows along the shore of Lake Mead, offering great views of the lake. All this combines to make the trail one of the best rides for families and sightseeing in all of Las Vegas.

Start: At the parking lot just below the Alan Bible Visitor Center

Distance: 7.5 miles

Riding time: Advanced riders, 1 hour; intermediate riders, 1.5 hours; beginning riders, 2.5 hours

Fitness effort: Physically easy as the grade on the terrain for most of the ride is level

Difficulty: Technically easy with one short climb halfway through the ride

Terrain: Wide trail, mostly dirt and loose gravel

Map: *National Park Service: Lake Mead*, nps .gov/lake/planyourvisit/hikerr.htm

Nearest town: Boulder City

Other trail users: Hikers, walkers, and runners.

Dog friendly: Yes, but coyotes are often seen in the area

Trail contact: Alan Bible Visitor Center; 601 Great Basin Hwy., Boulder City; (702) 293-8906

Getting there: Take U.S. Highway 93 toward the Hoover Dam (Boulder City). Turn onto Lakeshore Road and follow it to the parking lot just below the Alan Bible Visitor Center. GPS: N36 00.707'/ W114 47.609'

The Ride

The trailhead is just south of the parking lot below the Alan Bible Visitor Center. It starts out as a cement trail, but quickly turns into a dirt trail when you follow the "trail" sign as it breaks off the cement trail. This dirt trail takes you to the entrance of the main trail, which is a large metal gate. If the gate is not open, the trail cannot be ridden. Once on the trail, simply follow it as it winds its way into the mountains above Lake Mead, offering spectacular views of the lake to the left. Because the road that makes up the Historic Railroad Tunnel Trail was once used by trains to transport supplies, the dirt road that makes up the trail is very wide and relatively flat. And while the trail does climb as it makes its way through the tunnels, that climb is gradual and relatively easy.

There are five tunnels on the trail. Each tunnel is 18 feet wide and 27 feet high. The width and height were needed to allow massive pieces of pipe, turbine, and construction equipment to pass through unobstructed. Many of the tunnels were reinforced with timbers that were meant to prevent rock from falling onto the train. Unfortunately, the original timbers in tunnel two burned down in 1990; however, they were replaced by the National Park Service. The timbers in tunnel five were also burned in 1978, after which the tunnel was sealed. In 2001 the walls were reinforced with shotcrete and the tunnel reopened.

Just before you reach the first tunnel, a look down the ravine to the right will reveal several concrete plugs that were taken out of the Hoover Dam to install the turbines. This ravine, which is filled with the large, loose rocks removed as the tunnels were dug out, follows the trail for most of the way. The trail takes an easy climb

TUNNELS TO THE DAM

On December 30, 1929, President Herbert Hoover signed the bill authorizing the construction of a dam to tame the mighty Colorado River. The next problem was how to get those materials to the construction site. A total of five tunnels, each approximately 300 feet long and 25 feet in diameter, were burrowed and blasted into the mountains leading to the construction site. The size was needed to ensure the turbines used at the dam would fit through the tunnels. Once the system was complete in 1931, 71 people kept nine steam and four gas locomotives operating on a twenty-four-hour basis. The tracks were abandoned after the completion of the dam in 1935, although trains still ran up until 1961. A year later, in 1962, the tracks were taken up and sold for scrap, along with the Oregon fir trees used as ties. In 1984 the trail was placed on the National Register of Historic Places and is the only remaining section of the Hoover Dam Railroad system that is not highly disturbed or under water. The trail which now follows the tracks once used by the nine steam and four gas locomotives has been designated as a National Historic Trail. In 1977 Clint Eastwood and Sondra Locke filmed the move "The Gauntlet" in a section of the trail. In the scenes filmed at the tunnels, the couple is on a motorcycle being chased by an assassin in a helicopter.

through the five tunnels, following the very road used by the railroad back in the 1930s.

About 2 miles into the ride, at the end of the last tunnel, is another, smaller metal gate. At this point the trail switches owners, going from land owned by the National Park Service onto land owned by the Bureau of Reclamation. As a word of warning, this gate is closed at sunset and not opened again until the morning. You should not go onto the trail if you cannot be back at the gate before sunset, because the Bureau of Reclamation will not open the gate again once it is closed for the night and it is illegal for you to be on their land at night. If you don't make it back on time, you'll have to ride to an asphalt parking lot just off the road to the Hoover Dam and then climb the Great Basin Highway, back to the trailhead.

A wood truss–supported tunnel along the trail

The trail is largely downhill after the second gate. Remember to plan for the time it will take to climb back out when you decide if you have enough time to ride the entire trail. The trail loops at the end, allowing you to follow it back to the trailhead. There is a small portion of the trail which must be walked—mainly because it is very steep, but also because the signs tell you to walk. There is also a shortcut that you can take toward the end of the trail. This trail, which leads to the walking portion, is much steeper than the main trail.

Take the time to read the plaques posted along the trail. Some plaques provide valuable information about the animals you might see. While other plaques tell the story of the railroad construction, complete with vintage photographs taken when the railroad was being built. Also, because the trail is so easy to ride, you'll have time to look upward into the rocks, as well as downward toward the lake. If you do so you're bound to see animals such as big horn sheep, antelope, ravens, owls, lizards, and ground squirrels. In some areas along the trail, people have created offshoot hiking trails. These trails are illegal and should not be taken. Towards the end of the trail just

Historic Railroad Tunnel Trail

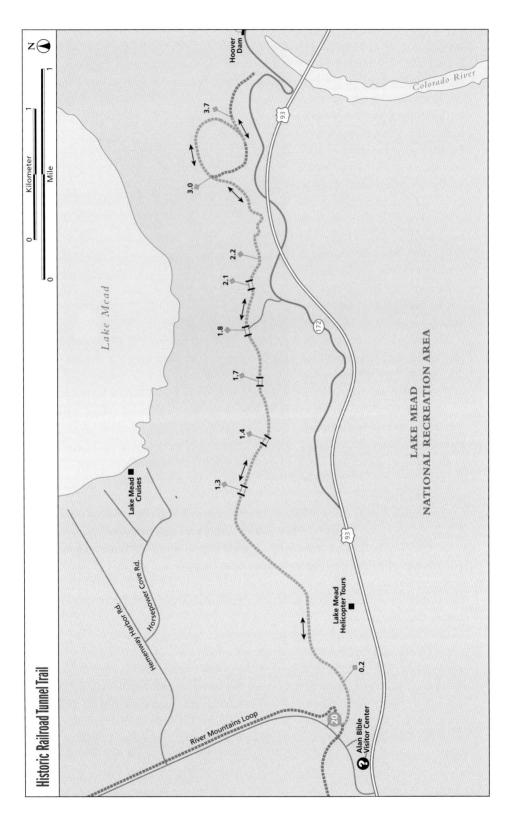

N

Kilometer
0   1

Mile
0   1

Lake Mead

Hoover Dam

Colorado River

93

3.7

3.0

2.2

2.1

1.8

1.7

1.4

1.3

Lake Mead Cruises

Hemenway Harbor Rd.

Horsepower Cove Rd.

172

93

Lake Mead Helicopter Tours

0.2

River Mountains Loop

20

Alan Bible Visitor Center

LAKE MEAD NATIONAL RECREATION AREA

to the east of the second set of gates, there is a parts boneyard. Here you can see the large pieces of equipment used to build the turbines powered by the dam. Looking at these pieces of equipment, it's easy to see why the tunnels were built so wide and tall.

Miles and Directions

0.0 Start at the trailhead just above the parking lot. Follow the trail as it heads left.

0.2 Enter large metal gates.

1.3 Go through the first tunnel. This tunnel is not very long and you can see the second tunnel as you enter.

1.4 Go through the second tunnel.

1.7 Go through the third tunnel.

1.8 Go through the fourth tunnel.

2.1 Go through the fifth tunnel. This is the longest of all the tunnels.

2.2 Go through the second gate, entering Bureau of Reclamation land.

2.8 Pass through another metal gate. Watch out for trucks on this portion of the trail.

3.0 Stay straight. Do not take the shortcut off to the right.

3.4 The trail splits; stay straight. Do not take the walking trail. In 0.2 mile, take the trail to the left.

3.7 Take the walking trail back up to the main trail, then follow the trail to the right back to the trailhead.

7.5 Arrive back at the trailhead.

Ride Information

Local Events and Attractions

Lake Mead Cruises: A popular attraction on Lake Mead is a cruise on a Mississippi-style paddleboat; lakemeadcruises.com.

Six Tunnel's to Hoover Dam: This annual run through the tunnels of Hoover Dam takes place every year on St. Patrick's Day. There is a half marathon and two-person relay, 5K run/walk, and a 1-mile stroll. There are even prizes for best costume; mountainmanevents.com.

Restaurants

Boulder Pit Stop: Best hamburgers in town; located a short distance from the trail; 802 Buchanan Blvd.; (720) 293-7080; boulderpitstop.com

Boulder Dam Brewing Company: Local brewery and restaurant started by Seattle native Todd Cook; 453 Nevada Way; (702) 243-2739; boulderdambrewing.com

21 Anthem East Trail

The Anthem East Trail makes its way into the hills and valleys of the Sloan Canyon right behind houses, a school, and a park. Even though the trail is close to many homes, when riding the trail, it is easy to forget you are anywhere near an established community.

Start: At Anthem Hills Park
Distance: 4.4 miles
Elevation gain: 413 feet
Riding time: Advanced riders, 45 minutes; intermediate riders, 1 hour; beginning riders, 1.5 hours
Fitness level: Physically moderate, but after the initial climb and descent, the trail gets relatively easy
Difficulty: Technically easy to moderate with a difficult climb at the beginning of the trail

Terrain: Asphalt and dirt trail
Map: Bureau of Land Management; blm.gov/nv/st/en/fo/lvfo/blm_programs/blm_special_areas/sloan_canyon_nca/trails.html
Nearest Town: Henderson
Other trail users: Hikers, runners, and horseback riders
Dog friendly: Yes
Trail contact: BLM Southern Nevada District Office; 4701 North Torrey Pines Dr., Las Vegas; (702) 515-5000

Getting there: Take the Bruce Woodbury Beltway (I-215) to the Eastern Avenue exit. Turn right onto Eastern, left onto Reunion Drive, and left onto McCullough Hills Parkway. Take the first left and then the right to Anthem Hills Park. Park at the trailhead. GPS: N35 58.974'/W115 05.027'

The Ride

The Anthem East Trail is so named because it makes its way into the hills of Sloan Canyon behind the Anthem community. Even though you are riding in the hills just behind a well-established community, you get the feeling you are riding your trusty steed, just like the cowboys of old, out in the open desert. In fact, when on this trail, it's easy to forget you are anywhere near Las Vegas. That is, of course, once you get back into the hills. Before that you are presented with wonderful views of the Las Vegas Valley as it opens up in front of you.

The trail starts in the parking lot at Anthem Hills Park. The trailhead is clearly marked and there is a covered bench right next to the trail. The first part of the trail is asphalt and is heavily used by people just walking along the trail, so be courteous and move out of the way for people on the trail. Not far up the trail you'll find a hiking trail to the right called Bear Paw Trail. This is a fun trail that can be hiked before starting your bike ride; however, do not take your bike on this trail. Located at a couple of spots on the asphalt trail are scenic overlooks that give great views of the Las Vegas Valley. These are great places to stop and take in those views.

A rider makes his way down the Anthem East Trail.

About halfway up the trail the asphalt path splits. It's best not to take the split to the right. Although it will lead you to the dirt part of the trail, you'll have to climb a steep hill to get there. Instead, continue on the left split to the top of the hill. When the asphalt dead ends at a dirt road, cross the dirt road and pick up the little-bit-wider-than-single-track trail. Take this trail to the left and follow it as it climbs up the hill. The large dirt road is commonly used by horseback riders who ride along the trail as well.

A little over a half mile into the trail, the road turns to a dirt trail that winds its way up into the hills. As it travels through the canyon, the trail makes its way into and out of a wash that runs through the canyon. There are signs along the trail warning of riding in the wash while it is raining. Be sure to heed these signs. Flash floods are common in the Mojave Desert and these washes are where the water flows. Faster than you can imagine, water can come rushing down a wash, sweeping away everything in its path—including bike riders and their bikes.

When riding in the wash, be sure to keep a firm grip on the bike's handlebars and continue pedaling. This particular wash, in many places, is filled with deep gravel that can bog down the bike and make it hard to move. It is not uncommon for the front tire to jump from one groove in the gravel to another, causing the handlebars to turn sharply, which can cause you to fall.

When riding the Anthem East Trail, it is important to follow the trail markers. There are many unofficial trails that have been blazed in this area. Not only are these

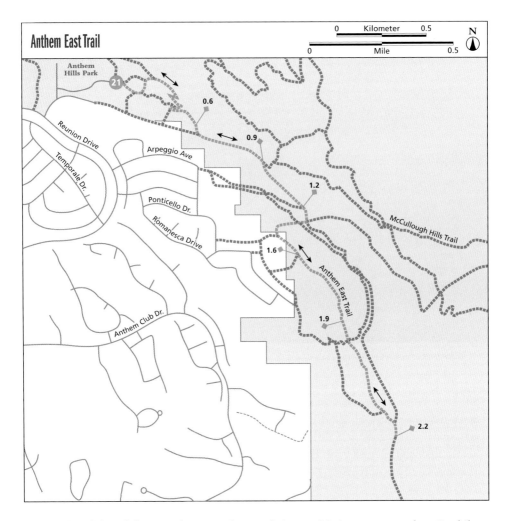

trails illegal, but following them can be confusing and it is easy to get lost. Luckily, the Anthem East Trail is simple to follow because it is well marked with square, rusty metal markers that have the name of the trail as well as directional arrows. As long as you follow these markers, you'll be fine.

Once you reach the top of the hill, about a mile into the ride, the trail turns to the right and starts a tricky downhill section. Follow this trail as it narrows and snakes its way through the black rocks that decorate the canyon. Close to the end of this downhill section, the trail widens as it drops into the wash. Follow the trail across the wash, then take the sharp right turn and head up onto the hill, following the trail to the left as it climbs up the hill. At the top of the hill, take the single track to the right. About 2 miles into the ride, the trail makes its way back down into the wash. Follow the trail through the wash up to the other side. The trail ends where the single track comes out of the wash and meets the dirt road. You'll know you are at the end of the trail because there is a marker with the name of the trail but no directional arrow. Here you turn and ride back.

Be careful not to be fooled by the dirt road. This road travels through Sloan Canyon and at times is actually part of the trail. The dirt road continues to travel up the hill, back into the canyon. If you want to make the trail longer, you can take the road. Just be aware, the dirt road is not as well groomed as the trail and is not intended to be ridden as part of the trail.

Miles and Directions

0.0 Start at the Anthem Hills Trailhead. Take the asphalt road next to the covered bench.

0.2 Stay straight. Do not take the trail to the right.

0.5 Follow the trail to the left. Do not take the trail to the right. At 0.6 mile, cross the dirt road and take the narrower trail. Turn left and follow that trail up the hill.

0.9 Follow the narrower single-track trail to the right at the trail marker. Begin a tricky downhill section along the side of the hill.

1.2 Cross the wash, following the trail markers. Pick up the trail to the right and climb the hill. Do not follow the dirt road to the right or the left.

1.3 Follow the trail as it turns left at the trail marker. Continue straight at the trail marker at 1.4 miles and climb to the top of the hill. Do not take the road to the right.

1.6 Follow the single-track trail to the right and start another downhill section. Stay straight at the trail marker at 1.8 miles. Do not take the trail to the right.

1.9 Follow the trail as it goes down into the wash. Continue straight into the wash at the trail marker at 2.0 miles.

2.1 Stay straight. Do not take the offshoot trail to the right.

2.2 Cross the wash and meet up with the dirt road. Turn around and head back the way you came, following trail markers to the trailhead.

4.4 Arrive back at the trailhead.

Ride Information

Local Events and Attractions

Henderson Pavilion: The largest outdoor amphitheater in Nevada is a state-of-the-art venue for both visual and performing arts; cityofhenderson.com.
Henderson Multigenerational Center/Aquatic Complex: The 84,120-square-foot facility has a demonstration kitchen, jogging track, adult lounge, and dance room, as well as an outdoor aquatic complex; cityofhenderson.com.

Restaurants

Crepe Expectations: 9500 S. Eastern Ave., Suite 150, Las Vegas; (702) 583-4939; crepeexpectations.com
Island Sushi and Grill: Hawaiian and Japanese cuisine; 9400 S. Eastern Ave., Las Vegas; (702) 221-1600; islandsushiandgrill.com

22 McCullough Hills Trail

This well-groomed dirt trail winds its way into the hills of Sloan Canyon National Conservation Area, offering a completely different view of the Nevada desert, one where volcanic action played a large part. The trail is one of the few multipurpose trails in the southern part of the valley that accommodates hikers, mountain bike riders, and equestrian enthusiasts.

Start: At McCullough Hills Trailhead
Distance: 14.8 miles
Elevation gain: 831 feet
Approximate riding time: Advanced riders, 1.5 hours; intermediate riders, 2 hours; beginning riders, 3.5 hours
Fitness Effort: Physically moderate
Difficulty: Technically easy to moderate, the trail isn't technical, but there are many climbs and the trail is rather long
Terrain: Well-groomed dirt; however, rocks placed intentionally in the washes have the potential of causing pinch flats, so bring extra tubes.
Map: Bureau of Land Management; blm.gov/nv/st/en/fo/lvfo/blm_programs/blm_special_areas/sloan_canyon_nca/trails.html
Nearest Town: Henderson
Other trail users: Hikers, runners, and horseback riders.
Dog friendly: Yes
Trail contact: BLM Southern Nevada District Office; 4701 North Torrey Pines Dr., Las Vegas; (702) 515-5000

Getting there: Take the Great Basin Highway south to the Horizon Drive Exit. Turn right on Horizon Drive and then left on Horizon Ridge Parkway. Turn right on Mission Drive and follow the road to the McCullough Hills Trailhead on the left. GPS: N35 59.870'/W114 59.872'

The Ride

In 2002, Congress set aside 48,438 acres of land with the intent of protecting a portion of Southern Nevada's Mojave Desert for the "benefit and enjoyment of present and future generations." The area became known as the Sloan Canyon National Conservation Area. A portion of Sloan Canyon is known as the North McCullough Wilderness and it is through this wilderness that the McCullough Hills Trail runs.

The McCullough Hills Trail is a good place to start for anyone looking to get into mountain biking. Unlike most mountain bike trails, this trail is fairly wide. In fact, it's wide enough for bikers to ride side-by-side. This means it is not considered single track. Additionally, the trail is well groomed and is, for the most part, free of many of the obstacles, such as rocks, commonly found on most mountain bike trails. In fact, about the only time you encounter rocks is in the washes, where they have been placed intentionally to prevent the trail from becoming washed out. Riding over these rocks creates the potential of causing pinch flats, so it is wise to bring extra tubes or to use tubes with some type of flat repellent.

While the trail is relatively easy, it does have some tricky parts. There are some steep climbs and sharp turns—some of which are fairly difficult to navigate. However, most climbs are gradual and have been designed with flat spots, making the climb easier. Located at two points on the trail are shaded benches designed to provide a break in the long trail. These benches are strategically positioned to provide great views of the Las Vegas and Henderson Valleys. Each rest stop is also complete with a hitching post for horses. The structure providing shade is artistically designed so it fits in nicely with the desert landscape.

The McCullough Hills Trail is well marked for the first 7 miles. Markers are made of metal posts that have been allowed to rust. The markers are strategically placed to help riders stay on the correct trail. The trail itself starts at the McCullough Hills Trailhead—an area specifically designed for people using the trail. There is a small parking lot, a restroom, a map kiosk, and a drinking fountain. The trail starts on the south side of the parking lot right behind the map kiosk and turns right into the hills.

The trail is easy to follow, mainly because of its width. All offshoot trails are much narrower and shouldn't be followed. In most cases where there is a question about where the trail heads, there is a trail marker with directional arrows showing the way. Follow the trail as it makes its way up into the hills. The first three miles are a gradual

Mile marker on the McCullough Hills Trail

climb and the next mile is an alternating climb and downhill section. A little over 4 miles into the ride you'll find a set of switchbacks. There is also a sign warning riders of the switchbacks. Follow them as the trail climbs up the hill and then turns to the right as it makes its way over the top of the hill. Once you're at the top of the hill, follow the trail as it winds down into the valley. The Las Vegas Valley, including the Strip, will start to open up in front of you at this point. Follow the trail as it starts to climb after mile marker 6.

Shortly after this marker, the wide trail meets up with a convergence of single-track trails. There is a trail marker here, but it is a little confusing and doesn't really tell you which trail to take. There is only about a half mile of the trail remaining and the terrain gets difficult and confusing from here. I would recommend stopping at this point and heading back. However, if you wish to continue, take the single-track trail to the left and follow it as it curves to the right. Be careful to stay on the correct trail as the trail splits not far after the turn. If you keep to the right, you'll be on the proper trail. You should be able to see the trail marker for mile 7 a short distance ahead.

Follow the trail as it climbs the hill and then goes down the other side. The trail ends at the marker a little less than 7.5 miles into the ride. In my opinion, the extra portion of the trail is not worth the ride, so I'd turn back at either the marker at the bottom of the hill or the point where the wide trail stops.

Miles and Directions

0.0 Start at the McCullough Hills Trailhead behind the map kiosk.

0.2 Stay straight and climb the hill. Do not take the trail to the right.

0.6 Climb the hill and continue with the short downhill section. At 0.7 mile, cross the wash—which is also used by horseback riders—at the trail marker.

0.9 Cross the dirt road at the trail marker and then follow the trail left, crossing the dirt road a second time at the next trail marker.

1.2 Follow the trail left. Do not take the offshoot trail to the right.

1.5 Follow the trail right, crossing the wash at 1.9 miles.

2.1 Follow the trail up the small hill. Do not take the trail to the right. Continue on the trail, staying straight at the next trail marker at 2.2 miles. Do not take the trail to the left.

2.5 Pass the shaded rest area. In 0.1 mile, take the drop and the climb on the other side.

3.4 Stay straight as the trail levels out a bit. Do not take the offshoot trail to the right.

4.7 Pass the elevation marker, marking the highest point on the trail—3,120 feet—then start a downhill section. Do not take the offshoot trail to the right.

5.4 Pass the second shaded rest area and head into the downhill switchbacks.

5.6 Cross the wash and the dirt road at the trail marker, then follow the trail up the hill.

6.1 Stay straight and cross the dirt road at the marker.

6.9 The wide trail ends at the convergence of single-track trails. I recommend turning back at this point. Option: If you continue, take the trail to the left and stay on it as it curves to the right. Do not follow the trail that offshoots from that trail on the left.

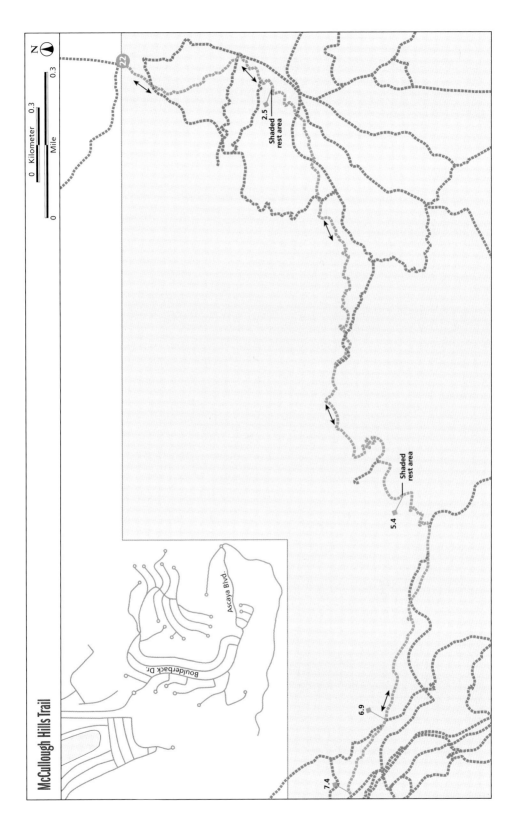

McCullough Hills Trail

N

0 Kilometer 0.3

0 Mile 0.3

22

Shaded rest area

2.5

Shaded rest area

5.4

6.9

7.4

Boulderback Dr.

Ascaya Blvd.

7.2 Climb the steep and rocky section up the hill for 0.1 mile, then follow the trail down the hill on the other side. The trail is extremely rocky.

7.4 Stay straight at the trail marker and follow the trail down to the next marker. Here the trail ends. Turn around and ride back to the trailhead, following the trail markers.

14.8 Arrive back at the trailhead.

Ride Information

Restaurants

Settebello Pizzeria Napoletana: Located in the District, it serves official pizza from Italy; 140 S. Green Valley Pkwy., Henderson; (702) 222-3556; settebello.net

Lucille's Smokehouse Bar–B–Que: Located in the District; 2245 Village Walk Dr., Henderson; (702) 257-7427; lucillesbbq.com

Honorable Mentions

Several more trails didn't make the list, not because they aren't worthy, but because they either require a specific skillset or help getting to the trailhead—and in some cases both. Still, if you possess the skillset or are looking to possess the skillset, these trails are definitely worthy of your consideration.

A. Bootleg Canyon Downhill Trails

If cross-country riding isn't your thing. If your idea of a two-wheeled ride is something a bit more daring, adventurous, or dare I say, thrilling, then look no further than the downhill trails at Bootleg Canyon. In fact, it is these trails that helped put Bootleg Canyon on the map as a world-class system of trails. With titles like "reaper," "Armageddon," and "Kevorkian," it's little wonder these trails have been sought after by seasoned veterans and pro downhill enthusiasts alike. The trails have even been the site of Reaper Madness, a pro-rider qualifier for the Gravity Nationals. If downhill is your thing, Bootleg has all you can handle and more. If it's good enough for professional rides, it's good enough for everyone else.

The downhill trails at Bootleg Canyon are accessed by taking the dirt road that runs through the canyon to its final destination. From here you hike with your bike (often referred to as hike-a-bike) from the uppermost parking lot to the trailheads and head downward. While the trails are open all year round, for most of the year you have to get to the top of the canyon by your own resources. For part of the

Shuttle taking riders to the downhill trails in Bootleg Canyon

year—depending on the need—All Mountain Cyclery has a shuttle that will get you to the top for a price. If you do plan on riding when the shuttle isn't running, remember it's a long way up that steep, narrow dirt road, so you may want to have someone take you up there and pick you back up at the bottom. Either way, you're bound to find your thrill with the downhill trails atop Bootleg Canyon hill.

List of Bootleg Canyon Downhill Trails:

- Ginger
- Kevorkian
- Diva
- Reaper
- Armageddon
- Ona Lee
- Sidewinder
- Snake Back
- Poopchute

B. Boy Scout

Boy Scout is a trail that requires a certain amount of downhill skills to ride. It also requires a bike able to handle a trail that is not quite a full downhill trail, but definitely not a cross-country trail. The other problem with Boy Scout is that, like the downhill trails at Bootleg Canyon, you can only access it by taking the dirt road to the uppermost parking lot at the very top of the hill. This means you'll need someone to either take you to the top and pick you up at the bottom or you'll have to ride down the trail and walk or ride your bike back up the hill—a ride that is very, very steep.

Boy Scout can be accessed at the far east end of the upper parking lot. When the trail splits, take the trail to the right, merging with another trail a short distance ahead. When the trails split a second time, follow the trail to the left and begin the downhill ride. Boy Scout connects with Caldera about halfway through the ride and then with Inner Caldera towards the end of the trail. Boy Scout officially ends at the upper parking lot right before the last climb of the dirt road; however, if someone took you up to the very top and dropped you off, you may want to connect Boy Scout to East Leg for a longer, more challenging ride down to the restrooms.

C. Skyline

Like Boy Scout, Skyline is a trail that requires a certain amount of downhill skills to ride. It also requires a bike able to handle a trail that is not quite a full downhill trail, but definitely not a cross-country trail. The other problem with Skyline is that you can only access it by taking the dirt road to the uppermost parking lot at the very top of the hill. You'll need someone to either take you to the top and pick you up at the bottom or you'll have to ride down the trail and walk or ride your bike back up the hill—a ride that is very, very steep.

Skyline can be accessed at the far east end of the upper parking lot. When the trail splits, take the trail to the left to begin the downhill ride. Skyline rides the canyon wall well above Boy Scout, so beside the technical aspect, you have a height issue as well, making this trail doubly difficult. Skyline officially ends at the upper parking lot right before the last climb of the dirt road. It does not connect to any other trail; however, if someone took you up to the very top and dropped you off, you may want to connect Skyline to East Leg for a longer, more challenging ride down to the restrooms.

Cottonwood Valley and the Surrounding Area

Home to the Red Rock Canyon National Conservation Area—Nevada's first National Conservation Area—the southwest section of the valley is arguably the most scenic. Here you can find petroglyphs, wild burros, and some of the most colorful mountains in all of Nevada. This section of the valley is also possibly the most remote. Much of it is owned and controlled by the Bureau of Land Management, meaning there are few housing developments. However, it is also a well-used recreation area, is

Burros grazing in Blue Diamond

home to such treasures as Spring Mountain Ranch State Park, and is one of the few places where you can actually ride a bike along the same dirt once trodden by settlers making their way to California along the Old Spanish Trail. It is also here that you can find more than 140 miles of single-track trails in an area called Cottonwood Springs, or simply Cottonwood to locals.

There are two places to access the trails in Cottonwood. The first is a paved parking lot, with an actual restroom, that is also just off State Route 160. The second spot is in the nearby town of Blue Diamond, which is off State Route 159. Blue Diamond is a town of roughly 290 people with just about one wild burro per person. In fact, it is a common morning sight to see a herd of burros grazing or just lying around in the grass at the town's park. A sign welcoming visitors to the town boasts the elevation as "high," the population as "low," and the burros as a question mark.

Officially, the town of Blue Diamond can trace its roots back to the early 1920s as a corporate town for workers of the Blue Diamond Company, which owned the local gypsum mine. However, locals know the town's roots spread all the way back to the 1830s and '40s when the area that now houses Blue Diamond was the site of a watering stop and trading post for settlers traveling the Old Spanish Trail between Santa Fe, New Mexico, and California. In fact, records show a local tribe of Native Americans—the Paiutes—growing crops of pumpkins and melons as far back as 1872. In 1965, the Blue Diamond Company started selling bunk housing and homes to the public and the town became populated by people other than workers in the gypsum mines.

The town of Blue Diamond is very welcoming to mountain bike riders—any bike riders, in fact—so long as those riders obey the town rules. One of the biggest rules is where to park. Ample parking is available in the heart of the downtown area next to a local bike shop—McGhie's Bike Outpost. In order to keep cars off the streets and limit the interactions between visitors and burros, you should park your vehicle in this area and then ride out to the various trailheads.

Like Bootleg Canyon, the trails at Cottonwood are interconnected, and you could actually ride every trail in the valley without having to drive to a separate trailhead. And while each section of trail has its own name, rides are mainly created by joining several trails into one larger ride. Cottonwood is growing steadily in popularity mainly due to the fact that it is far less technical than its cousin to the east—Bootleg Canyon. Though no less enjoyable, this system of trails is more geared to the rider with beginning to intermediate skills; however, trails do exist that require a more advanced set of skills. As you would expect, with such a vast system of trails, the rides in this area are also much longer than are the rides in Bootleg Canyon, meaning that while they are less technical in terrain, they require their own set of unique skills and present their own level of challenge.

Local Bike Shops

Broken Spoke Bikes: 11700 West Charleston, #190; (702) 823-1680; brokenspoke bikeslv.com

Las Vegas Cyclery: 10575 Discovery Dr., Las Vegas; (702) 596-2953; lasvegas cyclery.com

McGhie's Bike Outpost: 16 Cottonwood, #B, Blue Diamond; (702) 875-4820; mcghies.com

Peloton Sports: 911 N. Buffalo Dr., #101, Las Vegas; (702) 363-1991; peloton sports.com

Pro Cyclery: 7034 W. Charleston, Las Vegas; (702) 228-9460; procyclery.com

REI: 710 S. Rampart Blvd., Las Vegas; (702) 951-4488; rei.com

Southern Highlands Cyclery: 10550 Southern Highlands Pkwy., Ste. 130; (702) 778-7786; southernhighlandscyclery.com

Southwest Bikes: 7290 West Azure, Ste. 110, Las Vegas; (702) 227-7433; southwest bikes.com

Sport Chalet: 8825 W. Charleston Blvd., Las Vegas; (702) 255-7570; sportchalet .com

Vegas Bike Store: 3955 S. Durango, Ste. B-1, Las Vegas; (702) 586-5500; vegas bikestore.com sponsors bike rides

Vegas Velo Bicycles: 691 N. Valle Verde Dr., Ste. 130; (702) 503-9005; vegasvelo .com

23 Landmine Loop

The Landmine Loop covers a large part of the Cottonwood system of trails as it runs behind the small town of Blue Diamond. The trail makes its way through Cottonwood just outside Red Rock National Conservation Area, below the La Madre Mountains and the area known as the Red Rock Escarpment—an area that provides spectacular views of Cottonwood and all it has to offer. Much of the ride is in the hills just behind Blue Diamond. In fact, the trail actually begins on one side of town and ends on the other. This trail is complete with a couple of steep, rocky climbs and a tricky downhill section at about the middle of the trail. Between the two is a nice, fun ride through an area of Joshua trees and dark reddish-brown dirt.

Start: Asphalt parking lot outside McGhie's Outpost
Distance: 7.7 miles
Elevation gain: 564 feet
Riding time: Intermediate to advanced riders, 1 hour; beginning riders, 1.5 hours
Fitness effort: Physically moderate to challenging, mainly due to the trail's length
Difficulty: Technically moderate to challenging with some technically difficult spots

Terrain: Mostly dirt, some large rocks, and loose gravel
Maps: There are no official maps to this region
Nearest town: Blue Diamond
Other trail users: Hikers and runners
Dog friendly: Yes, but there are commonly wild burros
Trail contact: McGhie's Bike Outpost, (702) 875-4820; Southern Nevada Mountain Bike Association, snmba.net

Getting there: Take Interstate 15 to the Blue Diamond Exit. Head west along Blue Diamond Road (State Route 160). Turn right onto State Route 159 and follow the road to the town of Blue Diamond. Turn left onto Castalia Street and head to the asphalt parking lot outside McGhie's Bike Outpost. GPS: N36 02.835'/W115 24.443'

The Ride

From the parking lot, pull out onto Castalia Street and turn left heading to Cottonwood Drive. Turn left again and follow Cottonwood Drive up the hill. While traveling up the street, don't be in a hurry to get to the trail. Take time to notice the houses in the area. Many of them are wonderfully decorated and quite quaint. A right turn on Cerrito Street will lead you to the trailhead at the top of the hill. Cerrito Street is a bit of a climb and you'll know you've found the trailhead when asphalt turns to dirt. There will also be several large rocks at the trailhead, which are meant to deter motorized vehicles from going on the trail.

When you reach the trailhead, you'll find a bit of a drop with a fairly steep, but short climb on the other side. Once up that side, continue straight when the trail splits. As the trail progresses, it makes its way up a very long, very steep hill. There are

A group of riders head up the first big climb

many rocky spots and some areas are covered with loose gravel. This can be a tricky hill, but it offers a great sense of accomplishment when you reach the top. At the top, just to the left, is a collection of rocks that riders like to arrange into various shapes. One time it may form the outline of a rider on a mountain bike and another time it may be formed into a large smiley face or a gigantic peace sign.

From here you'll continue around one of the hills outside Blue Diamond on a trail that has a long, storied history. It was once traveled by settlers heading west, looking to make a better life for themselves. So many people traveled the trail that it earned a name—The Old Spanish Trail. When the trail splits, follow it to the right. Shortly after that split, the trail will fork. You can take either trail because they meet up again a short distance ahead. The trail to the right is the Hurl. It climbs high into the hills and eventually ends at that long steep hill you just climbed. This guide follows the trail to the left. Both trails meet up ahead, so if you take the trail to the right, be sure to take the trail back down when it splits.

Not long after you take that split to the left, there is a short but tricky drop. Follow the trail as it makes its way around the bottom of the hills. As you continue, you'll encounter a wash full of gravel. Cross the wash and make an immediate right turn, climbing up the small ridge. Follow the trail, being sure not to take any offshoot trails on either side of the main trail.

The trail climbs gradually through the desert, offering stunning views of the Red Rock Escarpment—which is the name of the multicolored mountains just to

THE OLD SPANISH TRAIL

In 1829, merchant Antonio Armijo led a group of 60 men and 100 mules on a trek from Santa Fe, New Mexico, to Los Angeles, California. Looking to establish a trade route, Armijo chose trails blazed by trappers, traders, and mountain men, such as Jedidiah Smith. He also created his own trails, connecting those existing into one main trail that could be used over and over again. Armijo eventually arrived at the San Gabriel mission with his group, for the most part, intact—minus a few mules that were used for meat.

The trail quickly gained the reputation of being the "longest, most arduous pack mule route in the history of America." The distinction, however, did not stop it from being heavily used by pack mule trains carrying supplies from New Mexico to California. In 1843, John C. Fremont and Kit Carson were hired to survey the area. Fremont and Carson chose to stick closer to the Red Rock Mountains, taking advantage of the many mountain springs, as they made their way through Cottonwood Valley. The trail they mapped would eventually be named the Old Spanish Trail and then the Mormon Trail.

the west of the trail. You'll also ride right by some of the largest Joshua trees in the area. These trees are home to many birds, such as woodpeckers, who perch on the branches of the trees in search of grubs. At one point the trail makes its way back to the foot of the hills. Here you'll find a large gray rock that offers a tricky obstacle. Shortly after the rock obstacle, you'll find another fork in the trail. Take the trail to the right and follow it as it climbs up into the hills. While the terrain isn't difficult, the climb is fairly steep in many places.

After you climb to the top of the ridge next to the hill, cross what looks like a rock bridge and start a little downhill section. Toward the end of the downhill section, an offshoot trail can be seen to the right. This is Dave's Driveway. Stay straight. When the trail splits yet again at the trail marker, follow the offshoot to the right. Here the dirt turns a rich reddish-brown as you make your way to the crest of a road. When the trail intersects the road at the top of the crest, you'll find a map of the trails on a kiosk and a large Joshua tree that is commonly used as a landmark. From here, take the trail to the right as it veers off the dirt road.

On the other side of the crest, the trail goes downhill, following a wash. This portion of the trail has sections filled with soft sand and others filled with smooth, but large boulders. The trail is made even trickier by the many cacti that lay in wait on either side of the trail for you to make a wrong move. Once you get past the wash, the trail continues its downhill trek back to Blue Diamond. However, there is still one hill left to climb. As you begin the climb, looking to the left, you'll find an old car—possibly from the '30s or '40s—on its side, down in the valley. The car has been shot up time and again and has often been confused with the car driven by notorious bank robbers Bonnie and Clyde. The confusion is further enhanced by the fact that there is a trail in the area known as "Bonnie and Clyde." Rest assured that the bank-robbing duo never made it this far west.

After you complete the final climb, it is an easy downhill ride to the end of the trail. At one point, the trail splits again. You can take either trail as they meet up again a short distance ahead. The upper trail is more difficult and the lower trail is a bit easier. This guide follows the lower trail. After the trails meet back up, you are home free. That is, except for the final drop. This drop is a little intimidating, but if you have the courage to take the drop without using your brakes, you'll have enough momentum to easily make it up the other side. Once you've navigated the final obstacle, follow the trail as it curves to the right and makes its way into Blue Diamond. You'll come out on Cottonwood Drive and easily find the parking lot on your left.

Miles and Directions

0.0 Turn left onto Castalia Street and then left again onto Cottonwood Drive. At 0.2 mile, turn right onto Cerrito Street and climb the hill.

0.3 Take the trailhead to the right in the gravel area marked by large boulders and a trail marker. In 0.1 mile, stay straight. Do not take the offshoot trail to the right.

0.5 Begin the long, steep climb up the hill. At the top of the hill at mile 0.7, stay straight. When the trail splits, take either trail for a short downhill section. The trails will meet back up ahead. Stay straight when another trail on the right merges with the main trail at mile 0.8.

1.2 Head right at the trail marker. Stay left when the trail forks. Take a short drop over some rocks at mile 1.3.

1.4 Stay straight as the upper trail merges with the lower trail. In 0.1 mile, enter the wash and make a sharp right turn on the other side, followed by a quick climb up the ridge. The wash is full of deep gravel.

1.6 The trail splits twice. Stay to the right each time. When the trail merges to the right, stay straight.

2.4 Ride over the large gray rock. Speed is the key in navigating this obstacle.

2.5 When the trail forks, stay right and cross the wash. Follow the trail left and begin a steep climb.

2.9 Cross the rock "bridge" and climb the hill on the other side.

3.4 When two trails cross, take the trail to the right and climb.

4.2 Stay straight when the trail merges with Dave's Driveway on the right.

4.3 Merge onto the dirt road and turn right. Climb up the hill past the trail map.

4.4 Pick the trail back up at the crest of the road, to the right; do not follow the dirt road. In 0.2 mile, turn right and connect with the dirt road for a short distance. When the dirt road starts to go down, take the trail to the right.

4.9 Follow the trail through a wash. There are sections with soft dirt and sections with large, smooth rocks. This portion of the trail is tricky. Stay straight as the trail merges on the right at 5.1 miles.

5.2 End of tricky rock section; stay straight, then follow the trail to the right. Do not follow the wash straight.

Landmine Loop

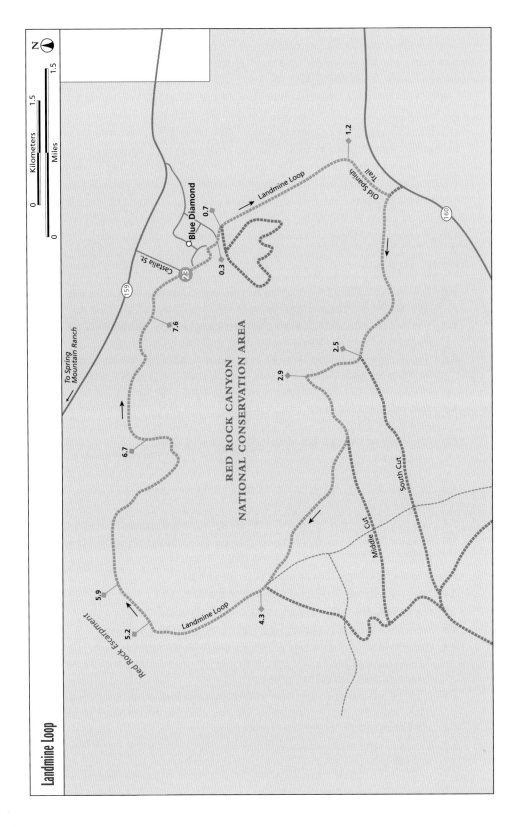

5.8 Stay straight. Do not take the offshoot trail to the left, which leads to an old shot-up car, lying on its side.

5.9 Stay straight as the offshoot trail on the left meets back up with the main trail. Start a steep climb. Follow the trail to the right at the top of the hill at mile 6.1 and begin a downhill section.

6.7 When the trail splits at the marker stay left. This is the lower trail. Stay straight when the upper and lower trails meet back up at mile 7.0.

7.5 Take the last deep drop and climb up the other side. Then follow the trail to the right.

7.6 When the trail meets up with a dirt road, follow the road to the right onto Cottonwood Drive.

7.7 Turn left onto Castalia Street and then take an immediate right into the parking lot.

Ride Information

Local Events and Attractions

Spring Valley Ranch State Park: Located close to Red Rock Canyon, this protected park was once a functioning ranch owned at various times by movie stars and famous billionaires, it is also home to some of the oldest buildings in the valley; parks.nv.gov.

Super Summer Theater: Located in the Spring Valley Ranch State Park is live theater nightly under the summer stars; supersummertheater.org.

Restaurant

Bonnie Springs Ranch Restaurant: American-style food located next to Bonnie Springs Ranch; 1 Gunfighter Ln., Bonnie Springs; (702) 875-4400; bonniesprings.com.

24 Landmine/Middle Cut Loop

This trail is an alternate route to the Landmine Loop, adding a little over a mile to the total ride. The ride offers an easy and enjoyable route through the middle of Cottonwood Valley, adding a fun downhill section before it meets back up with the Landmine Loop at the trail map kiosk and large Joshua tree that are commonly used as landmarks.

Start: Asphalt parking lot outside McGhie's Outpost
Distance: 8.8 miles
Elevation gain: 564 feet
Riding time: Intermediate to advanced riders, 1.5 hours; beginning riders, 2 hours
Fitness effort: Physically moderate to challenging, mainly due to the trail's length
Difficulty: Technically moderate to challenging with some technically difficult spots

Terrain: Mostly dirt, some large rocks, and loose gravel
Maps: There are no official maps to this region
Nearest town: Blue Diamond
Other trail users: Hikers and runners
Dog friendly: Yes, but there are commonly wild burros
Trail contact: McGhie's Bike Outpost, (702) 875-4820; Southern Nevada Mountain Bike Association, snmba.net

Getting there: Take Interstate 15 to the Blue Diamond Exit. Head west along Blue Diamond Road (State Route 160). Turn right onto State Route 159 and follow the road to the town of Blue Diamond. Turn left onto Castalia Street and head to the asphalt parking lot outside McGhie's Outpost. GPS: N36 02.835'/W115 24.443'

The Ride

Just like the Landmine Loop, the trail starts in the small town of Blue Diamond, beginning on one side of the town and ending on the other. Also like the Landmine Loop, the trail offers great views of the Cottonwood Valley and the Red Rock Escarpment. The difference between the two trails is that instead of staying on the trail that makes up the Landmine Loop, this route takes a detour when the Landmine Loop trail intersects the Middle Cut Trail, also known as North Cut and Middle Fork. Middle Cut, which is an easy, gradual climb, travels directly through the Cottonwood Valley offering wonderful views of the Las Vegas desert.

After the climb, Middle Cut meets up with another trail called Daytona (also called Little Daytona). This aptly named trail takes the rider on a fun, quick ride, eventually leading into a long downhill dash before meeting back up with the Landmine Loop at the large Joshua tree on the crest of a dirt road. From here, the trail follows Landmine Loop back to Blue Diamond.

From the parking lot, pull out onto Castalia Street and turn left heading to Cottonwood Drive. Turn left again and follow Cottonwood Drive up the hill. A right turn on Cerrito Street will lead you to the trailhead at the top of the hill. Cerrito Street is a bit of a climb and you'll know you've found the trailhead when asphalt turns to dirt. There will also be several large rocks at the trailhead, which are meant to deter motorized vehicles from going on the trail.

Follow the trail straight, not taking any offshoot trails and climb the long, steep climb up the hill. From here you'll continue on the trail as it makes its way around one of the hills outside Blue Diamond. This section is a welcomed downhill after the rigorous climb you just completed. Be sure to look up into the hills as you travel because it is a favorite spot for wild burros. When the trail splits a second time, follow it to the right. Shortly after that split, the trail will fork. The trail to the right is Hurl and eventually leads back to the large hill you just climbed. The trail to the left heads down into the wash, running alongside. Both trails meet up ahead, so if you take the trail to the right, be sure to take the trail back down when it splits.

Follow the trail as it makes its way around the bottom of the hills. As you continue, you'll encounter a wash full of gravel. Cross the wash and make an immediate right turn, climbing up the small ridge. From here, follow the trail, being sure not to take any offshoot trails on either side of the main trail.

Armina Grewell heading down the Middle Cut Trail

WILD BURROS

Just as you enter the town of Blue Diamond, you'll see a sign welcoming you to the town. The welcome is followed by some valuable information: "Elevation – High," "Population – Low," and "Burros - ?" Spend any time at all in Blue Diamond and you are bound to encounter a wild burro. This is because the town welcomes them as much, if not more, than they welcome mountain bikers. Burros can be seen walking the streets of the town in the evening and early-morning hours. They are most often found in the town's park, resting in or snacking on the cool grass.

Although they are plentiful in the hills of Cottonwood Valley, burros aren't native to the United States. They're actually native to Africa and were brought to the American continent by the Spanish in the late 1400s as pack animals. As gold and silver were discovered just outside of Las Vegas in the early 1800s, miners used these animals to pack their supplies into the mine and ore out of the mine. The miners eventually abandoned the area, often leaving their pack mules behind.

Wild, or feral, burros are well-suited to the Nevada desert and have thrived in the Red Rock Canyon. If you see one of these animals on your ride, enjoy their beauty from a distance. Most burros are not camera shy and love to have their photos taken—of course they haven't expressed that, but they do stand still when you take their picture, unless, of course, you get too close. When dealing with wild burros, remember they are wild animals. Unfortunately, many people ignore the signs and feed these animals. This combined with the fact that they are welcomed in Blue Diamond, make them comfortable around people, which can mistakenly make them seem docile. They are not. They have a strong kick and an even stronger bite. If one brays at you, take it as a warning to back off. And remember, feeding wild animals can make them dependent on a food source that is not reliable. Stop and look at them, take their picture, but let wild animals stay wild.

The trail climbs gradually through the desert, and at one point makes its way back to the foot of the hills. Here you'll find a large gray rock that provides a tricky obstacle. Speed is the key to successfully navigating this rock. Shortly after the rock obstacle, you'll find another fork in the trail. Take the trail to the right and follow it as it climbs up into the hills. While the terrain isn't difficult, the climb is fairly steep in many places.

After you climb to the top of the ridge next to the hill, cross what looks like a rock bridge and start a little downhill section. When the trail splits yet again at the trail marker, continue straight (note: Landmine Loop is the trail to the right). From here take a gradual climb through reddish-brown dirt following the trail until it dead ends at Daytona. Turn right onto Daytona and prepare for a fun, easy ride. When you see the wide dirt road, look for the trail on the other side. It is marked by a Bureau of Land Management trail marker—a long brown piece of plastic. Cross the road and take the trail onto a downhill section that allows you to go about as fast as you feel comfortable. The trail will eventually make its way to another dirt road. Keep your momentum up and use it to make the short but steep climb up the hill to the crest of the second dirt road. When the trail intersects the road at the top of the crest, you'll find a map of the trails on a kiosk and a large Joshua tree that is commonly used as a landmark. From here take the trail to the right as it veers off the dirt road. This is the Landmine Loop.

On the other side of the crest, the trail goes downhill, following a wash. This portion of the trail has sections filled with soft sand and others filled with smooth, but large boulders. The trail is made even trickier by the many cacti that lay in wait on either side of trail for you to make a wrong move. Once you get past the wash, the trail continues its downhill trek back to Blue Diamond. However, there is still one hill left to climb.

After you complete the final climb, it is an easy downhill ride to the end of the trail. At one point the trail splits again. You can take either trail as they meet up again a short distance ahead. The upper trail is more difficult and the lower trail is a bit easier. This guide follows the lower trail. Before you reach the end of the trail, there is one big last drop. Once you've navigated the final obstacle, follow the trail as it curves to the right and makes its way into Blue Diamond. You'll come out on Cottonwood Drive and easily find the parking lot on your left.

Miles and Directions

0.0 Turn left onto Castalia Street and then left again onto Cottonwood Drive. At 0.2 mile, turn right onto Cerrito Street and climb the hill.

0.3 Take the trailhead to the right in the gravel area marked by large boulders and a trail marker. In 0.1 mile stay straight. Do not take the offshoot trail to the right.

0.5 Begin the long, steep climb up the hill. At the top of the hill at mile 0.7, stay straight. When the trail splits, take either trail. Stay straight when another trail on the right merges with the main trail at mile 0.8.

1.2 Head to the right at the trail marker. Stay left when the trail forks.

1.4 Stay straight when the upper trail merges with the lower trail. In 0.1 mile, enter the wash and make a sharp right turn, then a quick climb up the ridge. The wash is full of deep gravel.

1.6 The trail splits twice. Stay to the right each time. When the trail merges to the right, stay straight.

2.4 Ride over the large gray rock. Speed is the key in navigating this obstacle.

2.5 When the trail forks, stay right and cross the wash, then head left and begin a steep climb.

2.9 Cross the rock "bridge" and climb the hill on the other side.

Landmine/Middle Cut Loop

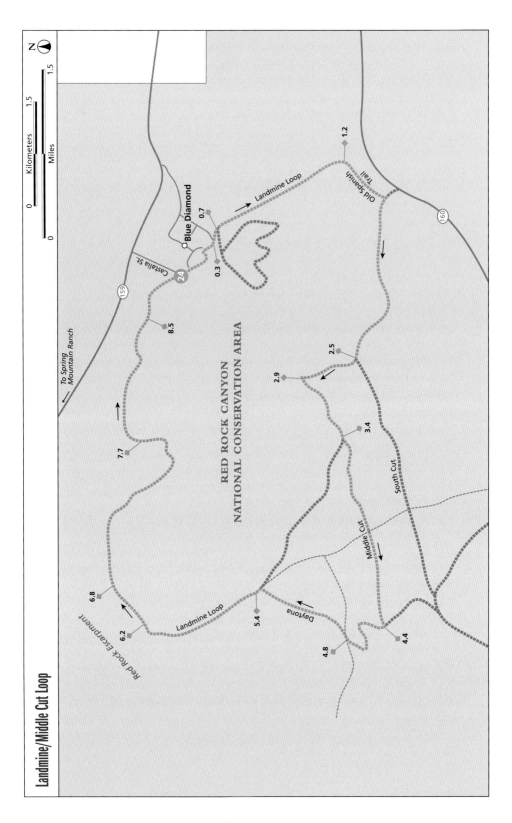

3.4 When two trails cross, continue straight. In 0.1 mile, cross the wash and make the short climb on the other side.

4.0 Cross the dirt road and in 0.2 mile, cross another wash. At 4.3 miles, cross the wash again.

4.4 When the trail dead ends, take the Daytona Trail to the right. In 0.1 mile, cross the wash and climb up the other side.

4.8 Cross the dirt road and look for the trail on the other side. Take that trail into a fun, easy downhill section that eventually makes its way up to the crest of a dirt road.

5.4 Turn left and merge onto the dirt road. Climb up the hill past the trail map. Pick the trail back up at the crest of the road, to the right; do not follow the dirt road.

5.8 Follow the trail into the quick drop with large rocks, then take the sharp right turn and begin a climb.

6.1 Stay straight as the trail merges on the right.

6.2 End of tricky rock section; stay straight, then follow the trail as it curves to the right. Do not follow the wash straight.

6.8 Stay straight. Do not take the offshoot trail to the left, which leads to an old shot-up car, lying on its side.

6.9 Stay straight as the offshoot trail on the left meets back up with the main trail. Start a steep climb. Follow the trail to the right at the top of the hill at mile 7.1 and begin a down-hill section.

7.7 Take the lower trail on the left when the trail splits at the marker. Stay straight as the upper and lower trails meet back up at mile 8.0.

8.5 Take the last deep drop. After the climb, follow the trail to the right.

8.6 When the trail meets up with a dirt road, follow the road to the right onto Cottonwood Drive.

8.8 Turn left onto Castalia Street and then take an immediate right into the parking lot.

Ride Information

Local Events and Attractions

Bonnie Springs Ranch: Visit an honest-to-goodness, old-fashioned Wild West town, complete with hangings, shootouts, and an official main street; bonniesprings .com.

Horseback Riding: If you'd like to see the scenery of the Red Rock Canyon from atop four hooves, you can do so at the Cowboy Trail Rides, just outside the National Conservation Area; cowboytrailrides.com.

Restaurant

Bonnie Springs Ranch Restaurant: American-style food located next to Bonnie Springs Ranch; 1 Gunfighter Ln., Bonnie Springs; (702) 875-4400; bonniesprings .com

25 Landmine Loop via Dave's Driveway

Dave's Driveway provides a challenging alternate route to the Landmine Loop. Once you've made Landmine's initial technical climb, you are rewarded with a nice easy ride through the valley before a technical downhill section. Dave's Driveway removes that easy ride and replaces it with a very technical climb over an extremely rocky section of the Cottonwood Hills, adding about a half mile to the trail. Due to the technical challenges this trail presents, only bikers with intermediate to advanced skills should take this alternate route to the Landmine Loop.

Start: Asphalt parking lot outside McGhie's Outpost
Distance: 8.1 miles
Elevation gain: 578 feet
Riding time: Advanced riders, 1 hour; intermediate riders, 1.5 hours
Fitness effort: Physically moderate to challenging with the Dave's Driveway section being challenging
Difficulty: Technically moderate to challenging with the Dave's Driveway section being challenging

Terrain: Mostly dirt with large rocks and loose gravel
Maps: There are no official maps to this region.
Nearest town: Blue Diamond
Other trail users: Hikers and runners
Dog friendly: Yes, but there are commonly wild burros
Trail contact: McGhie's Bike Outpost, (702) 875-4820; Southern Nevada Mountain Bike Association, snmba.net

Getting there: Take Interstate 15 to the Blue Diamond Exit. Head west along Blue Diamond Road (State Route 160). Turn right onto State Route 159 and follow the road to the town of Blue Diamond. Turn left onto Castalia Street and head to the asphalt parking lot outside McGhie's Bike Outpost. GPS: N36 02.835'/W115 24.443'

The Ride

From the parking lot, pull out onto Castalia Street and turn left heading to Cottonwood Drive. Turn left again and follow Cottonwood. A right turn on Cerrito Street will lead you to the trailhead at the top of the hill. Cerrito Street is a bit of a climb and you'll know you've found the trailhead when asphalt turns to dirt. There will also be several large rocks at the trailhead, which are meant to deter motorized vehicles from going on the trail.

When you reach the trailhead, continue straight, not taking any offshoot trails, as you make your way up the long, steep hill, around the hill and onto The Old Spanish Trail. When the trail splits a second time, follow it to the right. Shortly after that split, the trail will fork. The right trail is the Hurl. It climbs high into the hills and eventually ends at the steep hill you just climbed. The trail to the left heads down into the wash. The two trails meet up eventually, so if you take the trail to the right,

A group of riders head up Dave's Driveway.

be sure you follow the trail downward when that trail splits. This guide follows the trail to the left.

As you continue, you'll encounter a wash full of gravel. Cross the wash and make an immediate right turn, climbing up the small ridge. From here, you'll follow the trail, being sure not to take any offshoot trails on either side of the main trail. The trail climbs gradually through the desert. At one point the trail makes its way back to the foot of the hills. Here you'll find a large gray rock that offers a tricky obstacle. Shortly after the rock obstacle, you'll find another fork in the trail. Take the trail to the right and follow it as it climbs up into the hills. While the terrain isn't difficult, the climb is fairly steep in some places.

After you climb to the top of the ridge next to the hill, you'll cross what looks like a rock bridge and start a little downhill section. A short distance into the downhill section, you'll find the entrance to Dave's Driveway on the right. Most of Dave's Driveway is a long, steady, very technical climb complete with large rocks in some areas and many loose smaller rocks in other areas. Dave's Driveway heads high up into the hills, climbs over the top, before eventually heading back down into the valley and meeting back up with the Landmine Loop. When the trails intersect, head right. Here the dirt turns a rich reddish-brown as you make your way to the crest of a road. When the trail intersects the road at the top of the crest, you'll find a map of the trails on a kiosk and a large Joshua tree that is commonly used as a landmark. From here, take the trail to the right as it veers off the dirt road.

On the other side of the crest, the trail goes downhill, following a wash. This portion of the trail has sections filled with soft sand and others filled with smooth, but large boulders. The trail is made even trickier by the many cacti that lay in wait on either side of the trail for you to make a wrong move. Once you get past the wash, the trail continues its downhill trek back to Blue Diamond. However, there is still one hill left to climb. After you complete the final climb, it is an easy downhill ride to the end of the trail. Once you've navigated the final steep drop, follow the trail as it curves to the right and makes its way into Blue Diamond. You'll come out on Cottonwood Drive and easily find the parking lot on your left.

Miles and Directions

0.0   Turn left onto Castalia Street and then left again onto Cottonwood Drive. At 0.2 mile, turn right onto Cerrito Street and climb the hill.

0.3   Take the trailhead to the right in the gravel area marked by large boulders and a trail marker. In 0.1 mile, stay straight. Do not take the offshoot trail to the right.

0.5   Begin the long, steep climb up the hill. At the top of the hill at mile 0.7, stay straight. When the trail splits, take either trail for a short downhill section. The trails will meet back up ahead. Stay straight when another trail on the right merges with the main trail at mile 0.8.

1.2   Head right at the trail marker. Stay left when the trail forks. Take a short drop over some rocks at mile 1.3.

1.4   Stay straight as the upper trail merges with the lower trail. In 0.1 mile, enter the wash and make a sharp right turn, followed by a quick climb up the ridge. The wash is full of deep gravel.

1.6   The trail splits twice. Stay to the right each time. When the trail merges to the right, stay straight.

2.4   Ride over the large gray rock. Speed is needed to navigate this obstacle.

2.5   When the trail forks, stay right and cross the wash, then head left and begin a steep climb.

2.9   Cross the rock "bridge" and climb the hill on the other side.

3.2   Take Dave's Driveway turnoff to the right and begin a long gradual climb.

3.6   Take the short, steep drop that takes an immediate turn to the left at the bottom. The climb up the other side is very steep and rocky. Take the sharp left hairpin turn and head into another rocky climb.

4.1   Pass between the Joshua tree and the large rock, then head into a downhill section.

4.6   When the trail meets back up with Landmine Loop, turn right.

4.7   Merge onto the dirt road and turn right. Climb up the hill past the trail map.

4.8   Pick the trail back up at the crest of the road, to the right; do not follow the dirt road. In 0.2 mile, turn right and connect with the dirt road for a short distance. When the dirt road starts to go down, take the trail to the right.

6.2   Stay straight. Do not take the offshoot trail to the left.

6.3   Stay straight as the offshoot trail on the left meets back up with the main trail. Start a steep climb.

7.1   Stay left when the trail splits at the marker. This is the lower trail.

Landmine Loop via Dave's Driveway

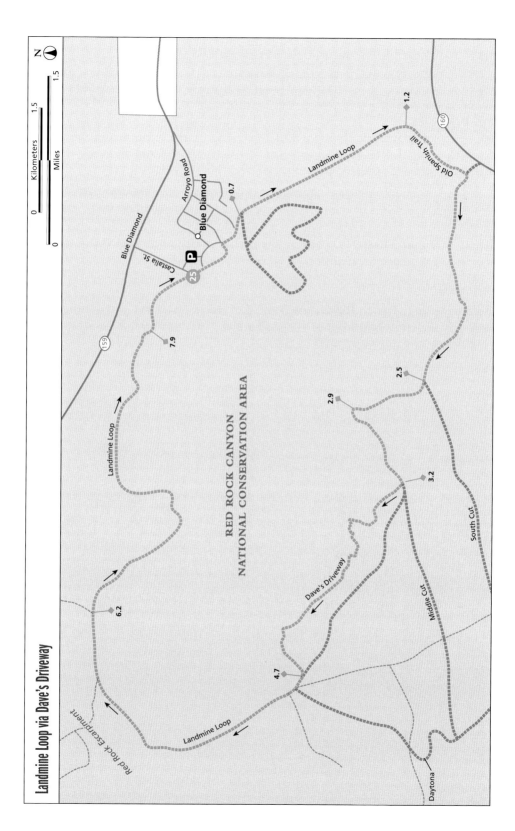

7.9 Take the last deep drop. After the climb, follow the trail to the right.

8.0 Follow the dirt road to the right onto Cottonwood Drive.

8.1 Turn left onto Castalia Street and then take an immediate right into the parking lot.

Ride Information

Local Events and Attractions

Spring Valley Ranch State Park: Located close to Red Rock Canyon, this protected park was once a functioning ranch owned at various times by movie stars and famous billionaires. It is also home to some of the oldest buildings in the valley; parks .nv.gov.

Super Summer Theater: Located in the Spring Valley Ranch State Park is live theater nightly under the summer stars; supersummertheater.org.

Restaurant

Bonnie Springs Ranch Restaurant: American-style food located next to Bonnie Springs Ranch; 1 Gunfighter Ln., Bonnie Springs; (702) 875-4400; bonniesprings .com.

26 Inner Loop via South Cut

The Inner Loop is a great trail that gives you a taste of everything Cottonwood has to offer. If you want to get to know the Cottonwood area, this is the trail for you. Not only will you have a fun ride, you'll get to see a large portion of the valley, and much of the Cottonwood trail system.

Start: Asphalt parking lot outside McGhie's Outpost

Distance: 9.7 miles

Elevation gain: 578 feet

Riding time: Intermediate to advanced riders, 2 hours; beginning riders, 2.5 hours

Fitness level: Physically moderate

Difficulty: Technically easy to moderate, with a couple of long gradual climbs and a tricky drop midway through the ride

Terrain: Mostly dirt, some large rocks, and loose gravel

Maps: There are no official maps to this region

Nearest town: Blue Diamond

Other trail users: Hikers and runners

Dog friendly: Yes, but there are commonly wild burros

Trail contact: McGhie's Bike Outpost, (702) 875-4820; Southern Nevada Mountain Bike Association, snmba.net

Getting there: Take Interstate 15 to the Blue Diamond Exit. Head west along Blue Diamond Road (State Route 160). Turn right onto State Route 159 and follow the road to the town of Blue Diamond. Turn left onto Castalia Street and head to the asphalt parking lot outside McGhie's Outpost. GPS: N36 02.835'/W115 24.443'

The Ride

From the parking lot, pull out onto Castalia Street and turn left heading to Cottonwood Drive. Turn left again and follow Cottonwood. A right turn on Cerrito Street will lead you to the trailhead at the top of the hill. Cerrito Street is a bit of a climb and you'll know you've found the trailhead when asphalt turns to dirt. There will also be several large rocks at the trailhead, which are meant to deter motorized vehicles from going on the trail.

When you reach the trailhead, continue straight, not taking any offshoot trails, as you make your way up the long, steep hill and onto The Old Spanish Trail. When the trail splits a second time, follow it to the right. Shortly after that split, the trail will fork. The right trail is the Hurl. It climbs high into the hills and eventually ends at the steep hill you just climbed. The trail to the left heads down into the wash. The two trails meet up eventually, so if you take the trail to the right, be sure you follow the trail downward when that trail splits. This guide follows the trail to the left.

As you continue, you'll encounter a wash full of gravel. Cross the wash and make an immediate right turn, climbing up the small ridge. From here, you'll follow the trail, being sure not to take any offshoot trails on either side of the main trail. The

Beth Rudolph heads down the Inner Loop.

trail climbs gradually through the desert. At one point the trail makes its way back to the foot of the hills. Here you'll find a large gray rock that offers a tricky obstacle. Shortly after the rock obstacle, you'll find another fork in the trail. Take the trail to the left and follow it as it climbs up into the hills. It only stays in the hills briefly before it heads back down into the valley, where it then makes a gradual climb as it heads toward Daytona, also called Little Daytona. There are several offshoot trails, so make sure you stay on the main trail whenever you encounter one of these trails. This section of the trail is called South Cut, but is also called Cactus Slalom because the trail snakes through a series of cactus that grow very close to the edge of the trail. For this reason, it is a good idea to take a couple spare tubes with you.

You'll cross a couple of dirt roads—usually the same dirt road—several times. The last time you cross a dirt road, you'll pick up the trail on the other side. Several trails converge in this area so be sure you take the right trail. You'll know you're on the right trail, because there will be a steep drop followed by an equally steep climb on the other side. This is the start of Daytona, a trail named for its twists, turns, and dips. This portion of the trail is a fun, easy ride, allowing you to go as fast as you feel comfortable.

Toward the end of this trail you'll encounter another dirt road. Look for the trail on the other side. It is marked by a Bureau of Land Management trail marker—a long brown piece of plastic. Cross the road and take the trail into a gradual descent that again allows you to go as fast as you feel comfortable. The trail will eventually make its way to another dirt road. Keep your momentum up and use it to make the short but steep climb up the hill to the dirt road. When the trail intersects the road at the top of the crest, you'll find a map of the trails on a kiosk and a large Joshua tree that is commonly used as a landmark.

Before you get to the crest of the dirt road, however, you'll see a trail on the other side. Take this trail, which is part of the Landmine Loop, and start a little downhill section through the valley. You'll be heading back toward where you started. At the point where two trails cross, turn to the left and climb the hill, then cross what looks like a rock bridge and start another downhill section. Towards the end of the downhill section you'll cross a wash and come out on the other side through some bushes. Here you'll find a familiar fork in the road—the one you encountered toward the beginning of the ride. Turn left and make your way back to the large gray rock obstacle. From there, follow the trail back the way you came initially, eventually going down the long steep hill you navigated at the beginning of the ride. When the trail ends, stay straight on Cerrito Street before turning left onto Cottonwood Drive. Take Cottonwood Drive back to the parking lot, turning right on Castalia Street and then an immediate right into the parking lot.

Miles and Directions

0.0 Turn left onto Castalia Street and then left again onto Cottonwood Drive. At 0.2 mile, turn right onto Cerrito Street and climb the hill.

0.3 Take the trailhead to the right in the gravel area marked by large boulders and a trail marker. In 0.1 mile, stay straight. Do not take the offshoot trail to the right.

0.5 Begin the long, steep climb up the hill.

0.8 Stay straight when another trail on the right merges with the main trail.

1.2 Stay left when the trail forks.

1.5 Enter the wash and make a sharp right turn, then a quick climb up the ridge. The wash is full of deep gravel.

1.6 The trail splits twice. Stay to the right each time. When the trail merges to the right, stay straight.

2.4 Ride over the large gray rock. Speed is the key in navigating this obstacle.

2.5 When the trail forks, stay left and begin a climb.

2.7 The trail splits twice, first on the left and then on the right. Stay straight each time.

2.8 Stay straight, as the trail splits again, following it to the right of the trail marker. Continue straight when the trail splits at mile 3.1 and climb the small hill.

3.5 Cross the dirt road and pick up the trail on the other side. You'll cross the same road in about a half mile.

3.7 Cross the dirt road a third time. Watch for cactus needles in this part of the trail.

4.0 Cross the wide dirt road and pick up the trail on the other side. Take the steep drop and the equally steep climb on the other side.

4.2 Stay straight; do not take the trail to the left. Begin a fun, fast section with lots of turns and little drops. Stay straight when the trail splits at 4.4 miles; do not take the trail to the right.

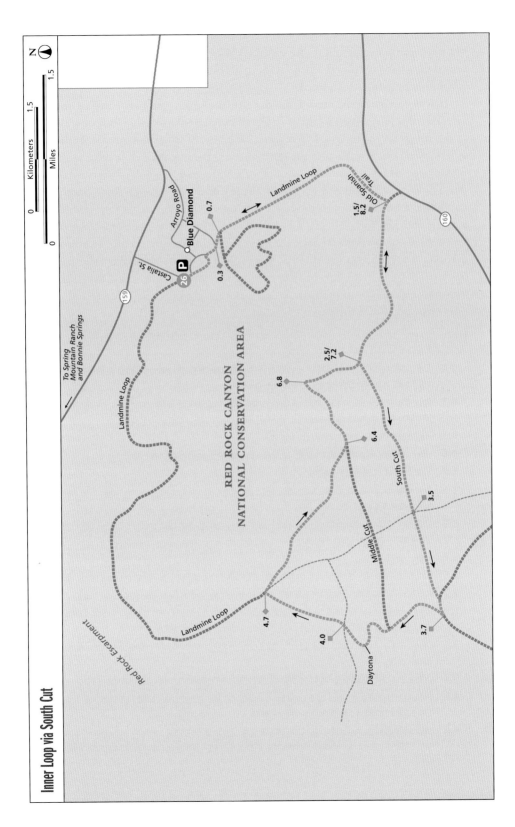

Inner Loop via South Cut

N

Kilometers
0   1.5   1.5

Miles
0   1.5

To Spring
Mountain Ranch
and Bonnie Springs

159

Castalla St.

Arroyo Road

Blue Diamond

P 26

0.7

0.3

Landmine Loop

Landmine Loop

Red Rock Escarpment

RED ROCK CANYON
NATIONAL CONSERVATION AREA

Landmine Loop

4.7

4.0

Daytona

3.7

Middle Cut

South Cut

3.5

6.4

6.8

2.5/
7.2

1.5/
8.2

Old Spanish
Trail

160

4.6 Follow the trail to the right, then climb the hill. Do not go straight when the trail seems to split. Stay to the right.

4.7 Cross the dirt road and pick up the trail on the other side at the trail marker. This begins a little downhill section.

5.3 Follow the trail as it turns to the left and meets up with a dirt road. Take the trail directly across the dirt road. This is the Landmine Loop. Stay straight at mile 5.4; do not take the trail to the left.

6.4 At the point where two trails cross, take the left trail and begin a short climb.

6.8 Cross the rock "bridge" and begin a downhill section.

7.2 Cross a wash and follow the trail through the bushes on the right. When the trail splits, go left. Navigate the large gray rock at mile 7.3.

8.0 When the trail splits, stay right. In 0.2 mile, follow the trail to the left. Do not take either of the offshoot trails to the right. Follow the trail into a gravel section. Turn right, cross the gravel, and pick up the trail on the other side. Stay straight at mile 8.3; do not take the trail to the left.

8.4 Take the steep climb with large rocks. When the upper and lower trail meet at mile 8.5, stay straight.

8.6 Follow the trail as it goes to the left. At mile 8.9, stay to the right when the trail seems to split.

9.0 When the two trails meet, stay straight, then follow the trail right down the steep hill.

9.3 Stay straight; do not take the trail to the left. Take the quick drop and then the short, but steep climb. Follow the trail as it curves left.

9.4 Head left onto Cerritos Street. In 0.1 mile, turn left onto Allegro Street and follow it to Cottonwood Drive.

9.7 Turn right onto Castalia Street and another immediate right into the parking lot.

Ride Information

Local Events and Attractions

Spring Valley Ranch State Park: Located close to Red Rock Canyon, this protected park was once a functioning ranch owned at various times by movie stars and famous billionaires. It is also home to some of the oldest buildings in the valley; parks .nv.gov.

Bonnie Springs Ranch: Visit an honest-to-goodness, old-fashioned Wild West town, complete with hangings, shootouts, and an official main street; bonniesprings .com.

Restaurants

Mountain Springs Saloon: Or, more specifically, the eating establishment behind the Mountain Springs Saloon; 19050 US 160, Las Vegas; (702) 875-4266; mountain springssaloon.com

Montana Meat Company: American-style food and steaks; 9135 S. Durango Dr., Las Vegas; (702) 407-0362; montanameatco.com

27 Inner Loop via Rubber Ducky

Inner Loop is actually supposed to be ridden through Rubber Ducky, also known as Ducky. This route adds more distance to the ride and is a little more difficult than the South Cut route. Rubber Ducky is a very popular trail in Cottonwood mainly because there is a large Joshua tree toward the end of the trail, just off to the side, from which bikers like to hang rubber ducks of all types and sizes. Whether this prompted the name of the trail or was a result of the trail being originally named "Ducky," is left for others to debate. If you do choose to leave a rubber ducky on the tree, make sure you do it in a way that does not harm the tree itself. Also, if you see a ducky that has fallen to the ground, please pick it up and pack it out with you. Remember, ride leaving no trace.

Start: Asphalt parking lot outside McGhie's Outpost
Distance: 10.4 miles
Elevation gain: 578 feet
Riding time: Intermediate to advanced riders, 2 hours; beginning riders, 2.5 hours
Fitness level: Physically moderate
Difficulty: Technically easy to moderate, with a couple of long gradual climbs and a tricky drop midway through the ride

Terrain: Mostly dirt, some large rocks, and loose gravel
Maps: There are no official maps to this region
Nearest town: Blue Diamond
Other trail users: Hikers and runners
Dog friendly: Yes, but there are commonly wild burros
Trail contact: McGhie's Bike Outpost, (702) 875-4820; Southern Nevada Mountain Bike Association, snmba.net

Getting there: Take Interstate 15 to the Blue Diamond Exit. Head west along Blue Diamond Road (State Route 160). Turn right onto State Route 159 and follow the road to the town of Blue Diamond. Turn left onto Castalia Street and head to the asphalt parking lot outside McGhie's Outpost. GPS: N36 02.835'/W115 24.443'

The Ride

From the parking lot, pull out onto Castalia Street and turn left heading to Cottonwood Drive. Turn left again and follow Cottonwood Drive up the hill. A right turn on Cerrito Street will lead you to the trailhead at the top of the hill. Cerrito Street is a bit of a climb and you'll know you've found the trailhead when asphalt turns to dirt. There will also be several large rocks at the trailhead, which are meant to deter motorized vehicles from going on the trail.

When you reach the trailhead, continue straight, not taking any offshoot trails, as you make your way up the long, steep hill and onto the Old Spanish Trail. When the trail splits a second time, follow it to the right. Shortly after that split, the trail will fork. The right trail is the Hurl. It climbs high into the hills and eventually ends at the steep hill you just climbed. The trail to the left heads down into the wash. The two trails meet up eventually, so if you take the trail to the right, be sure you follow the trail downward when that trail splits. This guide follows the trail to the left.

As you continue, you'll encounter a wash full of gravel. Cross the wash and make an immediate right turn, climbing up the small ridge. Be sure not to take any offshoot trails on either side of the main trail as it climbs gradually through the desert. At one point the trail makes its way back to the foot of the hills. Here you'll find a large gray rock that offers a tricky obstacle. Shortly after the rock obstacle, you'll find another fork in the trail. Take the trail to the left and follow it as it climbs up and over a short hill.

Twice along the route, the trail meets up with a trail on the left. The first is Lawn-mower. Continue straight at this intersection. When a similar intersection happens in a short distance, take the trail to the left. This trail is marked Ducky, but it will also be marked as Rubber Ducky. The trail you were on is the South Cut Trail, also called Cactus Slalom.

Rubber Ducky heads up into the hills, riding the valley that lays between two hills. The first part of this section is a bit of a climb, complete with several rock obstacles and big dips into the valley. The climb continues through most of the ride, following along the wash that lays between the two hills. Towards the end of the trail, a large Joshua tree can be seen off to the side. The tree is often covered with rubber ducks of all types and sizes. The trail eventually climbs to the top of the hill where it dead ends at the Old Spanish Trail. Turn right and head to the point where several trails converge at a dirt road. Cross the dirt road and head into a steep drop followed by an equally steep climb on the other side. This is the start of Daytona, also called Little Daytona, a trail named for its twists, turns, and dips. This portion of the trail is a fun, easy ride, allowing you to go as fast as you feel comfortable.

Towards the end of this trail you'll encounter another dirt road. Look for the trail on the other side. It is marked by a Bureau of Land Management trail marker—a long brown piece of plastic. Cross the road and take the trail into a gradual descent that again allows you to go as fast as you feel comfortable. The trail will eventually make its way to another dirt road. Keep your momentum up and use it to make the short but steep climb up the hill to the dirt road. When the trail intersects the road at the top of the crest, you'll find a map of the trails on a kiosk and a large Joshua tree that is commonly used as a landmark.

Before you get to the crest of the dirt road, however, you'll see a trail on the other side. Take this trail, which is part of the Landmine Loop, and start a little downhill section through the valley. You'll be heading back toward where you started. When two trails cross, turn to the left and begin a climb. After you climb to the top of a hill, cross what looks like a rock bridge and start another downhill section. Towards the end of the downhill section, cross a wash and come out on the other side through some bushes. Here you'll find a familiar fork in the road—the one you encountered toward the beginning of the ride. Turn left and make your way back to the large gray

The Joshua tree where riders hang rubber ducks

rock obstacle. From there, follow the trail back the way you came initially, eventually going down the long steep hill you navigated at the beginning of the ride. When the trail ends, stay straight on Cerrito Street before turning left onto Cottonwood Drive. Take Cottonwood Drive back to the parking lot, turning right on Castalia Street and then an immediate right into the parking lot.

Miles and Directions

0.0 Turn left onto Castalia Street and then left again onto Cottonwood Drive. At 0.2 mile, turn right onto Cerrito Street and climb the hill.

0.3 Take the trailhead to the right in the gravel area marked by large boulders and a trail marker. In 0.1 mile stay straight. Do not take the offshoot trail to the right.

0.5 Begin the long, steep climb up the hill.

0.7 At the top of the hill, stay straight. When the trail splits, take either trail for a short downhill section. The trails will meet back up ahead. Stay straight when another trail on the right merges with the main trail at mile 0.8.

1.2 Head right at the trail marker. When the trail forks, stay left.

1.5 Enter the wash and make a sharp right turn, then a quick climb up the ridge. The wash is full of deep gravel.

1.6 The trail splits twice. Stay to the right each time. When the trail merges to the right, stay straight.

2.4 Ride over the large gray rock. Speed is the key in navigating this obstacle.

2.5 Stay left when the trail forks and begin a climb over a rock section.

2.7 The trail splits twice, first on the left and then on the right. Stay straight each time.

2.8 Take the Rubber Ducky Trail to the left and head into a climb. The trail to the right is South Cut, or Cactus Slalom.

3.2 When the trail splits, stay right, eventually dropping into the wash. The trail to the left is Wounded Knee.

3.4 When the trail splits, stay left following the wash. The trail to the right is a connector trail to Mustang.

3.6 Pass the rubber ducky-decorated Joshua tree and head into a long gradual climb out of the wash to the crest of the hill.

3.8 When the trail dead ends at The Old Spanish Trail, go right. Stay straight when the two trails meet a short distance ahead.

3.9 When the trails split at a triangle, stay right and head into a downhill section. Left leads to the Late Night Trail. When the trails split again, stay left following Mustang and heading towards Daytona. The trail to the right is a connector trail leading to Landmine.

4.2 Cross the dirt road and continue the downhill section. In 0.1 mile, pass the large Joshua tree and begin a gradual climb.

4.3 Stay right when the trails merge.

4.7 Cross the wide dirt road and pick up the trail on the other side. Take the steep drop and the equally steep climb on the other side.

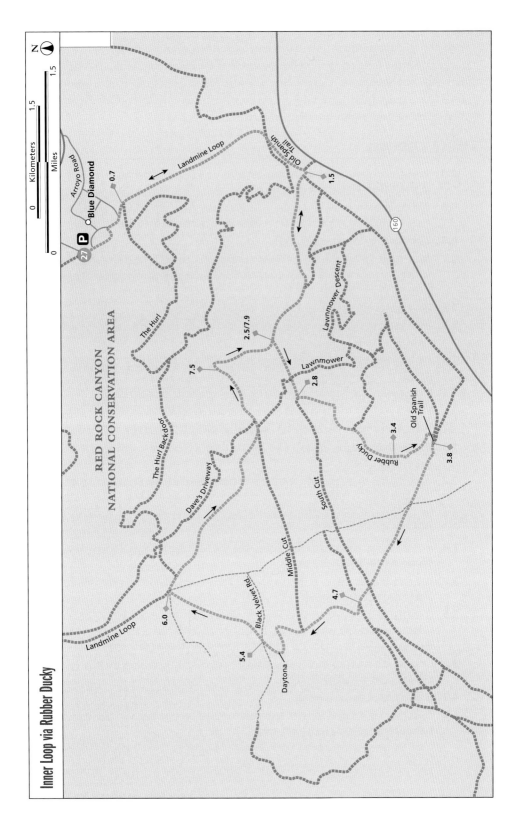

Inner Loop via Rubber Ducky

RED ROCK CANYON
NATIONAL CONSERVATION AREA

Blue Diamond

Arroyo Road

Landmine Loop

Old Spanish Trail

160

Lawnmower Descent

Lawnmower

The Hurl

The Hurl Backdoor

Dave's Driveway

Rubber Ducky

Old Spanish Trail

South Cut

Middle Cut

Black Velvet Rd.

Daytona

Landmine Loop

0.7

1.5

2.5/7.9

7.5

2.8

3.4

3.8

4.7

5.4

6.0

27

P

N

Kilometers
0   1.5

Miles
0   1.5

4.9 Stay straight; do not take the trail to the left. Begin a fun, fast section with lots of turns and little drops. Stay straight when the trail splits at 4.4 miles; do not take the Middle Cut trail to the right.

5.4 Cross the dirt road and pick up the trail on the other side at the trail marker. This begins a little downhill section.

6.0 Turn left and meet up with a dirt road. Take the trail directly across the dirt road. This is the Landmine Loop. Stay straight at mile 5.4; do not take Dave's Driveway to the left.

7.1 At the point where two trails cross, turn left and begin a short climb.

7.9 Cross a wash and follow the trail through the bushes on the right. Go left when the trail splits; navigate the large gray rock at mile 8.0.

8.5 When the trail splits, stay right. In 0.2 mile, follow the trail left. Do not take either of the offshoot trails to the right. Follow the trail into a gravel section. Turn right, cross the gravel, and pick up the trail on the other side. Stay straight at mile 8.3; do not take the trail to the left.

9.7 When the two trails meet, stay straight, then follow the trail to the right down the steep hill.

10.0 Stay straight; do not take the trail to the left. Take the quick drop and then the short, but steep climb on the other side. Follow the trail as it curves left.

10.1 Turn left onto Cerritos Street. In 0.1 mile, turn left onto Allegro Street and follow it to Cottonwood Drive.

10.4 Turn right onto Castalia Street and then another immediate right into the parking lot.

Ride Information

Local Events and Attractions

Spring Valley Ranch State Park: Located close to Red Rock Canyon, this protected park was once a functioning ranch owned at various times by movie stars and famous billionaires. It is also home to some of the oldest buildings in the valley; parks .nv.gov.

Bonnie Springs Ranch: Visit an honest-to-goodness, old-fashioned Wild West town, complete with hangings, shootouts, and an official main street; bonniesprings .com.

Restaurants

Bonnie Springs Ranch Restaurant: American-style food located next to Bonnie Springs Ranch; 1 Gunfighter Ln., Bonnie Springs; (702) 875-4400; bonniesprings .com

Montana Meat Company: American-style food and steaks; 9135 S. Durango Dr., Las Vegas; (702) 407-0362; montanameatco.com

28 Middle Cut Loop

This trail is an alternate route to the Landmine Loop, adding a little over a mile to the total ride. The ride offers an easy and enjoyable route through the middle of Cottonwood Valley, then gives you a fun downhill section before it meets back up with the Landmine Loop and eventually heads back to Blue Diamond.

Start: Asphalt parking lot outside McGhie's Outpost

Distance: 9.6 miles

Elevation gain: 564 feet

Riding time: Intermediate to advanced riders, 1.5 hours; beginning riders, 2 hours

Fitness effort: Physically moderate to challenging

Difficulty: Technically moderate to challenging, with a technical climb at the beginning of the ride and a tricky downhill towards the end of the ride

Terrain: Mostly dirt, some loose gravel and rocks

Maps: There are no official maps to this region

Nearest town: Blue Diamond

Other trail users: Hikers and runners

Dog friendly: Yes, but there are commonly wild burros

Trail contact: McGhie's Bike Outpost, (702) 875-4820; Southern Nevada Mountain Bike Association, snmba.net

Getting there: Take Interstate 15 to the Blue Diamond Exit. Head west along Blue Diamond Road (State Route 160). Turn right onto State Route 159 and follow the road to the town of Blue Diamond. Turn left onto Castalia Street and head to the asphalt parking lot outside McGhie's Outpost. GPS: N36 02.835'/W115 24.443'

The Ride

From the parking lot, pull out onto Castalia Street and turn left heading to Cottonwood Drive. Turn left again and follow Cottonwood Drive up the hill. A right turn on Cerrito Street will lead you to the trailhead at the top of the hill. Cerrito Street is a bit of a climb and you'll know you've found the trailhead when asphalt turns to dirt. There will also be several large rocks at the trailhead, which are meant to deter motorized vehicles from going on the trail.

Follow the trail straight, not taking any offshoot trails and make the long, steep climb up the hill. From here, you'll continue on the trail as it makes its way around one of the hills outside Blue Diamond. This section is a welcomed downhill after the rigorous climb you just completed. Be sure to look up into the hills as you travel as it is a favorite spot for wild burros. When the trail splits a second time, follow it to the right. Shortly after that split, the trail will fork. The trail to the right is Hurl and eventually leads back to the large hill you just climbed. The trail to the left heads down into the wash, running alongside. Both trails meet up ahead, so if you take the trail to the right, be sure to take the trail back down when it splits.

Aaron Osborne gets air on the Middle Cut Loop.

Follow the trail as it makes its way around the bottom of the hills. As you continue, you'll encounter a wash full of gravel. Cross the wash and make an immediate right turn, climbing up the small ridge. Be sure not to take any offshoot trails on either side of the main trail. The trail climbs gradually through the desert, and at one point makes its way back to the foot of the hills. Here you'll find a large gray rock that provides a tricky obstacle. Speed is the key to navigating this obstacle. Shortly after the rock obstacle, you'll find another fork in the trail. Take the trail to the right and follow it as it climbs up into the hills. While the terrain isn't difficult, the climb is fairly steep in many places.

After you climb to the top of the ridge next to the hill, cross what looks like a rock bridge and start a little downhill section. When the trail splits yet again at the trail marker, continue straight. Landmine Loop is the trail to the right. From here you'll take a gradual climb through reddish-brown dirt as the trail makes its way to Daytona. When the trail dead ends, turn right onto Daytona and prepare for a fun, easy ride. When you see the wide dirt road, look for the trail on the other side. It is marked by a Bureau of Land Management trail marker—a long brown piece of plastic. Cross the road and take the trail into a gradual descent that allows you to go about as fast as you feel comfortable. The trail will eventually make its way to another dirt road. Keep your momentum up and use it to make the short but steep climb up the hill to the crest of the second dirt road. When the trail intersects the road at the top of the crest, you'll find a map of the trails on a kiosk and a large Joshua tree that is commonly used as a landmark.

Do not head to the crest of the road. Instead, cross the dirt road and pick up the trail on the other side. Head back down into the valley as the trail once again travels through reddish-brown dirt through the Joshua trees into a slight downhill section down Landmine Loop. When the trail again meets the point where Landmine Loop intersects with Middle Cut, continue straight and take the gradual climb to the top of the hill. At the crest of the hill, follow the trail over a couple rock obstacles and down the back side. This is a tricky, fairly technical downhill section. Cross the wash and head left along South Cut when the trails intersect. You'll climb a short hill and head down the other side to the point where Landmine Loop split off to the left. Stay to the right, cross the wash, head over the large rock obstacle, and follow the trail back to the trailhead.

Miles and Directions

0.0 Turn left onto Castalia Street and then left again onto Cottonwood Drive. At 0.2 mile, turn right onto Cerrito Street and climb the hill.

0.3 Take the trailhead to the right in the gravel area marked by large boulders and a trail marker. In 0.1 mile, stay straight. Do not take the offshoot trail to the right.

0.5 Begin the long, steep climb up the hill. Stay straight at the top of the hill. Stay straight when another trail on the right merges with the main trail at mile 0.8.

1.2 Follow the trail right at the trail marker. When the trail forks, take the left trail.

1.6 The trail splits twice. Stay to the right each time. When the trail merges to the right, stay straight.

2.4 Ride over the large gray rock. Speed is the key to navigating this obstacle.

2.5 When the trail forks, take the trail to the right.

2.9 Cross the rock "bridge," then climb the hill.

3.4 When two trails cross, continue straight. In 0.1 mile, cross the wash and make the short climb on the other side.

4.0 Cross the dirt road and in 0.2 mile, cross another wash into a bit of a steep climb. At 4.3 miles, cross the wash again.

4.4 When the trail dead ends, take Daytona to the right. In 0.1 mile, cross the wash and climb the other side.

4.8 Cross the dirt road and pick up the trail on the other side. Take that trail into a fun, easy downhill section that eventually makes its way up to the crest of a dirt road.

5.4 Turn left and meet up with a dirt road. Take the Landmine Loop trail directly across the dirt road. Stay straight at mile 5.6; do not take Dave's Driveway to the left.

6.4 When the two trails cross, stay straight and begin the climb to the top of the hill.

6.7 Go over the rock ledge and head down the back side of the hill into a series of steep switchbacks and rock ledges.

6.9 Cross the wash when the trails meet up and head left.

7.2 Stay right when the trails meet and head into the wash. Go over the large rock obstacle and follow the trail back to the trailhead.

9.6 Arrive back at the parking lot.

Middle Cut Loop

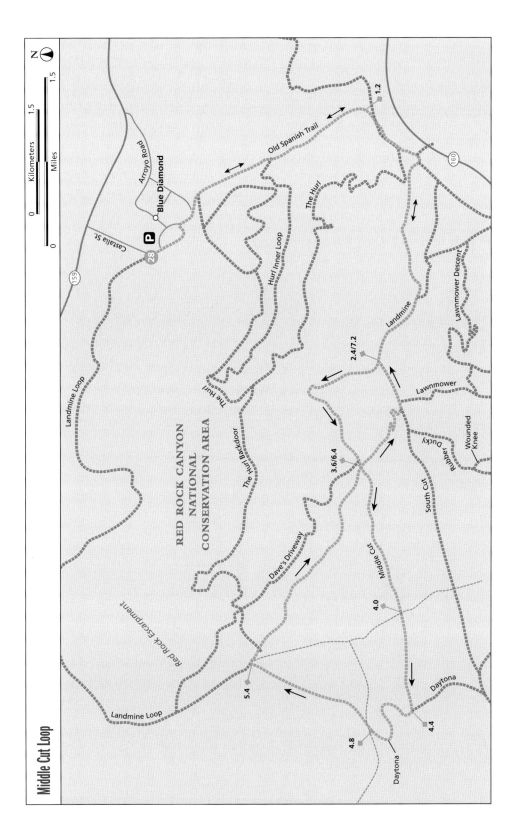

Ride Information

Local Events and Attractions

Bonnie Springs Ranch: Visit an honest-to-goodness, old-fashioned Wild West town, complete with hangings, shootouts, and an official main street; bonniesprings .com.

Horseback Riding: If you'd like to see the scenery of the Red Rock Canyon from atop four hooves, you can do so at the Cowboy Trail Rides, just outside the National Conservation Area; cowboytrailrides.com.

Restaurant

Bonnie Springs Ranch Restaurant: American-style food located next to Bonnie Springs Ranch; 1 Gunfighter Ln., Bonnie Springs; (702) 875-4400; bonniesprings .com

29 Blue Diamond Loop

The Blue Diamond Loop is a trail that combines much of the Inner Loop with the end of the Landmine Loop, making for a rather lengthy, but enjoyable ride. Before the ride is over, you'll find you've been on just about every trail in the Cottonwood Valley. You would be hard pressed to find a ride that shows you more of this beautiful valley and the colorful mountains that make up the Red Rock Escarpment surrounding the valley.

Start: Asphalt parking lot outside McGhie's Outpost

Distance: 10.2 miles

Elevation gain: 578 feet

Riding time: Intermediate to advanced riders, 3 hours; beginning riders, 3.5 hours

Fitness level: Physically moderate to challenging

Difficulty: Technically moderate to challenging, with a couple of long gradual climbs and a tricky drop midway through the ride, and a technical downhill section

Terrain: Mostly dirt, some large rocks, and loose gravel

Maps: There are no official maps to this region

Nearest town: Blue Diamond

Other trail users: Hikers and runners

Dog friendly: Yes, but there are commonly wild burros

Trail contact: McGhie's Bike Outpost, (702) 875-4820; Southern Nevada Mountain Bike Association, snmba.net

Getting there: Take Interstate 15 to the Blue Diamond Exit. Head west along Blue Diamond Road (State Route 160). Turn right onto State Route 159 and follow the road to the town of Blue Diamond. Turn left onto Castalia Street and head to the asphalt parking lot outside McGhie's Outpost. GPS: N36 02.835'/W115 24.443'

The Ride

From the parking lot, pull out onto Castalia Street and turn left heading to Cottonwood Drive. Turn left again and follow Cottonwood Drive. A right turn on Cerrito Street will lead you to the trailhead at the top of the hill. Cerrito Street is a bit of a climb and you'll know you've found the trailhead when asphalt turns to dirt. There will also be several large rocks at the trailhead, which are meant to deter motorized vehicles from going on the trail.

When you reach the trailhead, continue straight, not taking any offshoot trails, as you make your way up the long, steep hill and onto The Old Spanish Trail. When the trail splits a second time, follow it to the right. Shortly after that split, the trail will fork. The right trail is the Hurl. It climbs high into the hills and eventually ends at the steep hill you just climbed. The trail to the left heads down into the wash. The two trails meet up eventually, so if you take the trail to the right, be sure you follow the trail downward when that trail splits. This guide follows the trail to the left.

A rider on the Daytona portion of the Blue Diamond Loop

As you continue, you'll encounter a wash full of gravel. Cross the wash and make an immediate right turn, climbing up the small ridge. Be sure not to take any offshoot trails on either side of the main trail. The trail climbs gradually through the desert and at one point makes its way back to the foot of the hills. Here you'll find a large gray rock that offers a tricky obstacle. Shortly after the rock obstacle, you'll find another fork in the trail. Take the trail to the left and follow it as it climbs up and over a short hill.

Follow this trail until you come to a split in the trail that resembles a triangle, about 2.7 miles into the ride. This is the trailhead for Lawnmower. Take the tail to the left and begin a long steep climb complete with lots of loose rocks and several rock obstacles. When the trails split, stay straight, heading onto the Lawnmower Saddle, also known as Wounded Knee, until it meets up with Rubber Ducky, then turn left at Rubber Ducky.

Rubber Ducky heads up into the hills, riding the valley that lays between two hills. The climb continues through most of the ride, following along the wash that lays between the two hills. Toward the end of the trail a large Joshua tree can be seen off to the side. The tree is often covered with rubber ducks of all types and sizes. The trail eventually climbs to the top of the hill where it dead ends at the Old Spanish Trail. From here, turn right and head to the point where several trails converge. Cross the dirt road and head into a steep drop followed by an equally steep climb on the other side. This is the start of Daytona, also called Little Daytona, a trail named for its twists, turns, and dips. This portion of the trail is a fun, easy ride, allowing you to go as fast as you feel comfortable.

Toward the end of this trail, you'll encounter another dirt road. When you see the dirt road, look for the trail on the other side. It is marked by a Bureau of Land Management trail marker—a long brown piece of plastic. Cross the road and take the trail into a gradual descent that again allows you to go as fast as you feel comfortable. The trail will eventually make its way to another dirt road. Keep your momentum up and use it to make the short but steep climb up the hill to this dirt road. When the trail intersects the road at the top of the crest, you'll find a map of the trails on a kiosk and a large Joshua tree that is commonly used as a landmark.

On the other side of the crest, the trail goes downhill, following a wash. This portion of the trail has sections filled with soft sand and others filled with smooth, but large boulders. The trail is made even trickier by the many cacti that lay in wait on either side of the trail for you to make a wrong move. Once you get past the wash, the trail continues its downhill trek back to Blue Diamond. However, there is still one hill left to climb. As you begin the climb, looking to the left you'll find an old car—possibly from the '30s or '40s—on its side, down in the valley. The car has been shot up time and again and has often been confused with the car driven by notorious bank robbers Bonnie and Clyde. The confusion is further enhanced by the fact that there is a trail in the area known as "Bonnie and Clyde." Rest assured that the bank-robbing duo never made it this far west.

After you complete the final climb, it is an easy downhill ride to the end of the trail. At one point, the trail splits again. You can take either trail as they meet up again a short distance ahead. The upper trail is more difficult and the lower trail is a bit easier. After the trails meet back up, you are home free. That is, except for the final drop. This drop is a little intimidating, but if you have the courage to take the drop without using your brakes, you'll have enough momentum to easily make it up the other side. Once you've navigated the final obstacle, follow the trail as it curves to the right and makes its way into Blue Diamond. You'll come out on Cottonwood Drive and easily find the parking lot on your left.

Miles and Directions

0.0 Turn left onto Castalia Street and then left again onto Cottonwood Drive. At 0.2 mile, turn right onto Cerrito Street and climb the hill.

0.3 Take the trailhead to the right in the gravel area marked by large boulders and a trail marker. In 0.1 mile stay straight. Do not take the offshoot trail to the right.

1.2 Turn right at the trail marker. When the trail forks, take the left trail.

1.5 Enter the wash and make a sharp right turn, then a quick climb up the ridge. The wash is full of deep gravel.

1.6 The trail splits twice. Stay to the right each time. When the trail merges to the right, stay straight.

2.4 Ride over the large gray rock. Speed is key in navigating this obstacle.

Blue Diamond Loop

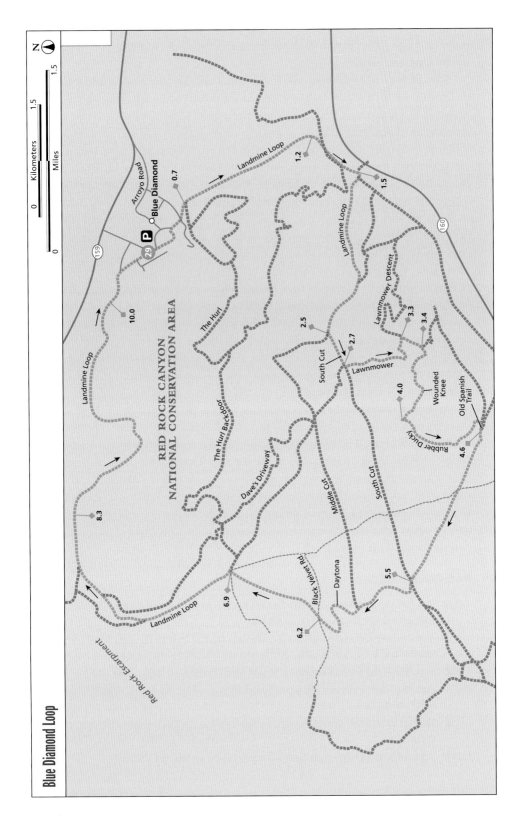

2.5 When the trail forks, take the left trail and begin a climb over a rock section.

2.7 When the trail splits, take the Lawnmower Trail left and begin a long steep climb with sections full of loose rocks.

3.3 When the trail dead ends, turn right and follow Wounded Knee as it climbs and then heads down to Rubber Ducky.

3.4 When the trail seems to split, stay straight. The trail to the left is Lawnmower Climb.

4.0 When the trails split again, take the Rubber Ducky Trail left and begin a long climb.

4.2 When the trail splits, stay left following along the wash. The trail to the right is a connector trail to Mustang.

4.4 Pass the rubber ducky–decorated Joshua tree and follow the trail as it makes a long gradual climb out of the wash to the crest of the hill.

4.6 When the trail dead ends at The Old Spanish Trail, go right. Stay straight when the two trails meet a short distance ahead.

4.7 When the trails split at a triangle, stay right and head into a downhill section. Left leads to the Late Night Trail. When the trails split again, stay to the left following Mustang and heading towards Daytona. The trail to the right is a connector trail leading to Landmine.

5.0 Cross the dirt road and continue the downhill section. In 0.1 mile, pass the large Joshua tree and begin a gradual climb.

5.1 When the trails merge, stay right.

5.5 Cross the wide dirt road and pick up the trail on the other side. Take the steep drop and the equally steep climb on the other side.

5.7 Stay straight; do not take the trail to the left. Begin a fun, fast section with lots of turns and little drops. Stay straight when the trail splits. Do not take the Middle Cut Trail to the right.

6.2 Cross the dirt road and pick up the trail on the other side at the trail marker. This begins a little downhill section.

6.8 Merge onto the dirt road and turn right. Climb up the hill past the trail map.

6.9 Pick the trail back up at the crest of the road, to the right; do not follow the dirt road.

7.4 Follow the trail through a wash. This portion of the trail is tricky. Stay straight as the trail merges on the right.

7.7 Stay straight then follow the trail as it curves to the right. Do not follow the wash straight.

8.3 Stay straight. Do not take the offshoot trail to the left, which leads to an old shot-up car, lying on its side.

8.4 Stay straight as the offshoot trail on the left meets back up with the main trail. Start a steep climb.

9.2 Stay left when the trail splits at the marker. This is the lower trail. Stay straight as the upper and lower trails meet back up.

10.0 Take the last deep drop and follow the trail to the right.

10.1 When the trail meets up with a dirt road, follow the road to the right onto Cottonwood Drive.

10.2 Turn left onto Castalia Street and then take an immediate right into the parking lot.

Ride Information

Local Events and Attractions

Spring Valley Ranch State Park: Located close to Red Rock Canyon, this protected park was once a functioning ranch owned at various times by movie stars and famous billionaires. It is also home to some of the oldest buildings in the valley and one of the best places to go bird watching; parks.nv.gov.

Bonnie Springs Ranch: Visit an honest-to-goodness, old-fashioned Wild West town, complete with hangings, shootouts, and an official main street; bonniesprings.com.

Restaurants

Bonnie Springs Ranch Restaurant: American-style food located next to Bonnie Springs Ranch; 1 Gunfighter Ln., Bonnie Springs; (702) 875-4400; bonniesprings.com

Mountain Springs Saloon: Or, more specifically, the eating establishment behind the Mountain Springs Saloon; 19050 US 160, Las Vegas; (702) 875-4266; mountainspringssaloon.com

30 Lawnmower

Lawnmower takes you on a ride to the outskirts of the Cottonwood Valley. It starts at the parking lot in Blue Diamond, climbs The Old Spanish Trail, and then takes a connector trail that eventually hooks up with the Landmine Loop, before veering off to South Cut. From here the trail climbs high onto a hill that offers great views of the Las Vegas Valley and the Cottonwood trail system. After the long rocky climb, you are rewarded with a fun, fast downhill, called Lawnmower Descent, that intersects the connector trail to complete the loop.

Start: Asphalt parking lot outside McGhie's Outpost

Distance: 6.8 miles

Elevation gain: 338 feet

Riding time: Intermediate to advanced riders, 1 hour; beginning riders, 2 hours

Fitness level: Physically moderate to challenging

Difficulty: Technically moderate to challenging, with long gradual climbs and a technical downhill section

Terrain: Mostly dirt, with large rocks and many loose small rocks

Maps: There are no official maps to this region

Nearest town: Blue Diamond

Other trail users: Hikers and runners

Dog friendly: Yes, but there are commonly wild burros

Trail contact: McGhie's Bike Outpost, (702) 875-4820; Southern Nevada Mountain Bike Association, snmba.net

Getting there: Take Interstate 15 to the Blue Diamond Exit. Head west along Blue Diamond Road (State Route 160). Turn right onto State Route 159 and follow the road to the town of Blue Diamond. Turn left onto Castalia Street and head to the asphalt parking lot outside McGhie's Outpost. GPS: N36 02.835'/W115 24.443'

The Ride

From the parking lot, pull out onto Castalia Street and turn left heading to Cottonwood Drive. Turn left again and follow Cottonwood Drive. A right turn on Cerrito Street will lead you to the trailhead at the top of the hill. Cerrito Street is a bit of a climb and you'll know you've found the trailhead when asphalt turns to dirt. There will also be several large rocks at the trailhead, which are meant to deter motorized vehicles from going on the trail.

When you reach the trailhead, continue straight, not taking any offshoot trails, as you make your way up the long, steep hill and onto The Old Spanish Trail. When the trail splits a second time, follow it to the right. Shortly after that split, the trail will fork. The right trail is the Hurl. The trail to the left heads down into the wash. The two trails meet up eventually, so if you take the trail to the right, be sure you follow the trail downward when that trail splits. This guide follows the trail to the left.

A rider heads up the Lawnmower Trail.

As you continue, you'll encounter a wash full of gravel. Cross the wash and make an immediate right turn, climbing up the small ridge. When the trail splits, follow the trail to the left up the wide dirt road, which is The Old Spanish Trail. About 0.2 mile into the ride, take the offshoot trail to the right, which leads to a fun connector trail that seems to be downhill no matter which way you take it. At the end of the connector trail, cross the long rock ledge and hook up with the Landmine Loop.

Turn left and follow the Landmine Loop until you reach the large gray rock that offers a challenging obstacle. Ride over the rock and into the wash, taking the short climb on the other side. When the trail splits again, stay left and climb the hill, head over the large flat rocks and down the other side. Follow this trail until you come to a split in the trail that resembles a triangle, about 1.3 miles into the ride. This is the trailhead for the Lawnmower Trail. Take the trail to the left and begin a long steep climb complete with lots of loose rocks and several rock obstacles.

When the trail dead ends, turn left and follow the trail as it climbs the next hill. At the top of the hill, be sure to pause and take in the view. From here you can see the Cottonwood Valley, a good portion of the trail system, and even the Las Vegas Valley off in the distance. Then follow the trail into a tight right turn and descent into a series of switchbacks. Follow the descent until it dead ends a second time. Go left and follow the trail until it meets the connector trail, then turn right and follow the trail back to the trailhead.

Miles and Directions

0.0 Turn left onto Castalia Street and then left again onto Cottonwood Drive. At 0.2 mile, turn right onto Cerrito Street and climb the hill.

Lawnmower

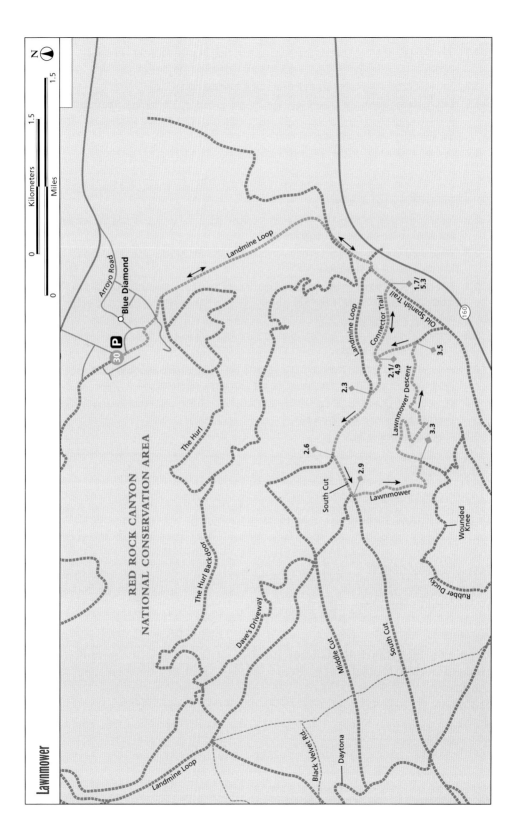

RED ROCK CANYON
NATIONAL CONSERVATION AREA

Blue Diamond

Arroyo Road

The Hurl

The Hurl Backdoor

Dave's Driveway

Middle Cut

Black Velvet Rd.

Daytona

South Cut

South Cut

Landmine Loop

Landmine Loop

Landmine Loop

Connector Trail

Old Spanish Trail

160

Lawnmower Descent

Lawnmower

Wounded Knee

Rubber Ducky

2.3

2.6

2.9

2.1/
4.9

3.5

3.3

1.7/
5.3

N

Kilometers

Miles

0   1.5

0   1.5

0.3 Take the trailhead to the right in the gravel area marked by large boulders and a trail marker. In 0.1 mile stay straight. Do not take the offshoot trail to the right.

1.2 Turn right at the trail marker. When the trail forks, take the left trail.

1.5 Enter the wash and make a sharp right turn, then a quick climb up the ridge. The wash is full of deep gravel. Follow the trail up the short, steep hill. When the trail splits, go left up the wide dirt road (The Old Spanish Trail).

1.7 Take the offshoot trail to the right and head down the connector trail to the Landmine Loop.

2.3 Cross the rock ledge that forms a bridge over the wash and turn left onto the Landmine Loop when the trail dead ends.

2.6 Navigate the large rock obstacle and cross the wash. When the trails split, take the left trail and head up the hill, over the large flat rock.

2.9 When the trail splits, take the Lawnmower Trail to the left and begin a long steep climb with sections full of loose rocks.

3.3 Take the quick left turn on the flat rocks. Do not head straight up the wash. The trail can clearly be seen on the left. Head into a quick right turn, then take the gradual, but steep climb.

3.5 When the trail dead ends, turn left. Head to the crest of the next hill, then begin a descent into a series of switchbacks.

4.7 Head left when the trails meet. In 0.2 mile, go to the right when the trail dead ends, and head back to the trailhead. You are on the connector trail you stated on.

5.3 When the trail dead ends at the Old Spanish Trail, turn left. Stay right when the trail splits, then head into and across the wash.

6.8 Arrive at the parking lot.

Ride Information

Local Events and Attractions

Bonnie Springs Ranch: Visit an honest-to-goodness, old-fashioned Wild West town, complete with hangings, shootouts, and an official main street; bonniesprings .com.

Horseback Riding: If you'd like to see the scenery of the Red Rock Canyon from atop four hooves, you can do so at the Cowboy Trail Rides, just outside the National Conservation Area; cowboytrailrides.com.

Restaurants

Bonnie Springs Ranch Restaurant: American-style food located next to Bonnie Springs Ranch; 1 Gunfighter Ln., Bonnie Springs; (702) 875-4400; bonniesprings .com

Mountain Springs Saloon: Or, more specifically, the eating establishment behind the Mountain Springs Saloon; 19050 US 160, Las Vegas; (702) 875-4266; mountain springssaloon.com

31 Lawnmower Saddle

Lawnmower Saddle is a fun ride that travels from Rubber Ducky to Lawnmower. It is called a saddle because the trail creates a reverse U—a kind of hump—meaning you ride one trail up to the top of the hump and another trail down the other side, just as if you were riding on a saddle. The trail climbs up Rubber Ducky for a short distance before heading to the left on a trail called Wounded Knee. This portion of the ride is a steady climb up the hill. At the top of the hill the trail heads down the other side toward Lawnmower, only this time when you get to Lawnmower, you get to go down what is a long steady climb the other way. While this trail is a bit longer than the Lawnmower to Lawnmower Descent Trail, it is a much easier ride.

Start: Asphalt parking lot outside McGhie's Outpost

Distance: 7.1 miles

Elevation gain: 337 feet

Riding time: Intermediate to advanced riders, 1 hour; beginning riders, 2 hours

Fitness level: Physically moderate to challenging

Difficulty: Technically moderate to challenging, with gradual climbs and a technical downhill section

Terrain: Mostly dirt, with large rocks and many loose small rocks

Maps: There are no official maps to this region

Nearest town: Blue Diamond

Other trail users: Hikers and runners

Dog friendly: Yes, but there are commonly wild burros

Trail contact: McGhie's Bike Outpost, (702) 875-4820; Southern Nevada Mountain Bike Association, snmba.net

Getting there: Take Interstate 15 to the Blue Diamond Exit. Head west along Blue Diamond Road (State Route 160). Turn right onto State Route 159 and follow the road to the town of Blue Diamond. Turn left onto Castalia Street and head to the asphalt parking lot outside McGhie's Outpost. GPS: N36 02.835'/W115 24.443'

The Ride

From the parking lot, pull out onto Castalia Street and turn left heading to Cottonwood Drive. Turn left again and follow Cottonwood Drive. A right turn on Cerrito Street will lead you to the trailhead at the top of the hill. Cerrito Street is a bit of a climb and you'll know you've found the trailhead when asphalt turns to dirt. There will also be several large rocks at the trailhead, which are meant to deter motorized vehicles from going on the trail.

When you reach the trailhead, continue straight, not taking any offshoot trails, as you make your way up the long, steep hill and onto The Old Spanish Trail. When the trail splits a second time, follow it to the right. Shortly after that split, the trail will fork. The right trail is the Hurl. The trail to the left heads down into the wash. The two trails meet up eventually, so if you take the trail to the right, be sure you follow the trail downward when that trail splits. This guide follows the trail to the left.

As you continue, you'll encounter a wash full of gravel. Cross the wash and make an immediate right turn, climbing up the small ridge. When the trail splits, follow the trail to the left up the wide dirt road, which is The Old Spanish Trail. About 1.7 miles into the ride, take the offshoot trail to the right, which leads to a fun connector trail that seems to be downhill no matter which way you take it. At the end of the connector trail, cross the long rock ledge and hook up with the Landmine Loop.

Turn left and follow the Landmine Loop until you reach the large gray rock that offers a challenging obstacle. Ride over the rock and into the wash, taking the short climb on the other side. When the trail splits again, stay left and climb the hill, head over the large flat rocks and down the other side. Follow this trail until you come to a split in the trail that resembles a triangle, about 2.8 miles into the ride. Continue straight until you reach the next triangle convergence of trails, then take Rubber Ducky, also called Ducky, to the left and head into a climb. At about 3.3 miles, when the trail splits again, take the Wounded Knee Trail to the left and make the steep climb on the trail full of loose rocks.

A rider heads over the Lawnmower Saddle.

Follow the trail as it climbs to the crest of the hill over a very rocky section. Once at the top of the hill, you may want to stop and take in the wonderful views of the Cottonwood Valley and the Las Vegas Valley off in the distance. On the other side of the hill begin a downhill section that eventually leads to the Lawnmower Trail at about 4.0 miles into the ride. Follow Lawnmower down to the point where the trail merges with South Cut and turn right. Follow the trail up the hill and down the other side. When the trail splits again, follow the trail to the right into and across the wash. Then go over the rock obstacle and follow the trail back to the connector trail, marked by a long, plastic, brown Bureau of Land Management marker. Cross the rock ledge and follow the connector trail to the point where it dead ends at The Old Spanish Trail. Turn left and then right when the trail splits again. Head into and across the wash and arrive at the dirt parking lot.

Miles and Directions

0.0 Turn left onto Castalia Street and then left again onto Cottonwood Drive. At 0.2 mile, turn right onto Cerrito Street and climb the hill.

0.3 Take the trailhead to the right in the gravel area marked by large boulders and a trail marker. In 0.1 mile stay straight. Do not take the offshoot trail to the right.

1.2 Turn right at the trail marker. When the trail forks, take the left trail.

1.5 Enter the wash and make a sharp right turn, then a quick climb up the ridge. The wash is full of deep gravel. Follow the trail up the short, steep hill. When the trail splits, go left up the wide dirt road (The Old Spanish Trail).

1.7 Take the offshoot trail to the right and head down the connector trail to the Landmine Loop.

2.3 Cross the rock ledge that forms a bridge over the wash and turn left onto the Landmine Loop when the trail dead ends.

2.6 Navigate the large rock obstacle and cross the wash. When the trails split, take the left trail and climb the hill, over the large flat rock.

2.8 When the trail splits, stay straight. Do not take the Lawnmower Trail to the left.

2.9 When the trail splits take the Rubber Ducky Trail to the left and begin a climb.

3.3 When the trails split again, take the Wounded Knee Trail to the left and begin a long, steep climb. The trail is full of loose rocks.

3.5 Follow the trail left as it crosses over to the next hill and begin a rocky climb to the crest of the hill.

3.8 Follow the trail left into a gradual downhill section.

3.9 When the trail seems to split, stay straight. The trail to the right is Lawnmower Climb.

4.0 When the trail splits again, take the Lawnmower Trail to the left. The trail to the right leads to Lawnmower Descent.

4.6 When the trail dead ends, take the South Cut Trail right. Climb the hill, over the flat rock obstacle, and down the other side. In 0.1 mile when the trails split, stay right, then head into the wash and over the large rock obstacle.

5.1 When the trail splits, take the connector trail to the right. Cross the rock bridge and follow the trail back to the trailhead.

5.3 When the trail splits, stay straight.

Lawnmower Saddle

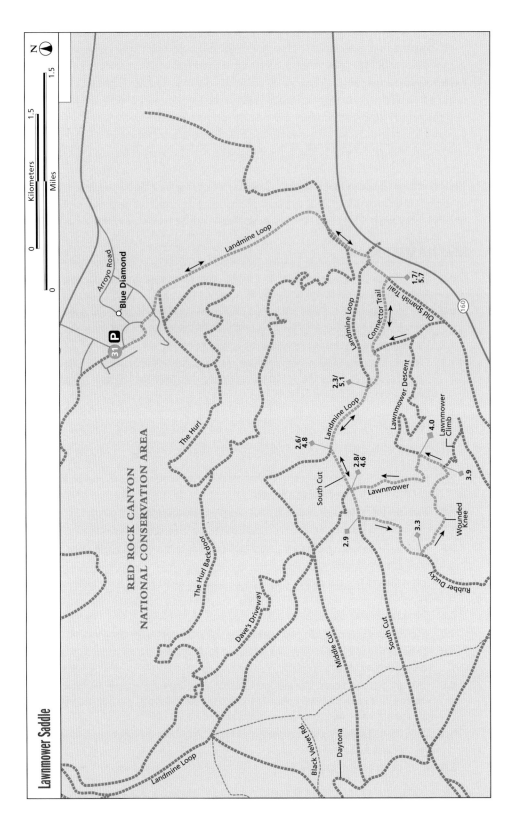

5.7 When the trail dead ends at The Old Spanish Trail, turn left. When the trail splits, follow the trail right into the wash.

7.1 Arrive at the parking lot.

Ride Information

Local Events and Attractions

Horseback Riding: If you'd like to see the scenery of the Red Rock Canyon from atop four hooves, you can do so at the Cowboy Trail Rides, just outside the National Conservation Area; cowboytrailrides.com.

Bonnie Springs Ranch: Visit an honest-to-goodness, old-fashioned Wild West town, complete with hangings, shootouts, and an official main street; bonniesprings .com.

Restaurants

Montana Meat Company: American-style food and steaks; 9135 S. Durango Dr., Las Vegas; (702) 407-0362; montanameatco.com

Bonnie Springs Ranch Restaurant: American-style food located next to Bonnie Springs Ranch; 1 Gunfighter Ln., Bonnie Springs; (702) 875-4400; bonniesprings .com

32 Lawnmower Descent via Lawnmower Saddle

This trail offers a fun alternative to the Lawnmower Trail which leads into the Lawnmower Descent. Instead of climbing Lawnmower, you take Rubber Ducky to Wounded Knee and then make the long gradual climb, eventually reaching the top of the hill. Once at the top you begin a descent down the other side, eventually leading into a technical downhill section before meeting up again with the connector trail that takes you back to the dirt road. The trail presents a challenging climb, accompanied by a very technical descent that is best suited to intermediate and advanced riders, but can be ridden by beginning riders.

Start: Asphalt parking lot outside McGhie's Outpost
Distance: 7.4 miles
Elevation gain: 338 feet
Riding time: Intermediate to advanced riders, 1 hour; beginning riders, 2 hours
Fitness level: Physically moderate to challenging
Difficulty: Technically moderate to challenging, with gradual climbs and a technical downhill section

Terrain: Mostly dirt, with large rocks and many loose small rocks
Maps: There are no official maps to this region
Nearest town: Blue Diamond
Other trail users: Hikers and runners
Dog friendly: Yes, but there are commonly wild burros
Trail contact: McGhie's Bike Outpost, (702) 875-4820; Southern Nevada Mountain Bike Association, snmba.net

Getting there: Take Interstate 15 to the Blue Diamond Exit. Head west along Blue Diamond Road (State Route 160). Turn right onto State Route 159 and follow the road to the town of Blue Diamond. Turn left onto Castalia Street and head to the asphalt parking lot outside McGhie's Outpost. GPS: N36 02.835'/W115 24.443'

The Ride

From the parking lot, pull out onto Castalia Street and turn left heading to Cottonwood Drive. Turn left again and follow Cottonwood Drive. A right turn on Cerrito Street will lead you to the trailhead at the top of the hill. Cerrito Street is a bit of a climb and you'll know you've found the trailhead when asphalt turns to dirt. There will also be several large rocks at the trailhead, which are meant to deter motorized vehicles from going on the trail.

When you reach the trailhead, continue straight, not taking any offshoot trails, as you make your way up the long, steep hill and onto The Old Spanish Trail. When the trail splits a second time, follow it to the right. Shortly after that split, the trail will fork. The right trail is the Hurl. The trail to the left heads down into the wash. The two trails meet up eventually, so if you take the trail to the right, be sure you follow the trail downward when that trail splits. This guide follows the trail to the left.

Resty Torres de Lima heads down the connector trail.

As you continue, you'll encounter a wash full of gravel. Cross the wash and make an immediate right turn, climbing up the small ridge. When the trail splits, follow the trail to the left up the wide dirt road, which is The Old Spanish Trail. About 1.7 miles into the ride, take the offshoot trail to the right, which leads to a fun connector trail that seems to be downhill no matter which way you take it. At the end of the connector trail, cross the long rock ledge and hook up with the Landmine Loop.

Turn left and follow the Landmine Loop until you reach the large gray rock that offers a challenging obstacle. Ride over the rock and into the wash, taking the short climb on the other side. When the trail splits again, stay left and climb the hill, head over the large flat rocks and down the other side. Follow this trail until you come to a split in the trail that resembles a triangle, about 2.8 miles into the ride. Continue straight until you reach the next triangle convergence of trails, then take Rubber Ducky, also called Ducky, to the left and head into a climb. At about 3.3 miles, when the trail splits again, take the Wounded Knee Trail to the left and make the steep climb on the trail full of loose rocks.

Follow the trail as it climbs to the crest of the hill over a very rocky section. Once at the top of the hill, you may want to stop and take in the wonderful views of the Cottonwood Valley. On the other side of the hill begins a downhill section that eventually leads to the Lawnmower Trail at about 4.0 miles into the ride. Pass the Lawnmower Trail and follow the trail as it climbs the next hill. At the top of the hill be sure to pause and take in the view. From here you can see the Cottonwood Valley, a good portion of the trail system, and even Las Vegas off in the distance. Then follow the trail into a tight right turn and descent into a series of switchbacks. Follow the descent until the trail dead ends a second time. Go left and follow the trail until it meets the connector trail, then turn right and follow the trail back to the trailhead.

Miles and Directions

0.0 Turn left onto Castalia Street and then left again onto Cottonwood Drive. At 0.2 mile, turn right onto Cerrito Street and climb the hill.

0.3 Take the trailhead to the right in the gravel area marked by large boulders and a trail marker. In 0.1 mile stay straight. Do not take the offshoot trail to the right.

1.2 Turn right at the trail marker. When the trail forks, take the left trail.

1.5 Enter the wash and make a sharp right turn, then a quick climb up the ridge. The wash is full of deep gravel. Follow the trail up the short, steep hill. When the trail splits, go left up the wide dirt road (The Old Spanish Trail).

1.7 Take the offshoot trail to the right and head down the Connector Trail to the Landmine Loop.

2.3 Cross the rock ledge that forms a bridge over the wash and turn left onto the Landmine Loop when the trail dead ends.

2.6 Navigate the large rock obstacle and cross the wash. When the trails split, take the left trail and head up the hill, over the large flat rock.

2.8 When the trail splits, stay straight. Do not take the Lawnmower Trail to the left.

2.9 When the trail splits take the Rubber Ducky Trail to the left and begin a climb.

3.3 When the trail splits again, take the Wounded Knee Trail to the left and begin a long, steep climb. The trail is full of loose rocks.

3.5 Follow the trail left and begin a rocky climb to the crest of the next hill.

3.8 Follow the trail left into a gradual downhill section.

3.9 When the trail seems to split, stay straight. The trail to the right is Lawnmower Climb.

4.0 When the trail dead ends, turn left. Head to the crest of the next hill, then begin a descent into a series of switchbacks.

4.6 Take the hairpin turn left over the rocky ledge, then continue along the side of the hill.

5.3 When the trails meet, head left. In 0.2 mile when the trail dead ends, go right and head back to the trailhead. You are on the Connector Trail you started on.

5.9 When the trail dead ends at The Old Spanish Trail, head left. When the trail splits, stay right, then head into and across the wash.

7.4 Arrive at the parking lot.

Ride Information

Local Events and Attractions

Spring Valley Ranch State Park: Located close to Red Rock Canyon, this protected park was once a functioning ranch owned at various times by movie stars and famous billionaires. It is also home to some of the oldest buildings in the valley; parks .nv.gov.

Lawnmower Descent via Lawnmower Saddle

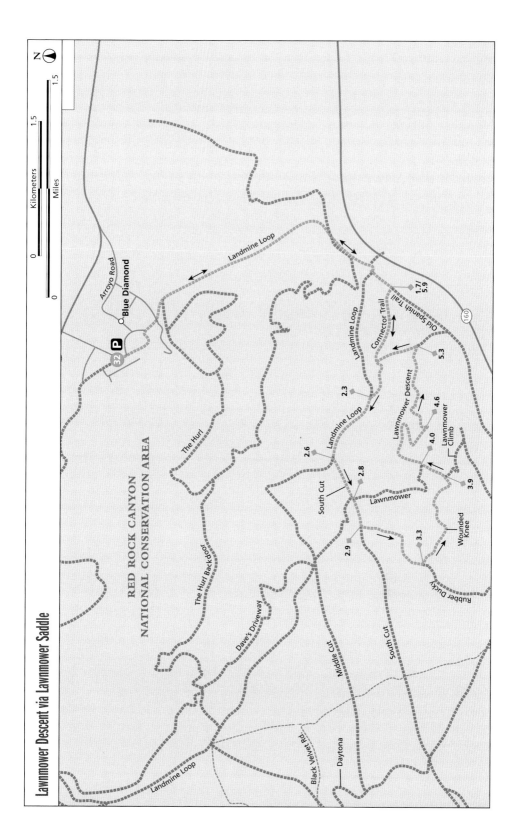

Super Summer Theater: Located in the Spring Valley Ranch State Park is live theater nightly under the summer stars; supersummertheater.org.

Restaurants

Mountain Springs Saloon: Or, more specifically, the eating establishment behind the Mountain Springs Saloon; 19050 US 160, Las Vegas; (702) 875-4266; mountain springssaloon.com

Montana Meat Company: American-style food and steaks; 9135 S. Durango Dr., Las Vegas; (702) 407-0362; montanameatco.com

33 The Hurl Inner Loop

While most of the trails in Cottonwood offer challenges in the moderate to intermediate range, there are some that can only be ridden by those with more advanced skills. One of these trails is the Hurl Inner Loop. This trail takes you up into the hills behind Blue Diamond on one of the most technically challenging trails in all the valley, before taking you back down on an equally technically challenging trail. If you want to test your skills, this is the ride for you.

Start: Asphalt parking lot outside McGhie's Outpost

Distance: 3.6 miles

Elevation gain: 543 feet

Riding time: Advanced riders, 1 hour; intermediate riders, 1.5 hours

Fitness effort: Physically challenging

Difficulty: Technically challenging, very technical trail with a steep, rocky climb and a very technical downhill

Terrain: Mostly dirt, large rocks, and loose gravel

Maps: There are no official maps to this region.

Nearest town: Blue Diamond

Other trail users: Hikers and runners

Dog friendly: Yes, but the trail is very steep and so are the drops

Trail contact: McGhie's Bike Outpost, (702) 875-4820; Southern Nevada Mountain Bike Association, snmba.net

Getting there: Take Interstate 15 to the Blue Diamond Exit. Head west along Blue Diamond Road (State Route 160). Turn right onto State Route 159 and follow the road to the town of Blue Diamond. Turn left onto Castalia Street and head to the asphalt parking lot outside McGhie's Bike Outpost. GPS: N36 02.835'/W115 24.443'

The Ride

The Hurl Inner Loop is a very technical trail that is much better suited to those riders with intermediate to advanced skills. Even then, many riders will find themselves having to hike-a-bike in a couple areas. One of those is a very steep, very rocky climb up the side of the hill behind the town of Blue Diamond. In fact, except for the equally technical downhill section, this trail is an almost constant climb, starting with one of the steepest climbs in the valley and leading to another one of the steepest and certainly one of the most technical climbs in all of Cottonwood. If you're looking for a fun challenging ride that will test your skill set, if not your mettle, this trail is for you.

From the parking lot, pull out onto Castalia Street and turn left heading to Cottonwood Drive. Turn left again and follow Cottonwood Drive up the hill. While traveling up the street, don't be in a hurry to get to the trail. Take time to notice the houses in the area. Many of them are wonderfully decorated and quite quaint. A right turn on Cerrito Street will lead you to the trailhead at the top of the hill. Cerrito Street is a bit of a climb and you'll know you've found the trailhead when asphalt

A particularly difficult portion of the Hurl Inner Loop

turns to dirt. There will also be several large rocks at the trailhead, which are meant to deter motorized vehicles from going on the trail.

When you reach the trailhead you'll find a bit of a drop with a fairly steep, but short climb on the other side. As the trail progresses, it makes its way up a very long, very steep hill. There are many rocky spots and some areas are covered with loose gravel. Turn right at the top of the very steep climb and head into another equally steep but shorter climb to the very top of the hill, then head down the other side into a series of technical switchbacks. When the trail splits at the bottom of the hill, head right into the drop and then left when the trail splits a second time.

From here you'll start a climb up into the hills behind the town of Blue Diamond. The climb is gradual and the trail is well groomed most of the way, but don't get comfortable, because about a mile into the ride the trail dips into a wash before beginning another steep climb. You'll hit a short downhill section before heading into another long, very steep climb up the side of the hill. This, in fact, is one of the most technically difficult climbs in all of Cottonwood. The trail is littered with small loose rocks that are bested only by large difficult rock obstacles that combine to make this trail about as challenging a trail as you're likely to find anywhere. At just the point when you think the climb cannot get worse, it steepens. About 2.0 miles into the ride you'll turn left when the trail splits and take the steep drop into the wash followed by a very technical descent along the ridge of the adjacent hill. You'll eventually wind up on the trail right at the end of the second steep hill you climbed previously, before heading down the first steep hill you climbed and back into the town of Blue Diamond.

Miles and Directions

0.0   Turn left onto Castalia Street and then left again onto Cottonwood Drive. At 0.2 mile, turn right onto Cerrito Street and climb the hill.

0.3   Take the trailhead to the gravel area on the right lined with large boulders and a trail marker. In 0.1 mile, take the drop and the small climb up the other side. Stay straight. Do not take the offshoot trail to the right.

0.7   Turn right at the top of the steep hill and continue the climb, then head down the other side of the hill.

0.9   When the trail splits, turn right and head into the dip. When the trail splits again a short distance ahead, stay left and begin a climb.

1.4   The trail gets steeper. Navigate the large rocks and continue straight when the trail splits.

1.7   Cross the wash and head into the long, steep, technical climb.

2.1   When the trail spits, go left, head into the tight switchbacks, and begin the long, gradual, technical descent that snakes along the foothills.

2.7   Watch for the large rock jetting out into the trail.

3.0   When the trail seems to dead end, drop off the rocks and head up the large, flat rock on the other side of the dip to find the trail.

The Hurl Inner Loop

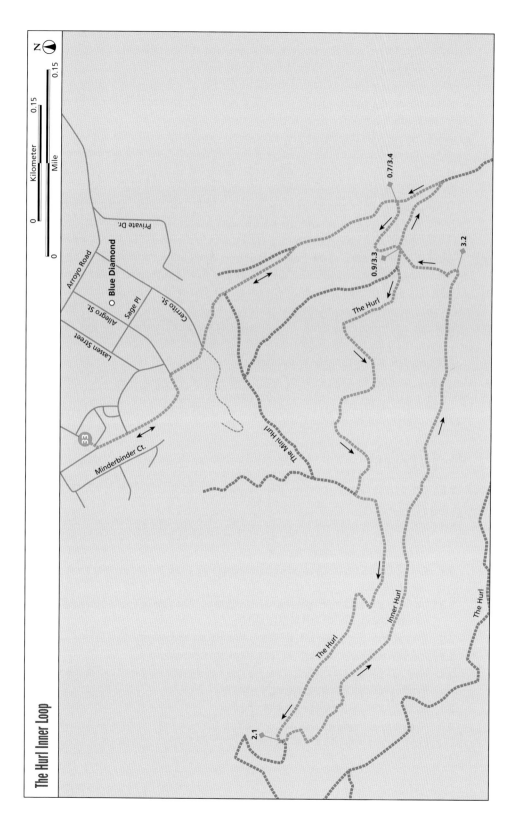

Blue Diamond

Arroyo Road

Private Dr.

Lassen Street

Allegro St.

Sage Pl

Cerrito St.

Minderbinder Ct.

33

The Mini Hurl

The Hurl

Inner Hurl

The Hurl

The Hurl

2.1

3.2

0.9/3.3

0.7/3.4

N

Kilometer

Mile

0

0.15

0

0.15

3.2 Take the switchback to the left and begin the final steep descent. In 0.1 mile, go right when the trails intersect. Stay left when the trails merge in 0.1 mile.

3.4 When the trail splits, stay right and head back down the steep hill to the trailhead.

3.6 Arrive back at the parking lot.

Ride Information

Local Events and Attractions

Spring Valley Ranch State Park: Located close to Red Rock Canyon, this protected park was once a functioning ranch owned at various times by movie stars and famous billionaires. It is also home to some of the oldest buildings in the valley; parks .nv.gov.

Bonnie Springs Ranch: Visit an honest-to-goodness, old-fashioned Wild West town, complete with hangings, shootouts, and an official main street; bonniesprings .com.

Restaurants

Bonnie Springs Ranch Restaurant: American-style food located next to Bonnie Springs Ranch; 1 Gunfighter Ln., Bonnie Springs; (702) 875-4400; bonniesprings .com

Mountain Springs Saloon: Or, more specifically, the eating establishment behind the Mountain Springs Saloon; 19050 US 160, Las Vegas; (702) 875-4266; mountain springssaloon.com

34 The Hurl

The hurl is probably the most aptly named trail in all of Cottonwood. Apt because if you miss on this trail, you will go hurling down the side of the hill. This trail is even more difficult than its inner counterpart. In fact, it follows that same route, but instead of taking the long gradual descent back to the trailhead, this trail heads up to the very tip top of the hill and back down the other side. While the trail is one of the most technical in all of Cottonwood, you are rewarded for your efforts with some of the most gorgeous views there are of the Red Rock Escarpment, the Cottonwood Valley, and the Las Vegas Valley.

Start: Asphalt parking lot outside McGhie's Outpost

Distance: 6.1 miles

Elevation gain: 654 feet

Riding time: Advanced riders, 1.5 hours; intermediate riders, 2 hours

Fitness effort: Physically challenging

Difficulty: Technically challenging, very technical trail with a steep, rocky climb and a very technical downhill

Terrain: Mostly dirt, large rocks, and loose gravel

Maps: There are no official maps to this region.

Nearest town: Blue Diamond

Other trail users: Hikers and runners

Dog friendly: Yes, but the trail is very steep and so are the drops

Trail contact: McGhie's Bike Outpost, (702) 875-4820; Southern Nevada Mountain Bike Association, snmba.net

Getting there: Take Interstate 15 to the Blue Diamond Exit. Head west along Blue Diamond Road (State Route 160). Turn right onto State Route 159 and follow the road to the town of Blue Diamond. Turn left onto Castalia Street and head to the asphalt parking lot outside McGhie's Bike Outpost. GPS: N36 02.835'/W115 24.443'

The Ride

Like the Hurl Inner Loop, The Hurl is a very technical trail that is much better suited to those riders with intermediate to advanced skills. However, if you're looking to test your skills and are willing to be rewarded with some of the most amazing views in all of Cottonwood, this trail is for you. Almost twice as long as the Hurl Inner Loop, this trail differs from that trail in that after you have made the long, steep climb to the top, you get to climb a bit more, to the very top of the hill and then make your way down into the valley on the other side of the hill at The Old Spanish Trail. While at the top of the hill, however, some of the most colorful mountains in all of Nevada, the Red Rock Escarpment, lay out before you. Take the time to pause and take in the view before you head down the fun ride on the other side.

From the parking lot, pull out onto Castalia Street and turn left heading to Cottonwood Drive. Turn left again and follow Cottonwood Drive up the hill. While traveling up the street, don't be in a hurry to get to the trail. Take time to notice the houses in the area. Many of them are wonderfully decorated and quite quaint. A right turn on Cerrito Street will lead you to the trailhead at the top of the hill. Cerrito Street is a bit of a climb and you'll know you've found the trailhead when asphalt turns to dirt. There will also be several large rocks at the trailhead, which are meant to deter motorized vehicles from going on the trail.

When you reach the trailhead, you'll find a bit of a drop with a fairly steep, but short climb on the other side. As the trail progresses, it makes its way up a very long, very steep hill. There are many rocky spots and some areas are covered with loose gravel. Turn right at the top of the very steep climb and head into another equally steep but shorter climb to the very top of the hill, then head down the other side into a series of technical switchbacks. When the trail splits at the bottom of the hill, head right into the drop and then left when the trail splits a second time.

From here you'll start a climb up into the hills behind the town of Blue Dia-mond. The climb is gradual and the trail is well groomed most of the way, but don't get comfortable, because about a mile into the ride, the trail dips into a wash before beginning another steep climb. You'll hit a short downhill section before heading into another long, very steep climb up the side of the hill. This is, in fact, one of the most

Stan Takashima coming down the back side of the Hurl

technically difficult climbs in all of Cottonwood. The trail is littered with small loose rocks that are bested only by large difficult rock obstacles that combine to make this trail about as challenging a trail as you're likely to find anywhere. At just the point when you think the climb cannot get worse, it steepens.

About 2.0 miles into the ride, you'll turn right when the trail splits and continue your climb up to the very top of the hill. From here, after you've taken in the magnificent views, you'll head over to the crest of the adjacent hill before heading down the back side of the hill, eventually catching up with The Old Spanish Trail. As you make your way to the left around the base of the hill, head back to the original steep hill you climbed, only this time head down that hill and back to the parking lot.

Miles and Directions

0.0 Turn left onto Castalia Street and then left again onto Cottonwood Drive. At 0.2 mile, turn right onto Cerrito Street and climb the hill.

0.3 Take the trailhead to the gravel area on the right lined with large boulders and a trail marker. In 0.1 mile, take the drop and the small climb up the other side. Stay straight. Do not take the offshoot trail to the right.

0.7 Turn right at the top of the steep hill and continue the climb, then head down the other side of the hill.

0.9 When the trail splits, turn right and head into the dip. Stay left when the trail splits again a short distance ahead and begin a climb.

1.4 The trail gets steeper. Navigate the large rocks and continue straight when the trail splits.

1.7 Cross the wash and head into the long, steep, technical climb.

2.1 When the trail splits, go right and continue the climb to the top of the hill.

2.6 Stay straight when the trail splits at the top of the second hill and head downhill. The trail to the right is the Hurl Backdoor.

3.3 Take the sharp right and continue the descent.

3.5 When the trail seems to disappear, head straight over the large, flat rock and pick up the trail on the other side.

4.5 When the trail dead ends, turn left.

4.7 Stay straight when the trails merge.

5.0 Stay straight when the trails merge then stay left when the trail splits. The trail to the right is Molly's.

6.1 Arrive at the parking lot.

Ride Information

Local Events and Attractions

Super Summer Theater: Located in the Spring Valley Ranch State Park is live theater nightly under the summer stars; supersummertheater.org.

The Hurl

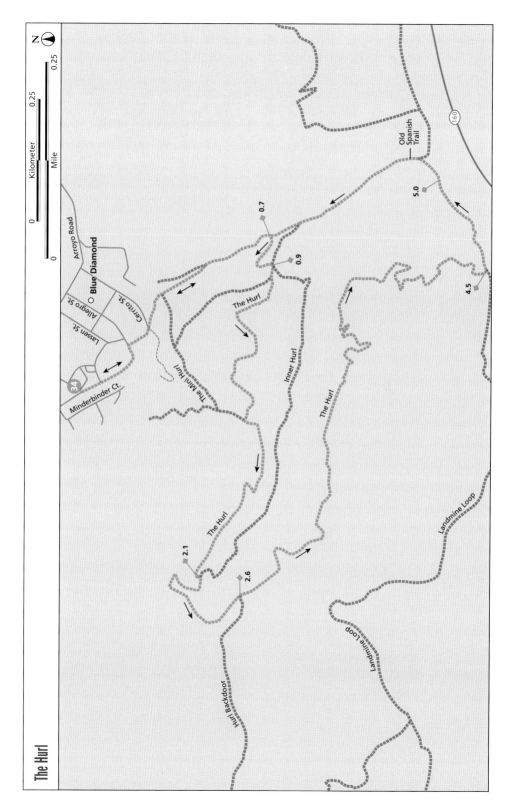

Arroyo Road

Blue Diamond

Lassen St.
Allegro St.
Cerrito St.

Minderbinder Ct.

34

The Mini Hurl

The Hurl

The Hurl

Inner Hurl

The Hurl

Hurl Backdoor

Landmine Loop

Landmine Loop

Old Spanish Trail

160

0.7

0.9

2.1

2.6

4.5

5.0

N

Kilometer
0   0.25   0.25

Mile
0   0.25

Horseback Riding: If you'd like to see the scenery of the Red Rock Canyon from atop four hooves, you can do so at the Cowboy Trail Rides, just outside the National Conservation Area; cowboytrailrides.com.

Restaurants

Mountain Springs Saloon: Or, more specifically, the eating establishment behind the Mountain Springs Saloon; 19050 US 160, Las Vegas; (702) 875-4266; mountain springssaloon.com

Montana Meat Company: American-style food and steaks; 9135 S. Durango Dr., Las Vegas; (702) 407-0362; montanameatco.com

35 The Mini Hurl Loop

The ride is a shorter version of the Hurl Loop, offering different views of Cottonwood Valley. This trail is a favorite of the many wild burros that live in the area and it is not uncommon to find them walking down the trail on their way to Blue Diamond.

Start: Asphalt parking lot outside McGhie's Outpost
Distance: 2.3 miles
Elevation gain: 140 feet
Riding time: Advanced riders, 30 minutes; intermediate to beginning riders, 1 hour
Fitness level: Physically easy to moderate
Difficulty: Technically easy to moderate
Terrain: Mostly dirt, some large rocks, and loose gravel

Maps: There are no official maps to this region
Nearest town: Blue Diamond
Other trail users: Hikers, runners, and horse-back riders
Dog friendly: Yes, but there are commonly wild burros
Trail contact: McGhie's Bike Outpost, (702) 875-4820; Southern Nevada Mountain Bike Association, snmba.net

Getting there: Take Interstate 15 to the Blue Diamond Exit. Head west along Blue Diamond Road (State Route 160). Turn right onto State Route 159 and follow the road to the town of Blue Diamond. Turn left onto Castalia Street and head to the asphalt parking lot outside McGhie's Outpost. GPS: N36 02.835'/W115 24.443'

The Ride

This trail is a shorter version of another trail called The Hurl. As you might guess by its name, The Hurl is a much more difficult trail, requiring more advanced mountain bike skills. This version of the trail has some technical areas, but the trail can be ridden by those with all skill levels. The trail also offers views of some interesting rock formations, as it follows a natural wash up into the hills.

From the parking lot, pull out onto Castalia Street and turn left heading to Cottonwood Drive. Turn left again and follow Cottonwood Drive up the hill. A right turn on Cerrito Street will lead you to the trailhead at the top of the hill. Cerrito Street is a bit of a climb and you'll know you've found the trailhead when asphalt turns to dirt. There will also be several large rocks at the trailhead, which are meant to deter motorized vehicles from going on the trail.

When you reach the trailhead, you'll find a bit of a drop with a fairly steep, but short climb on the other side. Once up that side, the trail splits. Take the trail to the right and begin a gradual climb up into the hills behind the town of Blue Diamond. As you climb the hill, there is an offshoot trail to the right and then to the left. Do not take either of these two trails. At the end of the loop, when you come down the hill, you'll be on the trail to the left.

A tricky portion of the Mini Hurl Loop

About a half mile into the ride the trail crosses the wash. Follow the trail into the wash and then into the short but steep climb up the other side. You'll now be on the opposite side of the wash. Follow the trail as it makes its way up a rock ledge. This is a tricky section and riders with a lower skill level may want to walk this section. Once you reach the top of the ledge, you'll find a convergence of trails. Take the trail to the left and follow it as it crosses the ledge and makes a gradual climb. As you cross the ledge, stay straight. Do not take the trail to the right that climbs the steep hill.

Once you cross the ledge the trail starts to climb before starting a downhill section. Follow the trail through these sections. The downhill section is a bit rocky, but it is a fun little section and comes right before a steep climb. Follow the trail as it makes the climb. When you come to a spot where several trails meet, take the trail to the left and head downhill. At the end of the downhill section, the trail begins a gradual climb to the original trail. Follow the trail until it dead ends at the original trail, then turn right and follow the trail down to the large drop. Take the drop and when the trail ends, stay straight on Cerrito Street before turning left onto Cottonwood Drive. Take Cottonwood Drive back to the parking lot, turning right on Castalia Street and then an immediate right into the parking lot.

Miles and Directions

0.0 Turn left onto Castalia Street and then left again onto Cottonwood Drive. At 0.2 mile, turn right onto Cerrito Street and climb the hill.

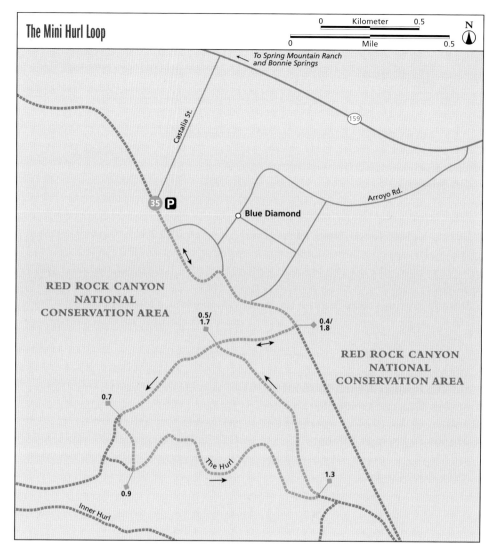

The Mini Hurl Loop

0   Kilometer   0.5

0   Mile   0.5

N

To Spring Mountain Ranch
and Bonnie Springs

159

Castalia St.

Arroyo Rd.

35 P

Blue Diamond

RED ROCK CANYON
NATIONAL
CONSERVATION AREA

0.5/
1.7

0.4/
1.8

RED ROCK CANYON
NATIONAL
CONSERVATION AREA

0.7

0.9

The Hurl

1.3

Inner Hurl

0.3 Take the trailhead to the gravel area on the right lined with large boulders and a trail marker. In 0.1 mile, take the drop and the small climb up the other side, then take the offshoot trail to the right.

0.5 Stay straight; do not take the offshoot trail to the right or the trail to the left a little farther ahead. In 0.1 mile, follow the trail right and drop into the wash. Cross the wash and make the short but steep climb up the ridge.

0.7 Go up the tricky rock ledge and follow the trail left. When the trail splits at mile 0.8, stay left and continue the climb.

0.9 When the trail dead ends at the Hurl trail, turn left and follow the trail down into the valley. This section is a bit tricky as the trail is filled with large rocks.

1.0 Take the small drop, then curve to the left. This is the end of the tricky rock section.

1.3 At the top of the climb, turn left when the trails meet and head downward toward the natural wash. At the bottom of the trail are two large boulders that create a tricky rock obstacle.

1.6 Cross the small wash and begin a gradual climb to the trail you took originally. When the trail dead ends at the original trail at 1.7 miles, turn right and head down to the large drop.

1.8 When the trails meet, go left, taking the quick drop and then the short but steep climb on the other side.

1.9 Turn left onto Cerritos Street and follow it to Cottonwood Drive.

2.3 Turn right onto Castalia Street and then another immediate right into the parking lot.

Ride Information

Local Events and Attractions

Spring Valley Ranch State Park: Located close to Red Rock Canyon, this protected park was once a functioning ranch owned at various times by movie stars and famous billionaires. It is also home to some of the oldest buildings in the valley; parks .nv.gov.

Bonnie Springs Ranch: Visit an honest-to-goodness, old-fashioned Wild West town, complete with hangings, shootouts, and an official main street; bonniesprings .com.

Restaurants

Bonnie Springs Ranch Restaurant: American-style food located next to Bonnie Springs Ranch; 1 Gunfighter Ln., Bonnie Springs; (702) 875-4400; bonniesprings .com

Mountain Springs Saloon: Or, more specifically, the eating establishment behind the Mountain Springs Saloon; 19050 US 160, Las Vegas; (702) 875-4266; mountain springssaloon.com

36 Beginner Loop

This trail has a great downhill section that makes for a fun, fast ride, so much so that the downhill portion of the trail is called Viagra. Of course, you have to pay for that downhill with a bit of a climb back to the trailhead. However, on the way, the trail offers great views of the Red Rocks Escarpment and you may even see a burro or two.

Start: Late Night parking lot off Nevada State Route 160
Distance: 3.8 miles
Elevation gain: 345 feet
Riding time: Advanced riders, 45 minutes; intermediate riders, 1 hour; beginning riders, 1.5 hours
Fitness level: Physically easy to moderate with a small portion of the trail being a fairly steep, but gradual climb
Difficulty: Technically easy to moderate

Terrain: Mostly dirt and loose gravel, with the downhill section following fairly deep, narrow ruts
Maps: There are no official maps to this region
Nearest town: Blue Diamond
Other trail users: Hikers and runners
Dog friendly: Yes, but there are commonly wild burros
Trail contact: McGhie's Bike Outpost, (702) 875-4820; Southern Nevada Mountain Bike Association, snmba.net

Getting there: Take Nevada State Route 160 past the Red Rock Conservation Area turnoff (SR 159). Follow the road as it curves to the right and to the left. Look for the asphalt parking lot to the right of the road. This the Late Night parking lot. The restroom is the only building in the area, so it is easy to spot. GPS: N36 00.674'/W115 25.879'

The Ride

Beginner Loop is a fun ride popular with many mountain bikers in the area. The majority of the ride is a great downhill section that you can take as slow or as fast as you feel comfortable. Of course, all that downhill riding does come with a price. Once you complete that portion, you'll have a gradual climb all the way back to the trailhead. Still, the climb is not difficult and the downhill section is worth the price of admission.

Beginner Loop begins at the Late Night parking lot just off State Route 160. A map of the trails in the area is carved into a large stone located just to the right of the restrooms. The map is not to scale and is only meant to give an overall idea of the trails. The trailhead for the Beginner Loop is just to the left of the restrooms. The first part of the trail, before you reach the downhill section, is a climb through loose rocks and gravel. The trail makes its way around the parking lot, eventually turning east at the trail marker and heading towards the Red Rock Escarpment.

About a half mile from the trailhead, the trail splits at another trail marker. Take the trail to the right into a short downhill section. Close to a mile into the ride you

A rider flies down the Beginner Loop. RESTY TORRES DE LIMA

cross a dirt road and continue straight. Be sure to look up into the hills as you might just spot a wild burro or two wandering around. You should also watch the trails, because these wild animals commonly walk along the trails and often leave little presents that you'll not want to ride through—especially if they're fresh.

The downhill section begins close to a mile into the ride, just after two separate trails turn into one. This section of the ride is known as Viagra. Shortly afterward, the trail splits again. Stay on the main trail to the right and take the drop, allowing momentum to get you up the other side. Shortly after the drop you'll see a dirt road. Cross the road and continue straight. The ruts in the trail get deep in this section and can be a little tricky to ride. Try to stay in the center so the ruts don't pull you up and off the trail.

A little more than two miles into the ride you'll see the dirt road again. Turn right and either ride down the dirt road or take the trail just to the right. They meet up about 30 or so feet ahead. Turn right at the trail marker and begin the climb back to the trailhead. Time to pay for the fun downhill section you just rode. This portion of the trail is Mustang. About a mile and a half up the trail, follow the trail to the right and head back to the trailhead.

Miles and Directions

0.0 Take the trail just to the left of the restrooms.

0.1 Turn right at the trail marker. In 0.2 mile, cross a wash and begin a climb.

0.5 Stay right when the trail splits at the trail marker and start a short downhill section. Take the small drop in 0.1 mile, then curve to the right and start a climb.

0.7 Pass through a section with large, sharp rocks, then head right.

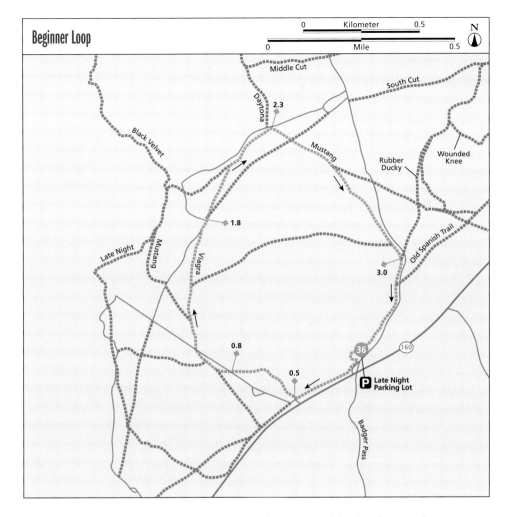

0.8   Cross the dirt road and continue straight. In 0.1 mile, stay right when the two trails meet and begin the downhill section.

1.0   When the trail splits, stay right and head down the drop.

1.1   Cross the dirt road a second time and continue straight into another drop. Take another short drop at mile 1.2.

1.8   Cross the dirt road and continue straight. Watch for the deep ruts.

2.3   Meet up with the dirt road and turn right. Follow the trail or the dirt road and take the trail to the right at the trail marker.

2.4   Cross the remnants of a dirt road and stay straight. When the trail splits at mile 2.7, stay right.

3.0   Start the steeper section of the climb. In 0.2 mile, head over the long rocks that form "stairs" up to the dirt road. Turn right to meet back up with the trail at the trail marker.

3.7   Take the trail right and follow it to the trailhead. You can also take the trail straight to the parking lot.

3.8 Arrive back at the trailhead.

Ride Information

Local Events and Attractions

Super Summer Theater: Located in the Spring Valley Ranch State Park is live theater nightly under the summer stars; supersummertheater.org.

Horseback Riding: If you'd like to see the scenery of the Red Rock Canyon from atop four hooves, you can do so at the Cowboy Trail Rides, just outside the National Conservation Area; cowboytrailrides.com.

Restaurants

Mountain Springs Saloon: Or, more specifically, the eating establishment behind the Mountain Springs Saloon; 19050 US 160, Las Vegas; (702) 875-4266; mountain springssaloon.com

Montana Meat Company: American-style food and steaks; 9135 S. Durango Dr., Las Vegas; (702) 407-0362; montanameatco.com

37 Late Night

The Late Night Trail is a more advanced version of the Beginner Loop, meaning it requires a higher skill set. Instead of making a quick circle, this trail heads out into the desert at the foothills of the Red Rock Escarpment combining a challenging ride with some of the best scenery you're likely to find in all of Cottonwood. It ends with the same climb up Mustang as does the Beginner Loop, meaning, in the end, you have to pay for that great scenery!

Start: Late Night parking lot off Nevada State Route 160
Distance: 5.0 miles
Elevation gain: 470 feet
Riding time: Advanced riders, 1 hour; intermediate riders, 1.5 hours; beginning riders, 2 hours
Fitness level: Physically moderate to challenging with a small portion of the trail being a fairly steep, but gradual climb
Difficulty: Technically moderate to challenging

Terrain: Mostly dirt and loose gravel, with a couple of tricky drops and climbs over large rocks
Maps: There are no official maps to this region
Nearest town: Blue Diamond
Other trail users: Hikers and runners
Dog friendly: Yes, but there are commonly wild burros
Trail contact: McGhie's Bike Outpost, (702) 875-4820; Southern Nevada Mountain Bike Association, snmba.net

Getting there: Take Nevada State Route 160 past the Red Rock Conservation Area turn off (SR 159). Follow the road as it curves to the right and to the left. Look for the asphalt parking lot to the right of the road. This the Late Night parking lot. The restroom is the only building in the area, so it is easy to spot. GPS: N36 00.674'/W115 25.879'

The Ride

The Late Night Trail starts at the Late Night parking lot, initially following the same trail as the Beginner Loop. However, instead of taking the first turnoff, or even the second turnoff, Late Night continues on the trail, crossing a couple of dirt roads, until it winds its way around a large dirt mound and heads into the desert. At the point where the trail turns to the right, you can see a collection of tunnels to the left. These tunnels provide an underpass to State Route 160 and eventually lead to the Dead Horse Loop. All of the trails are marked in this area, so it is easy to stay on the right trail.

As you travel along the trail, which is mainly a gradual descent, you'll cross a dirt road several times. The trail is easy to follow in this area and you can go just about as fast as you feel comfortable. You can also take a leisurely ride along the foothills of the Red Rock Escarpment and the Calico Hills—which is the name of the multicolored mountains just to the west of the trail. This way you can take the time to notice the beauty of your surroundings. These mountains have played host to thousands of

A rider heads down the Late Night Trail.

pioneers as they headed down The Old Spanish Trail on their way to California. The deep brownish-red dirt, Joshua trees, and thorny cactus are now home to hundreds of species of wildlife, especially wild burros.

About 2 miles into the ride the trail splits. Stay straight if you plan to ride the rest of the Late Night Trail. However, you can also take the trail to the right, which is often called the Inner Late Night Trail. This trail meets up with the Mustang Trail and the first half of the Beginner Loop on the trail known as Viagra. Mustang also runs from the Late Night parking lot and the Late Night Trail meets up with Mustang for the climb back to the parking lot. Mustang itself runs between Late Night and Viagra, hooking up with each trail at different points, making it a fun alternative trail to either the Beginner Loop or Late Night.

About a quarter mile after the trails split, you'll head into the first of two tricky descents into large gullies. You'll have to navigate large rocks on both the downhill and the climb on the other side and some of the climbs are pretty steep. Shortly after the first two gullies you'll drop into a third gully, only this time instead of climbing out of the gully you'll actually ride it downward. As you travel, the trail will split several times. Each time the trail splits, stay on the main trail. The trail will dip into and out of a wash. On the second dip, follow the trail straight and make the short, but steep climb out, crossing the dirt road and continuing down the trail. Be sure not to follow the trail to the left at the bottom of that drop as it is not the right trail and if you take it, you will no longer be on the Late Night Trail.

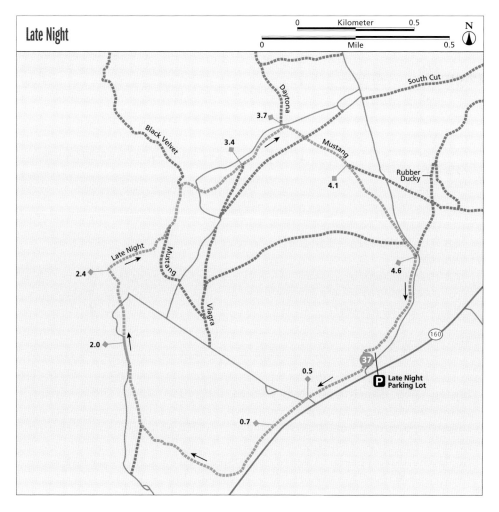

As you follow the trail downward, it will eventually meet at the convergence of trails. Mustang, Viagra, South Cut, and Late Night all meet here at the dirt road. The trail on the other side of the dirt road that heads down into the gully leads to Daytona. The trail to the right leads to Mustang and it is this trail that you will take as you make your way back to the trailhead. Do not take any of the offshoot trails as you climb to another dirt road. The first part of this trail is a fast easy shot, until you get to the short, but steep climb back to the parking lot. When you reach the dirt road, about halfway through the climb, follow the trail as it heads to the right. You can also take the road back to the parking lot, but the actual trail is better.

Miles and Directions

0.0 Take the trail to the left of the restrooms.

0.1	Take the trail right at the trail marker. In 0.2 mile, cross the wash and begin a long gradual climb.
0.5	Do not take the Viagra Trail to the right. In 0.2 mile, stay straight. Do not take the Mustang Trail to the right.
1.0	When the trail splits at the trail sign, stay right and head away from the highway towards the mountains.
2.0	Stay straight when the trail splits. The trail to the right is a connector to Mustang and Viagra.
2.2	Head into a gully. In 0.1 mile, head into another gully and then a third in another 0.1 mile.
2.5	Stay straight when the trail splits.
2.9	Stay straight when the trail splits. In 0.1 mile, when the trail splits again, stay right.
3.4	Stay straight when Late Night merges with Viagra.
3.7	Head right at the convergence of trails onto Mustang.
3.8	Cross the remnants of a dirt road and stay straight. When the trail splits at mile 4.1, stay right.
4.4	Start the steeper section of the climb. In 0.2 mile, head over the long rocks that form "stairs" up to the dirt road. Turn right to meet back up with the trail at the trail marker.
5.0	Arrive at the trailhead.

Ride Information

Local Events and Attractions

Spring Valley Ranch State Park: Located close to Red Rock Canyon, this protected park was once a functioning ranch owned at various times by movie stars and famous billionaires. It is also home to some of the oldest buildings in the valley; parks .nv.gov.

Super Summer Theater: Located in the Spring Valley Ranch State Park is live theater nightly under the summer stars; supersummertheater.org.

Restaurants

Mountain Springs Saloon: Or, more specifically, the eating establishment behind the Mountain Springs Saloon; 19050 US 160, Las Vegas; (702) 875-4266; mountain springssaloon.com

Montana Meat Company: American-style food and steaks; 9135 S. Durango Dr., Las Vegas; (702) 407-0362; montanameatco.com

38 Badger Pass/3 Mile Smile Loop

This trail has a downhill section that is so well liked it was given its own name. Of course, to be able to take that downhill section, you first have to make the gradual climb. Still, this gradual climb offers great views of the Cottonwood Valley and the Red Rocks Escarpment, making the climb well worth the trip.

Start: Late Night parking lot off Nevada State Route 160

Distance: 6.4 miles

Elevation gain: 682 feet

Riding time: Advanced riders, 1 hour; intermediate riders, 1.5 hours; beginning riders, 2.5 hours

Fitness level: Physically moderate to challenging, as most of the first half of the trail is a long gradual climb

Difficulty: Technically easy to moderate, the trail is well-groomed and there are few challenging obstacles

Terrain: Mostly dirt and loose gravel

Maps: There are no official maps to this region

Nearest town: Blue Diamond

Other trail users: Hikers, runners, and horseback riders

Dog friendly: Yes, but there are commonly wild burros and horses

Trail contact: McGhie's Bike Outpost, (702) 875-4820; Southern Nevada Mountain Bike Association, snmba.net

Getting there: Take Nevada State Route 160 past the Red Rock Conservation Area turn off (SR 159). Follow the road as it curves to the right and to the left. Look for the asphalt parking lot to the right of the road. This is the Late Night parking lot. The restroom is the only building in the area, so it is easy to spot. GPS: N36 00.674'/W115 25.879'

The Ride

This ride follows two trails, Badger Pass and 3 Mile Smile, to create an enjoyable, easily accessible loop. The trail starts on the southwest side of the parking lot. Here you'll find a small dirt trail that makes its way toward the asphalt road that leads to the parking lot. Cross the asphalt road and head into the wash towards the tunnels. Go through the tunnels, passing under State Route 160. The tunnels are divided into three tunnels and the center tunnel is the one most commonly used; however, you can use any one of the three. On the other side of the tunnel, follow the trail as it turns to the left and makes a quick, but steep climb. Stay straight at the trail marker, cross the dirt road and head up into the hills. There is a tricky rock section here.

After the rock section, follow the trail as it makes a gradual climb. While the climb levels out for a bit in certain parts, it is mostly a continuous gradual climb up into the hills. As you are climbing, be sure to pay attention to your surroundings. The Cottonwood Valley is full of all manner of interesting animals—of all shapes and sizes. You can easily find rabbits and lizards, but there are also many different types of birds and, if you're lucky, you might see a wild horse or burro. There are also snakes in this area that blend well into their surroundings. All of this can easily be missed if you pay too much attention to the trail and not enough to the desert around you.

About a mile and half into the ride, the trail splits. Take the trail to the left. Stay straight a short distance ahead when the two trails meet up. The trail will split again at the marker not far up the trail. Stay left and continue the climb up into the hills. As the trail continues, it hugs the bottom of the hills to the right. When you reach this point, you are about a half mile from the end of the climb. Follow the trail as it snakes around the hills and makes a final, steep climb before heading into the down-hill section. At the top of the hill where there is a convergence of trails, stay straight, not taking the trail to the left or the right.

Enter a series of switchbacks that can be tricky due to tight turns at the end of each switchback. At the bottom of the switchbacks, you have a choice. You can go right and head into a downhill section that is so popular with mountain bike riders that it has its own name: the 3 Mile Smile. As the name suggests, the downhill section lasts about three miles and is designed to make the rider smile. However, if you want

The Badger Pass/3 Mile Smile Loop offers great views of the Cottonwood Valley.

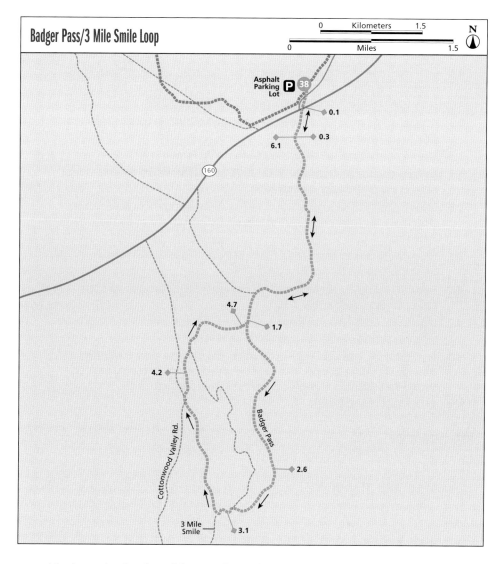

to ride the entire 3 miles of the 3 Mile Smile, you'll have to turn left and head up to the top of the hill, then turn and head back down.

Follow the trail as it makes its way up to a dirt parking lot. Pick up the trail directly ahead on the other side of the dirt lot and follow it across the wash. Here you'll have a bit of a gradual climb, but the trail will head downhill soon enough. Stay straight when the two trails merge into one and when the trail splits a short distance ahead, stay to the right. Two trails will merge again just ahead, so stay straight. When the trail nears some large rocks and a telephone pole, turn right and climb the rocks. Cross the dirt road and follow the trail to the left as it drops into the wash and heads toward the tunnels. Go through the middle tunnel, cross the asphalt road, and arrive at the trailhead.

Miles and Directions

0.0 Take the trail at the southwest side of the parking lot; cross the asphalt road into the wash.

0.1 Enter the middle tunnel and cross under SR 160. Climb the cement embankment and follow the trail right. Turn left in 0.1 mile and make a quick, but steep, climb. Stay straight at the trail marker, cross the dirt road, and head up into the hills.

0.3 Navigate a tricky rock section and begin a long, gradual climb. In 0.2 mile, cross a small gully and continue the climb.

1.5 Stay left when the trail splits. Stay straight when the trails meet in 0.1 mile.

1.7 Go left and start a climb when the trail splits at the trail marker. Take the small drop at mile 1.9 and climb through the large rocks.

2.6 Follow the trail as it hugs the bottom of the hills on the right and then makes a steep climb up the hill. At the convergence of trails at mile 3.0, stay straight and begin the downhill section.

3.1 Enter a series of switchbacks. At the bottom of the switchbacks in 0.3 mile, stay straight. The trail to the left is the top of the 3 Mile Smile.

4.2 Follow the trail up to a dirt parking lot and pick up the trail on the opposite side at the trail marker. Cross the wash at mile 4.3.

4.7 Stay straight when the two trails merge, then stay to the right when the trail splits in 0.1 mile. Stay straight when the two trails merge again at mile 4.9.

6.1 Turn right at the large rocks and telephone pole, and climb the rocks. Stay straight and cross the dirt road at mile 6.2, then follow the trail left as it drops into the wash. Go through the middle tunnel at mile 6.3 and cross the asphalt road.

6.4 Arrive back to the trailhead.

Ride Information

Local Events and Attractions

Bonnie Springs Ranch: Visit an honest-to-goodness, old-fashioned Wild West town, complete with hangings, shootouts, and an official main street; bonniesprings .com.

Horseback Riding: If you'd like to see the scenery of the Red Rock Canyon from atop four hooves, you can do so at the Cowboy Trail Rides, just outside the National Conservation Area; cowboytrailrides.com.

Restaurants

Bonnie Springs Ranch Restaurant: American-style food located next to Bonnie Springs Ranch; 1 Gunfighter Ln., Bonnie Springs; (702) 875-4400; bonniesprings .com

Mountain Springs Saloon: Or, more specifically, the eating establishment behind the Mountain Springs Saloon; 19050 US 160, Las Vegas; (702) 875-4266; mountain springssaloon.com

Honorable Mentions

Four more trails in the Cottonwood Valley or the surrounding area deserve your consideration when looking for trails to ride. Even though they didn't make the regular list, you'd be wise not to count them out.

D. The Hurl Backdoor

The Hurl Backdoor takes a difficult trail and makes it even harder. This is a trail that should really only be ridden by those with advanced skills. To reach the trail you first have to climb the first half of The Hurl, an aptly named, extremely technical trail that climbs high into the hills behind the town of Blue Diamond. Once you reach the top of the hills, The Hurl Backdoor takes you on a technical descent down the back of that very same hill, eventually meeting up with Dave's Driveway. From here you can either follow Dave's Driveway—another very technical trail—to the Landmine Loop or you can follow the downhill trail along the foot of the hill as it makes its way back to Blue Diamond. Of course, if your skills are that advanced, you may want to ride Dive's Driveway to the right, eventually meeting up with Landmine Loop on the other end and heading back toward Blue Diamond via The Old Spanish Trail. Either way, you'll find a ride that will test the skills of even the most advanced mountain biker.

E. Dead Horse Loop

The Dead Horse Loop is a 14-mile trail that heads under State Route 160 into the very outskirts of the Cottonwood Valley. It is a long trail that requires a great deal of gradual climbing, making it perfect for anyone looking to improve their climbing skills. The trail starts at the Late Night parking lot and heads west on the Late Night trail. When that trail turns to the right, a turn to the left will take you into the tunnels under State Route 160.

From here the trail turns to the right before heading south into the valley. The first part of the trail is an almost constant climb, but as you ride you'll be exposed to Mother Nature at her best. This area of the valley is home to all manner of animals and it is one of the best places to see wild horses. The trail, however, is a bit tricky. There are steep washes, a couple of double-track areas, and a section known fondly as Satan's Escalator—a series of steep switchbacks that even the best riders find themselves walking.

While the trail is a fun ride and the scenery is certainly worth the trip, the trail can be difficult to follow in some areas. At the end of the trail—a place called Wilson's Tank—the trail once again gets lost at the road. However, if you look to the other side, you'll find the trail again. This is actually the start of a very fun downhill section called 3 Mile Smile and it is this trail that will lead you back to the trailhead, eventually following Badger Pass to the Late Night parking lot.

F. Twilight Zone Loop

Twilight Zone Loop is a 10.6-mile trail located off Kyle Canyon Road heading towards Mount Charleston almost 40 miles north of Las Vegas along US 95. This is a great cross-country trail that makes its way through the high desert's rolling hills and washes. The Twilight Zone Loop is a good choice to make when the temperatures in Las Vegas start to climb into the 100s, because Mount Charleston is usually 20 to 30 degrees cooler. Of course, those temps are also cooler in the winter, making this trail much better for summer and spring riding. The trail starts on the northwest side of an old horse-riding parking area about 9 miles up Kyle Canyon Road and while the trail only changes about 700 feet in elevation during the entire ride, the trail itself is at a little over 4,000 feet, twice the elevation of Las Vegas. While the trail is open to mountain bikers, it is also used by hikers and horseback riders.

G. Bristlecone Loop

Bristlecone Loop is a 6-mile trail located high up in Mount Charleston almost 40 miles north of Las Vegas along US 95. This is actually one of the few trails in the Las Vegas area that qualifies as an actual "mountain" trail. In fact, it starts at 8,690 feet and eventually makes its way to 9,400 feet. This trail gives you a view of the Las Vegas Valley that you probably never thought possible. What the locals call Mount Charleston (officially named Charleston Peak) is the highest mountain in Clark County at 11,916 feet. Here you'll see ponderosa pine, white fir, and quaking aspen as well as a forest of ancient bristlecone pine. You can also see all manner of mountain wildlife, like the Mount Charleston chipmunk, which lives solely in the Spring Mountain area or the many butterflies that make the mountain their home.

This is a challenging trail that is off limits during the winter months because, believe it or not, the trail is covered in snow. The main reason this trail was included as an honorable mention is because it is a multiuse trail that is a favorite of hikers and birdwatchers, meaning there are frequently quite a few people on the trail at any given time. This tends to make the trail a bit congested. The other reason is that while the trail is well-groomed, it is not an easy trail to ride. While the views are spectacular, the climb is not easy and the altitude can be a bit much if you're not accustomed to such heights. Additionally, there are some rocky spots toward the top, making the trail difficult and a miscalculation could end in a disastrous fall down the side of the mountain.

The trailhead is located at the end of Lee Canyon Road and is clearly marked with signs. From here, take the fenced trail up towards the ski area. The trail follows the ridgeline of the mountain before reaching the Bonanza Trail junction. From the junction, head down the old road back to Lee Canyon Road and eventually down to the lower trailhead passing Scout Canyon and Lee Meadow along the way.

Oasis Valley Trails

The trails at Oasis Valley are probably the best-kept secret in all of Nevada and it's a shame because it is a secret definitely worth sharing. Just 6 miles outside of the town of Beatty, Nevada, lies Spicer Ranch, owned by Dave Spicer, an avid biker, both mountain and road, who understands the benefits that can only be gained by experiencing nature first hand. Dave also understands the economic opportunities that can be achieved when businesses work

The view of Oasis Valley and the Spicer Ranch

hand-in-hand with the state to create outstanding recreational experiences that are open to and can be enjoyed by all.

To this end, Dave created Trails-OV (a subsidiary of STORM-OV) with the express purpose of transforming the little town of Beatty, Nevada, into a recreational trails destination. He got the ball rolling by hiring a team to come to his ranch and assess the area, then he went through training with the International Mountain Bike Association and learned how to create trails that people would want to ride. In other words, he did it the right way. But that's not all he did. Along with the trails, Dave also created a parking lot on his land and a camping area—all open to the public and all free of charge—complete with a cooking area, a large tire swing, and working showers. It is important to note, however, that even though Dave has kindly opened his ranch to the public, the ranch and the trails on the ranch are not public land. They are still private property and should be respected as such.

Dave picked the right place. Beatty, Nevada, the one-time mining town named after its founder—Montillius Beatty—started in 1904 when gold was found in them thar' hills. Over the years, as mining played less and less of a role in the community, the little town has struggled at times to find its identity. But Beatty and the area surrounding it—the Oasis and Armargosa Valleys—are recreational dreamlands. Beatty is 10 minutes away from Death Valley, one of the most unique spots in the entire United States. It has some of the most peculiar rock formations anywhere in Nevada and is also home to one of the largest sand dunes in the entire state. Beatty has prehistoric fossils, hot springs, hiking, ATV and motorcycle trails, and an underground stream, and is one of the best places in Nevada to go bird watching. In truth, recreational opportunities already abound in and around Beatty, making mountain biking a perfect fit.

39 Spicer Ranch Trail

The Spicer Ranch Trail is one of three that are completely within the boundaries of Dave Spicer's working ranch. This trail is a perfect representation of what Dave Spicer is trying to accomplish with Trails-OV. It is a fun, easy trail that provides great views and allows the rider to experience everything the land and the ranch have to offer. If after riding the Spicer Ranch Trail you don't find yourself chomping at the bit to get on all the other trails in and around the ranch, you simply aren't riding properly.

Start: The parking lot just outside the cattle guard

Distance: 3.0 miles

Elevation gain: 281 feet

Riding time: Advanced riders, 45 minutes; intermediate riders, 1 hour; beginning riders, 1.5 hours

Fitness effort: Physically easy

Difficulty: Technically easy

Terrain: Well-groomed trail; mostly dirt with some small rocks; pasture

Map: Trails-OV.org

Nearest town: Beatty

Other trail users: Hikers and runners

Dog friendly: Yes, but it is a working ranch with horses, bulls, and cows

Trail contact: Spicer Ranch; Trails-OV.org

Getting there: If traveling from Las Vegas, take U.S. Highway 95 (Veteran's Memorial Highway) 115 miles north to Beatty, Nevada. Turn right on Main Street (still U.S. Highway 95) and follow it approximately 7 miles to Boiling Pot Road. Turn Right onto the Spicer Ranch and follow the signs to the parking lot. GPS: N36 59.8668'/W116 42.9173'

The Ride

The trailhead is to the east of the parking lot just on the other side of the cattle guard, which itself is just to the right of the kiosk. Cross the cattle guard and head along the dirt road to the left toward a sign directing you to the STORM Trail and camping area. STORM is the acronym for the non-profit organization Saving Toads Thru Off-Road Racing, Ranching, and Mining in Oasis Valley. Turn right as the dirt road makes its way to a metal gate. Remember, the Spicer Ranch is a working ranch complete with horses, cattle, and other livestock. Whenever a trail passes through a closed gate, you are welcome to open the gate to pass, just be sure to secure it behind you.

Follow the trail on the other side of the gate as it takes a sharp left into the fence. There is a green ramp that will allow you passageway through the fence. You will use several of these on this trail. On the other side of the ramp, the trail takes an immediate right and starts a gradual climb up the side of a small hill. You are now on the STORM Trail. While the trail is relatively easy to follow, it can be difficult to see in some spots, especially at the start of the trail. In these areas, the trail is marked with orange pin flags, so make sure to follow these markers.

Follow the trail as it makes its way left up and alongside the small hill. A pasture—often filled with horses—is on your left. At 0.3 mile, cross the wash and follow the trail as it makes its way around a foothill following the pasture. Do not turn to the right and pass through the gate. At about 0.6 mile the trail splits. The STORM trail continues on to the left, and the Spicer Ranch trailhead is to the right. Both trails are clearly marked by yellow signs, however, the turnoff can be missed if you don't pay close attention. If you are still following the pasture after you have passed the yellow sign marking the STORM Trail, then you have gone too far. The yellow sign marking the Spicer Ranch Trail is not at the point where the trail splits. It is off to the right.

Follow the Spicer Ranch Trail as is climbs a hill and heads toward the fence. Cross the fence at the green ramp and continue to follow the trail along the hill. At about a mile into the ride you'll enter a series of gradual switchbacks. Be careful of the soft dirt in this area and the steep drops to the right of the trail. Continue as the trail follows the foothills, climbing all the way. Be careful of the large rock protruding out into the trail. Another pasture is visible on the right. You will be riding through this pasture later in the loop.

At a little past a mile into the ride, cross over another fence using the green ramp. On the other side of the fence the trail splits. Stay straight. The trail that takes a sharp

The remains of an old homestead along the trail

left is the South Pond Trail. Cross the wash and follow the trail to the right. Just ahead the trail turns sharply to the left, before continuing the climb, eventually heading into a short downhill section, followed by a gradual climb up the other hill.

After the climb, the trail levels out for a short distance leading to a split in the trails. Do not take the Southgate Trail on the left. Head into a short, fun downhill section with easy gradual turns. At about 2.3 miles take the sharp turn to the left and follow the trail into the wash. A short distance ahead, the trail splits once again. Follow the sign to the Spicer Ranch Trail on the right. Do not take the Stirrup Trail on the left. Cross through the fence using the green ramp, then follow the trail to the left. The trail passes the remains of an old rock building as it hairpins to the right, following along the pasture. Head into the pasture. The trail can be a little difficult to follow, so it is important to look for the pin flags marking the trail. Remember, the ranch is a working ranch and there may be animals in the pasture. If you leave the animals alone, they will leave you alone as well. The pasture will most likely be wet.

After you leave the pasture, follow the trail as it turns to the left and continues along the ridge of a small hill. A short distance ahead the trail hairpins to the right, following the foothills, before heading into a wash. Enter a series of small dips and climbs as you make your way along the foothills. Turn left into a wash. Be sure to watch for the pin flags as this area can be a little difficult to follow. Also, the wash may be wet at times, so ride through carefully. Cross the wash and follow the trail up the small hill. The Spicer Ranch Trail officially ends at the dirt road marked with a yellow trail marker; however, you will have to turn left and follow the trail back to the parking lot. If the gate at the end of the road is closed, open it to allow yourself passage, just be sure to close and secure the gate behind you.

Miles and Directions

0.0 Cross the cattle guard and head to the left.

0.1 Follow the dirt road right towards the gate. Go through the gate, closing it behind you. Take the immediate left and use the green ramp to go through the fence, then take the immediate right, following the pin flags.

0.3 Cross the dry wash and head into a short climb. Do not turn right and go through the gate.

0.6 When the trail splits, stay right at the Spicer Ranch Trailhead. The trail is clearly marked with a yellow trail sign. A short distance ahead, cross through the fence with the green ramp, and follow the trail around the hill.

1.2 Make the short climb and cross over the fence using the green ramp. Then stay straight. Do not take the South Pond Trail to the left.

1.7 When the trail splits, stay right. There is a sign marking the Spicer Ranch Trail. Do not take the Southgate Trail to the left. Head into a fun downhill section.

2.3 When the trail splits, stay right, following the sign for the Spencer Ranch Trail. Do not take the Stirrup Trail to the left. Pass through the fence with the green ramp, then follow the trail left.

2.4 Pass the remains of an old rock building and take the hairpin turn to the right.

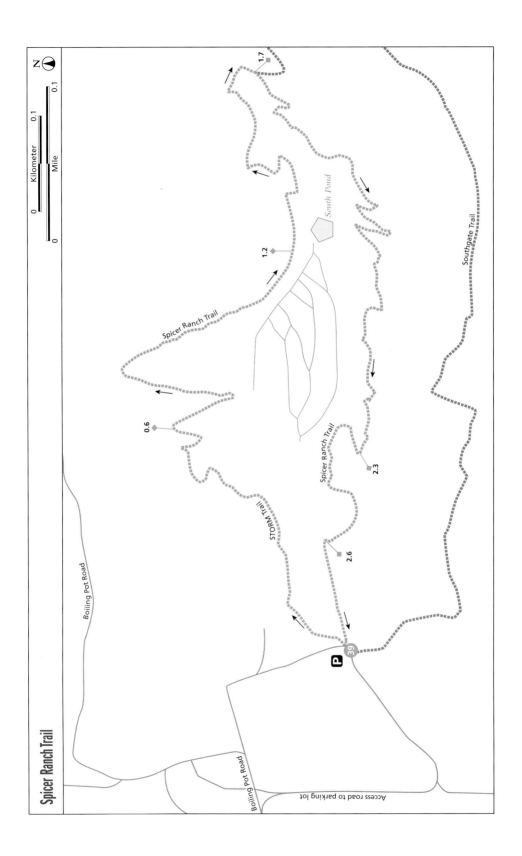

Spicer Ranch Trail

N

Kilometer
0   0.1   0.1

Mile
0   0.1

Boiling Pot Road

Spicer Ranch Trail

STORM Trail

Spicer Ranch Trail

Southgate Trail

South Pond

Boiling Pot Road

Access road to parking lot

P

39

0.6

1.2

1.7

2.3

2.6

2.5 Cross the pasture following the pin flags. Watch for cows and cow droppings. The pasture will usually be wet.

2.6 Once out of the pasture, turn left and continue along the ridge of the hill.

2.8 Head into the wash. Watch for pin flags as the trail can be hard to follow. Cross the wash and head up the small hill.

3.0 The Spicer Ranch Trail ends at the dirt road. The trail is marked with a yellow trail marker to the right. Take the dirt road left to the parking lot. Pass through another gate; be sure to close it behind you.

Ride Information

Local Events and Attractions

The Beatty Museum: Preserving and telling the story of Beatty and the historic Bullfrog Mining District; free admission; beattymuseum.org.

Scotty's Castle: Also known as Death Valley Ranch, this oasis in Grapevine Canyon was built in 1939, claimed by one man and built by another; nps.gov/deva/learn/historyculture/scottys-castle.htm.

Restaurants

KC's Outpost Eatery and Saloon: Best sandwiches in town; 100 E. Main, Beatty; (775) 553-9175

Mama Sara's Mexican Restaurant: Mexican food at its finest; 151 Highway 95 North, Beatty; (775) 553-9238

40 South Pond Trail

The South Pond Trail is named for—you guessed it—the pond on the south end of the property. This pond is often filled with all manner of ducks and water fowl throughout the year. Because the trail is one of the highest on the ranch, you get to look down and survey the area as you ride, affording yourself some very scenic views of not only the ranch and the pond, but the entire Oasis Valley.

Start: The parking lot just outside the cattle guard
Distance: 4.5 miles
Elevation gain: 394 feet
Riding time: Advanced riders, 1 hour; intermediate riders, 1.5 hours; beginning riders, 2 hours
Fitness effort: Physically moderate
Difficulty: Technically moderate, due to steady climbing

Terrain: Mostly dirt with some small rocks; pasture
Map: Trails-OV.org
Nearest town: Beatty
Other trail users: Hikers and runners
Dog friendly: Yes, but it is a working ranch with horses, bulls, and cows
Trail contact: Spicer Ranch; Trails-OV.org

Getting there: If traveling from Las Vegas, take U.S. Highway 95 (Veteran's Memorial Highway) 115 miles north to Beatty, Nevada. Turn right on Main Street (still U.S. Highway 95) and follow it approximately 7 miles to Boiling Pot Road. Turn Right onto the Spicer Ranch and follow the signs to the parking lot. GPS: N36 59.8668'/W116 42.9173'

The Ride

The trailhead is to the east of the parking lot just on the other side of the cattle guard. Cross the cattle guard and head along the dirt road to the left toward a sign directing you to the STORM Trail and camping area. Turn right as the dirt road makes its way to a metal gate. Remember, the Spicer Ranch is a working ranch. Whenever a trail passes through a closed gate, you are welcome to open the gate to pass, just be sure to secure it behind you.

Follow the trail on the other side of the gate as it takes a sharp left into the fence. There is a green ramp that will allow you passageway through the fence. On the other side of the ramp the trail takes an immediate right and starts a gradual climb up the side of a small hill. You are now on the STORM Trail. While the trail is relatively easy to follow, it can be difficult to see in some spots, especially at the start of the trail. In these areas, the trail is marked with orange pin flags, so make sure to follow these markers.

Follow the trail as it makes its way left up and alongside the small hill. At 0.3 mile cross the wash and follow the trail as it makes its way around a foothill following the

The South Pond filled with ducks

pasture. Do not turn to the right and pass through the gate. At about 0.6 mile, the trail splits. The STORM trail continues on to the left, and the Spicer Ranch trailhead is to the right. Both trails are clearly marked by yellow signs.

Follow the Spicer Ranch Trail as it climbs a hill and heads toward the fence. Cross the fence at the green ramp and continue to follow the trail along the hill. There is a small pond visible to the right. At about a mile into the ride, you'll enter a series of gradual switchbacks. Be careful of the soft dirt in this area and the steep drops to the right of the trail. Continue as the trail follows the foothills, climbing all the way.

At a little past a mile into the ride, cross over another fence using the green ramp. On the other side of the fence, the trail splits. Take the sharp left to the South Pond Trail. It is clearly marked with a yellow sign. Follow the trail as it makes a hairpin turn to the right. There are several small rock obstacles along the trail as you climb. About 1.5 miles into the trail, you'll encounter two tricky rock obstacles, one right after the other, before continuing the climb. When the trail seems to split, stay to the left. When the trail splits a second time, take either route as they meet back up about 15 feet ahead.

Follow the trail as it snakes its way to the crest of the next hill along the fence line. The body of water below you is the North Pond. Follow the trail as it eventually heads back on the back side of the hill, then start the long climb back up to the crest of the hill. Follow the trail down the other side until you reach the point where the trails meet back up, then head back down the trail you climbed previously.

When you meet back up with the Spicer Ranch Trail, you can either turn right and head back to the trailhead the way you came, or if you want a longer ride, turn left. This guide continues left. Cross the wash and follow the trail to the right. Just ahead, the trail turns sharply to the left, before continuing the climb, eventually heading into a short downhill section. Watch for the tight turn to the right, then follow the trail as it heads into the wash and then takes a gradual climb up the other hill.

After the climb, the trail levels out for a short distance leading to a split in the trails. Do not take the Southgate Trail on the left. Head into a short, fun downhill section with easy gradual turns. The trail makes its way toward the South Pond before climbing back up into the hills and heading down again.

When the trails split, you can either continue on the Spicer Ranch Trail to the right or you can take the Stirrup Trail to the left. Both trails will take you back to the parking lot. This guide takes the Stirrup Trail. Turn left and follow the trail through the wash along the base of the hills. The trail can be difficult to see, so look for the orange pin flags marking the trail.

When the trails split again, stay straight and head into the wash. This trail is marked as the Bottom Stirrup Loop. Do not take the Top Stirrup Loop Trail on the left. When the trails meet up again, follow the trail to the right. Do not climb the hill to the left. Take the sharp right turn and continue straight. Follow the trail as it dips into and climbs out of the wash. When the trails meet again, stay straight and head into the gully. Do not take the Canteen Trail on the left. Follow the trail as it heads right, traveling between the hill on the right and the old rock quarry on the left. The quarry is easily distinguished by the piles of dirt and rock. Then follow the trail to the parking lot.

Miles and Directions

0.0 Cross the cattle guard and head to the left.

0.1 Follow the dirt road right towards the gate. Go through the gate, closing it behind you. Take the immediate left and go through the fence using the green ramp, then take the immediate right, following the pin flags.

0.3 Cross the dry wash and head into a short climb. Do not turn right and go through the gate.

0.6 When the trail splits, head right at the Spicer Ranch Trailhead. The trail is clearly marked with a yellow trail sign. A short distance ahead, cross through the fence with the green ramp and follow the trail around the hill.

1.2 Make the short climb and cross over the fence using the green ramp. Take the South Pond Trail to the left and start the climb.

1.7 When the trail seems to split, stay left.

1.8 When the trail splits again, take either trail. They meet up again in about 15 feet. Then start a short downhill section.

2.2 When the trails meet, follow the trail down to the Sound Pond trailhead.

2.6 When the South Pond Trail meets the Spicer Ranch Trail, turn left.

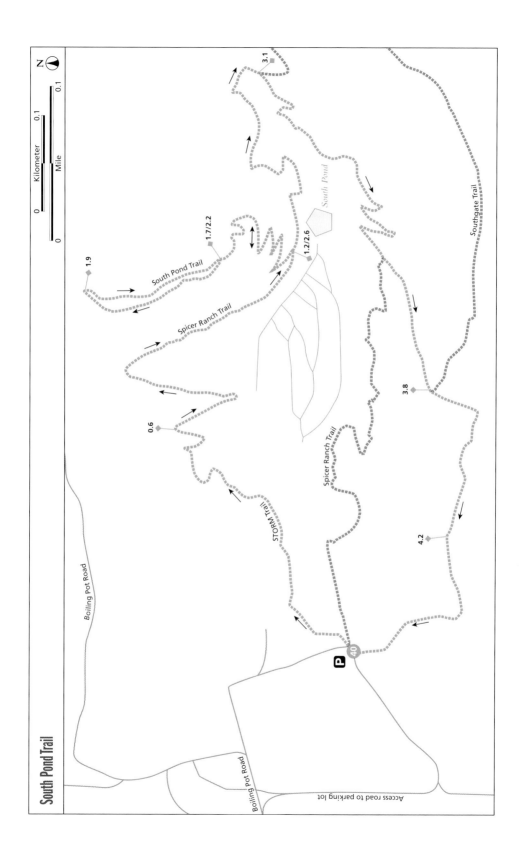

South Pond Trail

Boiling Pot Road

Access road to parking lot

Boiling Pot Road

STORM Trail

Spicer Ranch Trail

Spicer Ranch Trail

South Pond Trail

Southgate Trail

South Pond

0.6

1.9

1.7/2.2

1.2/2.6

3.1

3.8

4.2

40

N

Kilometer
0   0.1   0.1

Mile
0   0.1

3.1 When the trail splits, stay right. There is a sign marking the Spicer Ranch Trail. Do not take the Southgate Trail to the left. Head into a fun downhill section.

3.6 Take the hairpin turn right and continue the downhill section. When the trails split, take the Stirrup Trail to the left, then follow the trail into the wash.

3.8 When the trail splits again, stay straight, following the Bottom Stirrup Loop. Do not take the Top Stirrup Loop on the left. Cross the wash.

3.9 When the trails meet again, follow the Stirrup Trail to the right. Do not climb the hill to the left. Take the sharp right turn and continue straight.

4.2 Stay straight when the trails meet and head into the gully. Do not take the Canteen Trail to the left.

4.4 Turn left and follow the trail to the parking lot.

Ride Information

Local Events and Attractions

Rhyolite Ghost Town: Named after the silica-rich volcanic rock in the area, the town of Rhyolite once boasted a population of more than 10,000 and was at one time the 3rd largest city in Nevada; nps.gov/deva/learn/historyculture/rhyolite-ghost-town.htm.

Goldwell Open Air Museum: Started by a group of prominent Belgian artists, this collection of outdoor sculptures is a must-see-to-believe; goldwellmuseum.org/.

Restaurants

KC's Outpost Eatery and Saloon: Best sandwiches in town; 100 E. Main, Beatty; (775) 553-9175

Mama Sara's Mexican Restaurant: Mexican food at its finest; 151 Highway 95 North, Beatty; (775) 553-9238

41 Southgate Trail

The Southgate trail is an offshoot trail that hooks the Spicer Ranch Trail to the Junction Trail. While the first part of the trail is a long gradual climb, once you do reach the Junction Trail and head back, you're in for a fun, fast downhill ride along one of the largest washes in the Oasis Valley. This combination makes the Southgate Trail a great trail for anyone looking to hone skills. Because you can take the trail as fast as your skill level allows, the trail is perfect as a warmup to longer, more difficult rides.

Start: The parking lot just outside the cattle guard
Distance: 3.6 miles
Elevation gain: 339 feet
Riding time: Advanced riders, 45 minutes; intermediate riders, 1 hour; beginning riders, 1.5 hours
Fitness effort: Physically easy
Difficulty: Technically easy

Terrain: Mostly dirt with some small rocks; pasture
Map: Trails-OV.org
Nearest town: Beatty
Other trail users: Hikers and runners
Dog friendly: Yes, but it is a working ranch with horses, bulls, and cows
Trail contact: Spicer Ranch; Trails-OV.org

Getting there: If traveling from Las Vegas, take U.S. Highway 95 (Veteran's Memorial Highway) 115 miles north to Beatty, Nevada. Turn right on Main Street (still U.S. Highway 95) and follow it approximately 7 miles to Boiling Pot Road. Turn right onto the Spicer Ranch and follow the signs to the parking lot. GPS: N36 59.8668'/W116 42.9173'

The Ride

The trailhead is to the east of the parking lot just on the other side of the cattle guard. Cross the cattle guard and head along the dirt road to the left toward a sign directing you to the STORM Trail and camping area. Turn right as the dirt road makes its way to a metal gate. Remember, the Spicer Ranch is a working ranch. Whenever a trail passes through a closed gate, you are welcome to open the gate to pass, just be sure to secure it behind you.

Follow the trail on the other side of the gate as it takes a sharp left into the fence. There is a green ramp that will allow you passageway through the fence. On the other side of the ramp, the trail takes an immediate right and starts a gradual climb up the side of a small hill. You are now on the STORM Trail. While the trail is relatively easy to follow, it can be difficult to see in some spots, especially at the start of the trail. In these areas, the trail is marked with orange pin flags, so make sure to follow these markers.

At 0.3 mile cross the wash and follow the trail as it makes its way around a foothill following the pasture. Do not turn to the right and pass through the gate. At about

The bones of a dead burro rest alongside the trail.

0.6 mile, the trail splits. The STORM trail continues on to the left, and the Spicer Ranch trailhead is to the right. Both trails are clearly marked by yellow signs. Follow the Spicer Ranch Trail as it climbs a hill and heads toward the fence. Cross the fence at the green ramp and continue to follow the trail along the hill. There is a small pond visible to the right. The pasture will be disappearing behind you. The trail turns left just before the climb, then continues to follow the fence on the left. The pasture is now directly ahead of you.

At a little past a mile into the ride, cross over another fence using the green ramp. On the other side of the fence the trail splits. The trail that takes a sharp left is the South Pond Trail. It is clearly marked with a yellow sign. Stay straight, cross the wash, and follow the trail to the right. Watch for the tight turn to the right, then follow the trail as it heads into the wash and then takes a gradual climb up the other hill.

After the climb, the trail levels out for a short distance leading to a split in the trail. Take the Southgate Trail to the left and climb the crest of the hill, then follow the trail left as it heads away from the ranch toward Bureau of Land Management (BLM) land. Follow the trail as it continues to snake up the hill. This is a very gradual climb and actually looks like it should be steeper than it is. About 2.0 miles into the ride, Southgate meets the Junction Trail at a triangle of trails. All trails are marked with brown BLM trail markers. Take the sharp right and head into an easy gradual downhill section, eventually leading to a much steeper downhill.

Follow the trail as it takes a steep but gradual drop into the wash. At the bottom of the hill, the Southgate Trail officially ends. However, the trail meets up with the Stirrup Trail and that trail can be ridden back to the trailhead. Take the sharp right and head into the wash. Be careful coming down the hill because the wash is full of deep, soft gravel. Follow the trail as it snakes through the wash, eventually passing the bones of a long-dead burro on the right.

When the trails meet, stay straight. Do not take the Spicer Ranch Trail to the right. When the trails meet up a second time, follow the trail to the right. Do not climb the hill to the left. Take the sharp right turn and continue straight. Cross the wash again and make the short climb up the hill. Continue to follow the trail as it dips into and climbs out of the wash. When the trails meet again, stay straight and head into the gully. Do not take the Canteen Trail on the left. Follow the trail as it heads right, traveling between the hill on the right and the old rock quarry on the left. The quarry is easily distinguished by the piles of dirt and rock. Then follow the trail to the parking lot.

Miles and Directions

0.0 Cross the cattle guard and head to the left.

0.1 Follow the dirt road right towards the gate. Go through the gate, closing it behind you. Take the immediate left and go through the fence using the green ramp, then take the immediate right, following the pin flags.

0.3 Cross the dry wash and head into a short climb. Do not turn right and go through the gate.

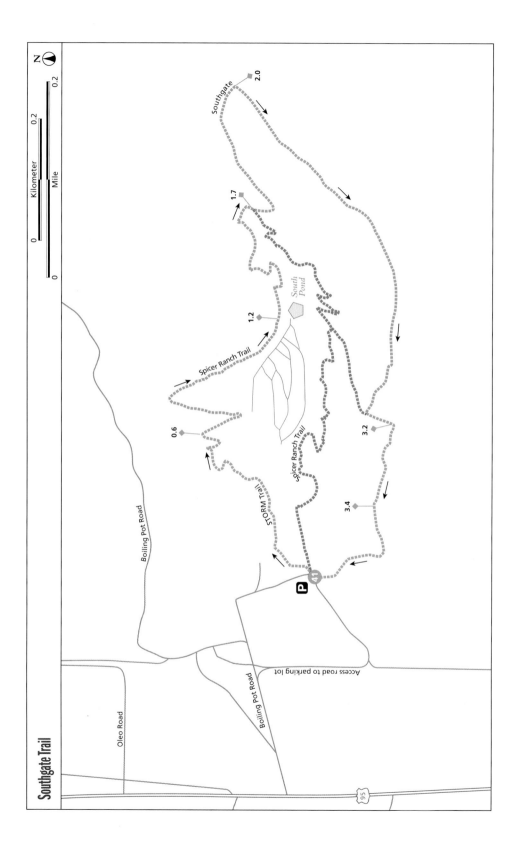

Southgate Trail

Boiling Pot Road

Oleo Road

Boiling Pot Road

Access road to parking lot

95

STORM Trail

Spicer Ranch Trail

Spicer Ranch Trail

South Pond

Southgate

0.6

1.2

1.7

2.0

3.2

3.4

P

N

Kilometer

Mile

0   0.2

0   0.2

0.6 When the trail splits, follow the trail right at the Spicer Ranch Trailhead. The trail is clearly marked with a yellow trail sign. A short distance ahead, cross through the fence with the green ramp and follow the trail around the hill.

1.2 Make the short climb and cross over the fence using the green ramp. Then follow the trail straight. Do not take the South Pond Trail to the left.

1.7 When the trail splits, take the Southgate Trail to the left and climb the crest of the hill. Then follow the trail left as it heads away from the ranch.

2.0 When Southgate meets the Junction Trail, take the sharp right and head into an easy downhill section.

2.9 Take the steep, but gradual drop into the wash. At the bottom of the hill, the Southgate Trail ends. Take the sharp right onto the Stirrup Trail and head into the wash, eventually passing the bones of a dead burro on the right.

3.0 When the trails meet up, stay straight. Do not take the Spicer Ranch Trail to the right.

3.1 When the trails meet again, follow the Stirrup Trail to the right. Do not climb the hill to the left. Take the sharp right turn and continue straight.

3.4 Stay straight when the trails meet and head into the gully. Do not take the Canteen Trail to the left.

3.6 Turn left and follow the trail to the parking lot.

Ride Information

Local Events and Attractions

Death Valley: Travel below sea level and experience the hottest, driest, and lowest point in the United States; www.nps.gov/deva/index.htm.

Scotty's Castle: Also known as Death Valley Ranch, this oasis in Grapevine Canyon was built in 1939, claimed by one man and built by another; nps.gov/deva/learn/historyculture/scottys–castle.htm.

Restaurants

Happy Burro Chili & Beer: This is the place for chilidogs and burgers after a long ride; 100 W. Main, Beatty; (775) 553-9099

Mel's Diner: Cash only; 600 US 95, Beatty; (775) 553-9003

42 Stirrup Trail

The Stirrup Trail is particularly fun because it has a great downhill section. Of course, before you get to ride that downhill, you first have to earn it with a bit of a climb. But don't worry, the climb is not strenuous and as you climb you get to travel through some great countryside. Then, having earned your downhill, you get to barrel down the trail as it dives into and across washes and along the foothills back to the trailhead. This is a fun, fast-paced ride that allows you to go as quickly as your skill level allows.

Start: The parking lot just outside the cattle guard

Distance: 3.2 miles

Elevation gain: 230 feet

Riding time: Advanced riders, 45 minutes; intermediate riders, 1 hour; beginning riders, 1.5 hours

Fitness effort: Physically easy to moderate

Difficulty: Technically easy to moderate

Terrain: Mostly dirt with some small rocks; pasture

Map: Trails-OV.org

Nearest town: Beatty

Other trail users: Hikers and runners

Dog friendly: Yes, but it is a working ranch with horses, bulls, and cows

Trail contact: Spicer Ranch; Trails-OV.org

Getting there: If traveling from Las Vegas, take U.S. Highway 95 (Veteran's Memorial Highway) 115 miles north to Beatty, Nevada. Turn right on Main Street (still U.S. Highway 95) and follow it approximately 7 miles to Boiling Pot Road. Turn Right onto the Spicer Ranch and follow the signs to the parking lot. GPS: N36 59.8668'/W116 42.9173'

The Ride

There are two access points to trails in the Oasis Valley. One is across the cattle guard following the STORM Trail. The other is adjacent to the cattle guard, directly across from the parking lot. It is from this point that you can access the Canteen Trail, the Junction Trail, the Lariat Loop, and the Stirrup Trail. The trails are actually laid out so you could access any trail from either access point, but this second access point is the way the trail is designed to be ridden. There is a yellow sign marking the trailhead and pin flags direct you along the way.

The trail makes its way past the old rock quarry, eventually heading into the back of the ranch. The Stirrup Trail is one of the trails in the Oasis Valley that is on both Bureau of Land Management (BLM) land and the Spicer Ranch, meaning it starts on the ranch and eventually makes its way to BLM land, before turning and heading back toward the ranch. The trail is relatively easy to follow and pin flags are located in places where it can be difficult to spot the trail.

At about 0.3 mile into the ride, the trail splits. The trail to the right is the Canteen Trail. Stay straight to remain on the Stirrup Trail. Both trails are clearly marked. At

A group of riders gets ready to head out on the trail. Dave Spicer

this point you'll drop in and out of washes as the trail heads eastward. At 0.5 mile, when the trail splits a second time, take the trail to the left and climb the crest of the hill. In this section, the trail looks much steeper than it is. There are also many burro trails in the area, so use the pin flags to make sure you stay on the main trail. Burro trails are well traveled and, for this reason, tend to look well groomed. This can make it a bit confusing; however, Stirrup is readily marked with pin flags in areas where it is not so easy to follow.

At 1.2 miles cross the wash and follow the trail to the right as it climbs back up to the foothills. When the trails meet up, stay straight. Do not take the trail to the left. In 1.6 miles when the Stirrup and Junction Trails meet at the triangle of trails, take the sharp turn to the left and begin the downhill section that eventually leads back to the trailhead. At almost two miles into the ride, the trail takes a steep drop into the wash, before crossing that wash and climbing the other side. At 2.2 miles Stirrup and Junction meet once again. Take the trail to the left and make the short, but steep climb up the hill before heading back into a downhill section. When the Stirrup Trail meets the Southgate Trail, take the sharp right and head into the wash. Be careful coming down the hill because the wash is full of deep, soft gravel. Follow the trail as it snakes through the wash, eventually passing the bones of a long dead burro on the right.

When the trails meet, stay straight. Do not take the Spicer Ranch Trail to the right. When the trails meet up a second time, follow the trail to the right. Do not climb the hill to the left. Take the sharp right turn and continue straight. Cross the wash again and make the short climb up the hill. Continue to follow the trail as it dips into and climbs out of the wash. When the trails meet again, stay straight and head into the gully. Do not take the Canteen Trail on the left. Follow the trail as it heads right, traveling between the hill on the right and the old rock quarry on the

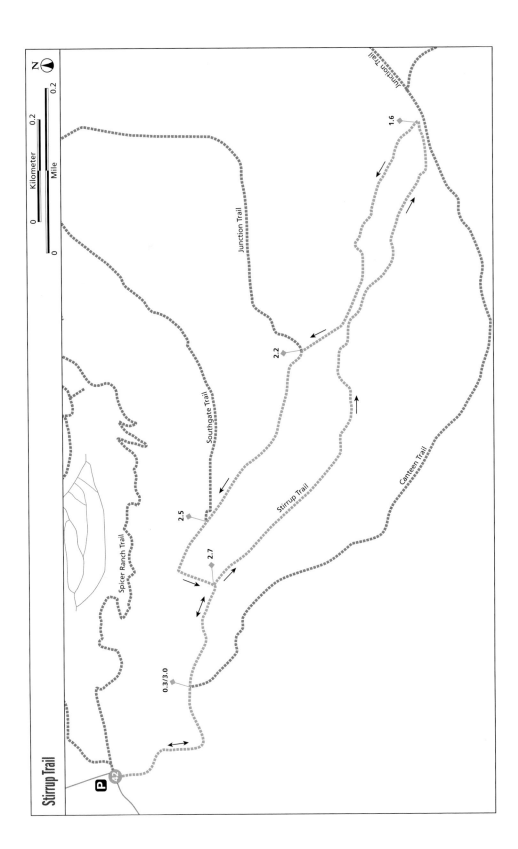

Stirrup Trail

Spicer Ranch Trail

Southgate Trail

Junction Trail

Stirrup Trail

Canteen Trail

Junction Trail

0.3/3.0

2.7

2.5

2.2

1.6

P

42

N

Kilometer

0   0.2

0   0.2

Mile

left. The quarry is easily distinguished by the piles of dirt and rock. Then follow the trail to the parking lot.

Miles and Directions

0.0 Start at the trail marker directly across from the parking lot. Do not cross the cattle guard. Follow the pin flags as the trail eventually heads east.

0.3 Stay straight when the trail splits. Do not take the Canteen Trail to the right.

0.5 When the trail splits, stay left, climbing the crest of the small hill.

1.6 When the Stirrup Trail meets the Junction Trail, take the sharp left turn and begin a downhill section.

1.9 Follow the trail as it takes a steep drop into the wash.

2.2 When the Stirrup Trail again meets the Junction Trail, follow Stirrup left and climb the hill before continuing the downhill ride.

2.5 Stay straight when Stirrup merges with the Southgate Trail. Take the sharp right onto the Stirrup Trail and head into the wash, eventually passing the bones of a dead burro on the right.

2.6 When the trails meet up, stay straight. Do not take the Spicer Ranch Trail to the right.

2.7 When the trails meet again, follow the Stirrup Trail right. Do not climb the hill to the left. Take the sharp right turn and continue straight.

3.0 Stay straight when the trails meet and head into the gully. Do not take the Canteen Trail to the left.

3.2 Turn left and follow the trail to the parking lot.

Ride Information

Local Events and Attractions

Beatty Museum: Learn the history of the town and surrounding area in this well-curated, free museum; beattymuseum.com.

Bailey's Hot Springs: What better way to relax after a hard ride than in a hot spring; www.baileyshotsprings.com.

Restaurants

KC's Outpost Eatery and Saloon: Best sandwiches in town; 100 E. Main, Beatty; (775) 553-9175

Death Valley Nut and Candy Company: Homemade ice cream, dried fruit and nuts, and jerky; 700 US 95, Beatty; (775) 553-2100

43 Canteen Trail

The Canteen Trail is one of the longer trails in the Oasis Valley system of trails. The trail got its name from an old canteen Dave Spicer found along the side of the trail as he was laying it out. The canteen made him wonder why it had been left behind and who had left it there. Of course, that question was never answered, but Dave left the canteen on the side of the trail as a reminder of a bygone era. This trail heads back to an old silica mine high into the hills and on the way provides some of the best views available of the Oasis Valley. As the terrain changes along the ride, you see colorful desert, stalwart Joshua trees, and landscape that in one place gives you the feeling of being on the surface of the moon.

Start: The parking lot just outside the cattle guard

Distance: 10.0 miles

Elevation gain: 416 feet

Riding time: Advanced riders, 1.5 hours; intermediate riders, 2 hours; beginning riders, 2.5 hours

Fitness effort: Physically moderate to challenging

Difficulty: Technically moderate to challenging

Terrain: Mostly dirt with some small rocks and deep gravel in some areas

Map: Trails-OV.org

Nearest town: Beatty

Other trail users: Hikers and runners

Dog friendly: Yes, but it is a working ranch with horses, bulls, and cows; burros also roam the area

Trail contact: Spicer Ranch; Trails-OV.org

Getting there: If traveling from Las Vegas, take U.S. Highway 95 (Veteran's Memorial Highway) 115 miles north to Beatty, Nevada. Turn right on Main Street (still U.S. Highway 95) and follow it approximately 7 miles to Boiling Pot Road. Turn right onto the Spicer Ranch and follow the signs to the parking lot. GPS: N36 59.8668'/W116 42.9173'

The Ride

The Canteen Trail is accessed by heading south directly across from the parking lot, not by going over the cattle guard. There is a yellow sign marking the trailhead and pin flags direct you along the way. The trail makes its way past the old rock quarry, eventually heading into the back of the ranch. At about 0.3 mile into the ride, the trail splits. Take the Canteen Trail to the right and begin a climb up into the hills. The Canteen Trail is one of the trails in the Oasis Valley that is on both Bureau of Land Management (BLM) land and the Spicer Ranch, meaning it starts on the ranch and eventually makes its way to BLM land and an old silica mine high up in the hills. In fact, the mine, which from a distance looks like a white spot on the top of the hill, is a reference point that helps you navigate as you ride southeast along the trail.

The very canteen that gave this trail its name

While the Canteen Trail is not a difficult trail, it is an almost constant climb through the hills toward the silica mine. There are some ups and down as the trail dips into and out of several washes and you travel along the foothills in many spots; still, the trail is uphill for almost the entire first half of the ride. This, however, does make the return trip to the trailhead a nice fun downhill ride. There are several burro trails along Canteen. In most cases the main trail is easy to spot, but in places where it is not so easy, pin flags mark the trail. Be sure to pay attention to these pin flag as burros are great groomers and the trails they use are typically groomed just as well as the Canteen Trail, which can make it a bit tricky to tell the difference at places and the flags are vital.

Just short of a mile into the trail, the silica mine comes into view at the top of the hill directly in front of you. From this distance, the mine just looks like a large white circle in the hill instead of an actual mine. In 1.3 miles the trail splits. Canteen continues to the left. The trail to the right is Spur and it eventually leads to the Lariat Loop. Stay straight when Canteen meets the Stirrup Trail in 0.3 mile and when the trails split again in another 0.1 mile, stay to the right. The trail on the left is Junction.

About 2.0 miles into the ride, the trail crosses a wash and makes a very steep climb up a hill. Here the trail seems to disappear, but it is easily found at the top of the short, but steep hill. Another 0.7 mile into the ride, the Lariat Loop Trail is off to the right on the other side of the wash. Stay straight and take the steep climb out of the wash. At 3.2 miles into the ride, the trail heads into a wash and then makes a right turn, following the wash. Here the terrain turns to soft, deep gravel. Follow the wash about 0.1 mile and pick the trail up again on the right side of the wash. You will cross the wash once again a short distance ahead, before climbing out of the wash on the other side.

The canteen that gives the trail its name is usually found about 3.5 miles into the ride. It is often on the right side of the trail. However, it does have a tendency to migrate and can be seen on the left side of the trail as well. When the trail meets the dirt road at about 4.1 miles, turn onto the dirt road and follow it up the steep hill. You may want to stop at the top of the hill and take in the views of the canyon just to the right of the road. The canyon, with its rocky cliffs, is not only beautiful, but unexpected as well.

Once you reach the top of the hill, you can simply head down the other side toward the large wash, called the Beatty Wash. Here you can see the silica mine high up the hill to your right. This is also a great place to get off your bike and explore. Just to the left of the wash is a mining tunnel and an old cabin, once used by the men who worked the silica mines. You can explore the cabin, but stay out of the tunnel as it is not safe. The road heads into the wash and you can follow it as long as you like. When you've reached as far as you want to go, simply turn your bike around, climb the hill on the dirt road, and head back to the trailhead with a fun, gradual downhill.

Miles and Directions

0.0 Start at the trail marker directly across from the parking lot. Do not cross the cattle guard. Follow the pin flags as the trail eventually heads east.

0.3 When the trail splits, take the Canteen Trail to the right.

1.3 Follow the trail left when the trail splits. Do not take the Spur Trail to the right.

1.7 Stay straight when the Stirrup Trail meets the Canteen Trail. Stay right a short distance ahead when the Junction Trail veers off to the left.

2.0 Cross the wash and make the steep climb up the short hill.

2.7 Stay straight when the trails split. Do not take the Lariat Loop to the right.

3.2 Drop into and follow the wash to the right. In 0.1 mile, pick the trail back up to the right.

4.1 When the trail meets the dirt road, follow the dirt road as it climbs up the hill.

4.9 At the top of the hill, follow the dirt road down into the wash.

5.0 Turn the bike around and return to the trailhead.

10.0 Arrive at the trailhead.

Ride Information

Local Events and Attractions

Marta Becket's Amargosa Opera House: Never feel alone in an opera house where the walls are adorned with 16th-century attendees; amargosaoperahouse.com. **Beatty Mudmound and Swiss Cheese Rocks:** One-of-a-kind rock formations where you can find the preserved remains of 480-million-year-old fossils. The

Canteen Trail

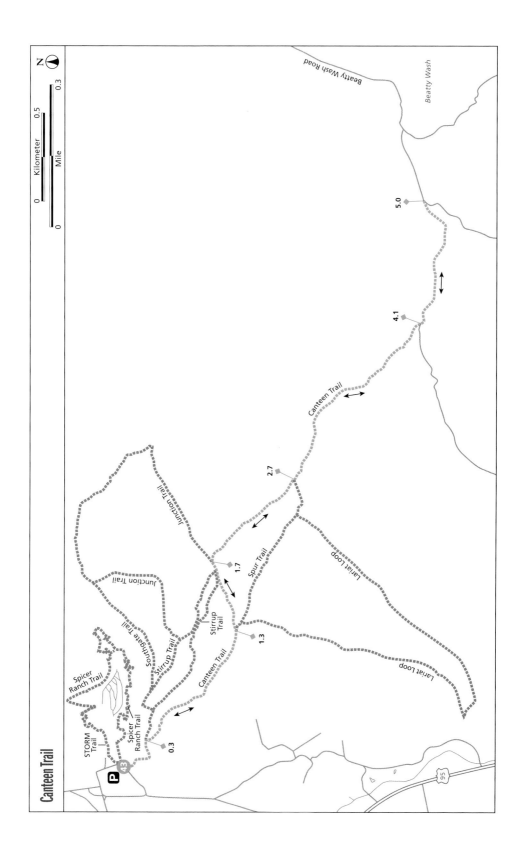

Spicer Ranch Trail

STORM Trail

Spicer Ranch Trail

Southgate Trail

Stirrup Trail

Junction Trail

Junction Trail

Stirrup Trail

Canteen Trail

Spur Trail

Lariat Loop

Lariat Loop

Canteen Trail

Beatty Wash Road

Beatty Wash

95

P

43

0.3

1.3

1.7

2.7

4.1

5.0

N

Kilometer

0   0.5

Mile

0   0.3

wind- and weather-worn Swiss cheese rocks have been compared to the limestone formations in Cappadocia, Italy.

Restaurants

KC's Outpost Eatery and Saloon: Best sandwiches in town; 100 E. Main, Beatty; (775) 553-9175

Death Valley Nut and Candy Company: Homemade ice cream, dried fruit and nuts, and jerky; 700 US 95, Beatty; (775) 553-2100

44 Lariat Loop

The Lariat Loop is a fun offshoot diversion from the Canteen Trail. This 4.4-mile trail jets off from Canteen, heading down into the valley before turning and meeting back up with Canteen via a great rolling trail known as Spur. At the end of this loop, you can either finish the ride along Canteen or you can just ride the Lariat Loop and head back to the trailhead afterward, as outlined in this guide. Either way, you'll find the loop an enjoyable ride with great scenic views, one well worth your time.

Start: The parking lot just outside the cattle guard
Distance: 5.7 miles
Elevation gain: 416 feet
Riding time: Advanced riders, 45 minutes; intermediate riders, 1 hour; beginning riders, 1.5 hours
Fitness effort: Physically easy to moderate
Difficulty: Technically easy to moderate

Terrain: Mostly dirt with some small rocks and loose gravel
Map: Trails-OV.org
Nearest town: Beatty
Other trail users: Hikers and runners
Dog friendly: Yes, but it is a working ranch with horses, bulls, and cows; burros also roam the area
Trail contact: Spicer Ranch; Trails-OV.org

Getting there: If traveling from Las Vegas, take U.S. Highway 95 (Veteran's Memorial Highway) 115 miles north to Beatty, Nevada. Turn right on Main Street (still U.S. Highway 95) and follow it approximately 7 miles to Boiling Pot Road. Turn right onto the Spicer Ranch and follow the signs to the parking lot. GPS: N36 59.8668'/W116 42.9173'

The Ride

The Lariat Loop is an offshoot of the Canteen Trail. Its trailhead is a little over a mile into the ride and is accessed from a connector trail known as Spur. The trailhead to the Canteen Trail can be found by heading south directly across from the parking lot. There is a yellow sign marking the trailhead and pin flags direct you along the way. The trail makes its way past the old rock quarry, eventually heading into the back of the ranch. At about 0.3 mile into the ride, the trail splits. Take the Canteen Trail to the right and begin a climb up into the hills.

While the Canteen Trail is not a difficult trail, it is an almost constant climb through the hills. There are some ups and downs as the trail dips into and out of several washes and you travel along the foothills in many spots. In 1.3 miles the trail splits. Canteen continues to the left. The trail to the right is Spur and it is this trail that eventually leads to the Lariat Loop. Shortly after the split the trail splits a second time. The trail to the right is the Lariat Loop. It is marked with a brown Bureau of Land Management (BLM) trail marker. The trail is easy to follow as it makes its way along the crest of the hill. About a mile into the ride, the trail moves to the edge of the crest

The trail markers for the Spur and Lariat Loop

as it follows to the left and heads down into and across the wash. Here it is important to follow the pin flags because the trail can be difficult to see in some places and there are many offshoot burro trails.

At about 3.6 miles into the ride, the Lariat Loop ends at the point where it connects to the Spur Trail. From here you can follow the trail to the right and eventually

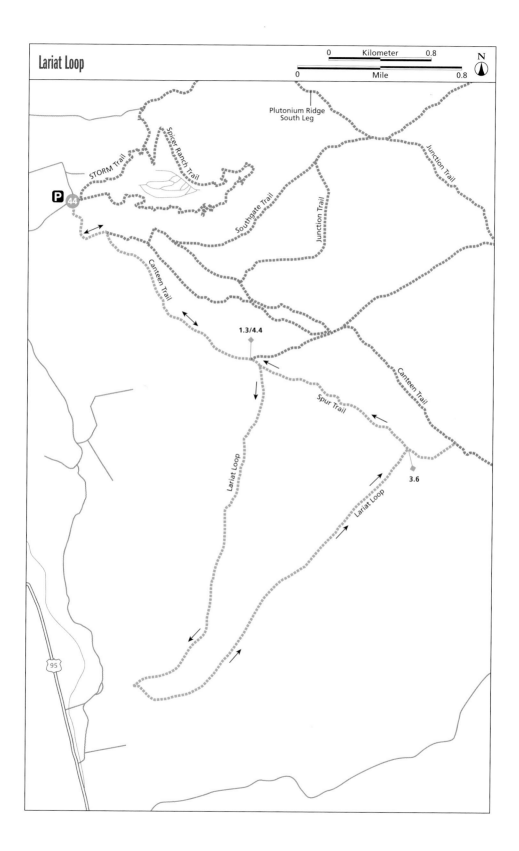

hook up with Canteen for a longer ride. You can also turn to the left and ride Spur back to the Lariat Loop trailhead. If you turn left, once you pass the trailhead to the Lariat Loop, continue on until you reach the Canteen Trail. From here you can follow Canteen back to the trailhead and the parking lot.

Miles and Directions

0.0 Start at the trail marker directly across from the parking lot. Do not cross the cattle guard. Follow the pin flags as the trail eventually heads east.

0.3 When the trails split, take the Canteen Trail right.

1.3 Follow the Spur Trail right when the trail splits, then take the Lariat Loop when it splits again a short distance ahead at the trail marker.

1.7 Take the dip into and cross the wash.

3.6 When the Lariat Loop ends, take the Spur Trail left.

4.4 Turn left and connect with the Canteen Loop.

5.7 Arrive at the trailhead.

Ride Information

Local Events and Attractions

Rhyolite Ghost Town: Named after the silica-rich volcanic rock in the area, the town of Rhyolite once boasted a population of more than 10,000; nps.gov/deva/learn/historyculture/rhyolite-ghost-town.htm.

Tom Kelly Bottle House: Made with a reported fifty-thousand bottles—mostly beer and wine—this house is one of the few buildings that remain in the town of Rhyolite; rhyolitesite.com.

Restaurants

Happy Burro Chili & Beer: This is the place for chilidogs and burgers after a long ride; 100 W. Main, Beatty; (775) 553-9099

Mama Sara's Mexican Restaurant: Mexican food at its finest; 151 Highway 95 North, Beatty; (775) 553-9238

45 Junction Trail

The Junction Trail is so named because it connects many trails in the Oasis Valley. This means the Junction Trail can be used to connect one trail to another, allowing you to extend your ride about as long as you'd like. The trail can also be ridden by itself, creating a nice loop that has a great downhill section when it connects to the Stirrup Trail.

Start: The parking lot just outside the cattle guard
Distance: 5.5 miles
Elevation gain: 129 feet
Riding time: Advanced riders, 45 minutes; intermediate riders, 1 hour; beginning riders, 1.5 hours
Fitness effort: Physically easy to moderate
Difficulty: Technically easy to moderate

Terrain: Mostly dirt with some small rocks
Map: Trails-OV.org
Nearest town: Beatty
Other trail users: Hikers and runners
Dog friendly: Yes, but it is a working ranch with horses, bulls, and cows; burros also roam the area
Trail contact: Spicer Ranch; Trails-OV.org

Getting there: If traveling from Las Vegas, take U.S. Highway 95 (Veteran's Memorial Highway) 115 miles north to Beatty, Nevada. Turn right on Main Street (still U.S. Highway 95) and follow it approximately 7 miles to Boiling Pot Road. Turn right onto the Spicer Ranch and follow the signs to the parking lot. GPS: N36 59.8668'/W116 42.9173'

The Ride

The Junction Trail is so named because it lies in the center of the system of trails that make up the Oasis Valley system of trails. In this position, the Junction Trail connects with the Plutonium Ridge Half Loop, the Canteen Trail, the Southgate Trail, and the Stirrup Trail. For this reason, the trail can be used to extend your ride, making any trail longer by connecting it to another trail. The Junction Trail can also be ridden by itself. This is done by first accessing the Canteen Trail. The trailhead can be found by heading south directly across from the parking lot. There is a yellow sign marking the trailhead and pin flags direct you along the way. The trail makes its way past the old rock quarry, eventually heading into the back of the ranch. At about 0.3 mile into the ride, the trail splits. Take the Canteen Trail to the right and begin a climb up into the hills.

While the Canteen Trail is not a difficult trail, it is an almost constant climb through the hills. There are some ups and down as the trail dips into and out of several washes and you travel along the foothills in many spots. In 1.3 miles the trail splits. Canteen continues to the left. The trail to the right is Spur and it eventually leads to the Lariat Loop. Stay straight when Canteen meets the Stirrup Trail in 0.3 mile and when the trails split again in another 0.1 mile, take the Junction Trail to the left.

At 2.5 miles into the ride, the trail intersects a dirt road. Head left onto the dirt road and pick up the trail to the right a little less than 0.1 mile ahead. In 0.3 mile, cross the dirt road again and head into another wash. At mile 2.9 stay straight when the Junction Trail and the Plutonium Ridge (south leg) Trail meet. Take the Junction Trail to the left when the trails split and do so again in 0.3 mile when the Southgate Trail meets the Junction Trail to the right. Stay straight at mile 4.1 when the Junction Trail meets the Stirrup Trail and follow the Stirrup Trail back to the trailhead.

Miles and Directions

0.0 Start at the trail marker directly across from the parking lot. Do not cross the cattle guard. Follow the pin flags as the trail eventually heads east.

0.3 When the trails split, take the Canteen Trail right.

1.3 Stay to the left when Canteen meets the Spur Trail.

1.7 Take the Junction Trail left and begin a gradual climb.

2.5 Turn left on the dirt road and pick the trail up again on the right a short distance ahead.

2.9 Stay straight when the Junction and Plutonium Ridge Trails meet. Take the Junction Trail left when the trails split.

It's common to see burros watching from above the trail.

Junction Trail

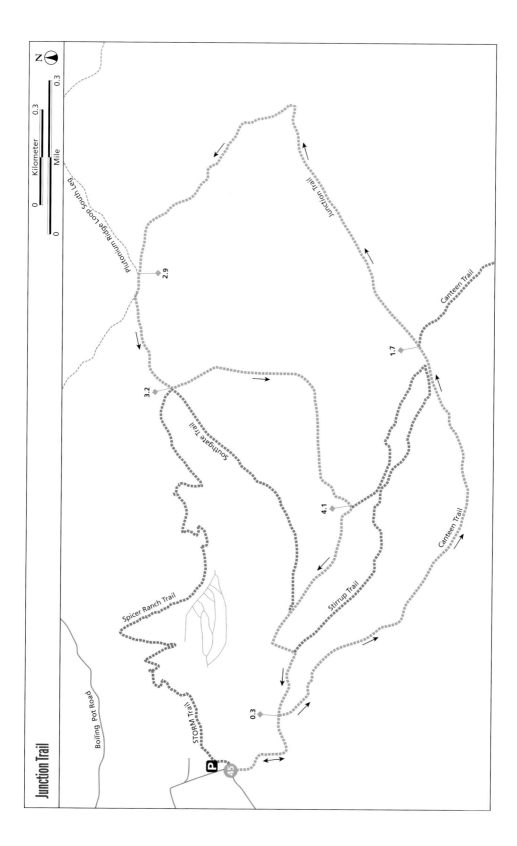

3.2 Take the Junction Trail left when the trails split. Do not take the Southgate Trail.

4.1 Stay straight when the Junction Trail meets the Stirrup Trail.

5.5 Arrive at the trailhead.

Ride Information

Local Events and Attractions

Marta Becket's Amargosa Opera House: Never feel alone in an opera house where the walls are adorned with 16th-century attendees; amargosaoperahouse.com.
Death Valley: Travel below sea level and experience the hottest, driest, and lowest point in the United States; nps.gov/deva/index.htm.

Restaurants

Happy Burro Chili & Beer: This is the place for chilidogs and burgers after a long ride; 100 W. Main, Beatty; (775) 553-9099
KC's Outpost Eatery and Saloon: Best sandwiches in town; 100 E. Main, Beatty; (775) 553-9175

46 Plutonium Ridge Loop

This trail is one of the longest official trails in the Oasis Valley system of trails. The first part of the trail is a continuous climb through almost the entire valley. The climb is rewarded, however, with some of the most scenic views you'll find and along the way you are exposed to all the beauty the desert landscape has to offer. Plus, after you take in the marvelous views, you are rewarded with a wonderful, gradual downhill ride back to the trailhead.

Start: The parking lot just outside the cattle guard
Distance: 9.7 miles
Elevation gain: 528 feet
Riding time: Advanced riders, 1.5 hours; intermediate riders, 2 hours; beginning riders, 2.5 hours
Fitness effort: Physically moderate to challenging; mainly due to the length of the trail and the washes you must ride through
Difficulty: Technically easy to moderate

Terrain: Well-groomed trail; mostly dirt with some small rocks; pasture, and areas of soft gravel
Map: Trails-OV.org
Nearest town: Beatty
Other trail users: Hikers and runners
Dog friendly: Yes, but it is a working ranch with horses, bulls, and cows; burros also roam the area
Trail contact: Spicer Ranch; Trails-OV.org

Getting there: If traveling from Las Vegas, take U.S. Highway 95 (Veteran's Memorial Highway) 115 miles north to Beatty, Nevada. Turn right on Main Street (still U.S. Highway 95) and follow it approximately 7 miles to Boiling Pot Road. Turn right onto the Spicer Ranch and follow the signs to the parking lot. GPS: N36 59.8668'/W116 42.9173'

The Ride

Las Vegas is known for three things: casinos, the mob, and the atomic bomb. One of those three extends all the way out of Las Vegas to the town of Beatty and the Oasis Valley. Plutonium Ridge got its name from the atomic testing that took place just to the east of the ridge of hills toward the back of the valley. Much of the area behind that ridge is owned by the United States government and it is this area that was used from the '50s on forward to test nuclear weapons—some above ground and some below. "I remember when a test went off as a kid," Dave Spicer recalls. "After the explosion you could see the ground rolling toward the ranch like a wave." Of course, that was many years ago and the tests no longer cause the ground to rise and fall like a wave heading to shore. While this ride doesn't go into the area where the tests occurred, it does travel close to the ridge that separates the Oasis Valley system of trails from the test site.

The Plutonium Ridge Loop is completely on BLM land and is accessed by traveling up the STORM Trail to a dirt road that takes you to the trailhead. The STORM

A large Joshua tree on the Plutonium Ridge Loop

Trail is accessed by crossing the cattle guard and heading along the dirt road to the left toward a sign directing you to the STORM Trail and camping area. Turn right as the dirt road makes its way to a metal gate. Remember, the Spicer Ranch is a working ranch complete with horses, cattle, and other livestock. Whenever a trail passes through a closed gate, you are welcome to open the gate to pass; just be sure to secure it behind you.

Follow the trail on the other side of the gate as it takes a sharp left into the fence. There is a green ramp that will allow you passageway through the fence. On the other side of the ramp the trail takes an immediate right and starts a gradual climb up the side of a small hill. You are now on the STORM Trail. While the trail is relatively easy to follow, it can be difficult to see in some spots, especially at the start of the trail. In these areas, the trail is marked with orange pin flags, so make sure to follow these markers.

Follow the trail as it makes its way left up and alongside the small hill. A pasture—often filled with horses—is on your left. At 0.3 mile cross the wash and follow the trail as it makes its way around a foothill following the pasture. Do not turn to the right and pass through the gate. At about 0.6 mile the trail splits. The STORM trail continues on to the left, and the Spicer Ranch trailhead is to the right. Both trails are clearly marked by yellow signs. Stay on the STORM trail as it heads around the hill, then follow the pin flags across the pasture. Remember, the pasture may be wet. Follow the trail on the other side of the pasture as it makes it way toward the fence, eventually heading through the fence at the green metal ramp.

When the trail intersects the dirt road, take the dirt road to the right and follow it as it climbs up the hill and down on the other side. When the trail meets a closed metal gate, follow the trail to the left and go around the gate on the down side of the hill. This trail allows you to go around the gate without having to open it. Follow the dirt road again, heading to the right when the road splits. A short distance up the road, you'll see the trailhead for the Plutonium Ridge Loop. The first trailhead is to the south leg of the loop. The north leg trailhead is a short distance ahead. The trail is intended to be ridden from the north leg to the south leg; however, you can ride it the other way if you wish. Riding a trail backwards can change the trail up, creating a whole new trail. This guide follows the north trailhead.

While this trail is easy to follow, it is bordered by several burro trails. Burros are great at grooming trails and their trails can look as groomed as the main trail, making it a bit difficult to follow the main trail at times. Whenever this occurs, pin flags have been placed to help identify the main trail. If you get on a burro trail by accident, don't panic; most of these trails meet back up with the main trail at times and you will be able to find the main trail.

About 2.2 miles into the ride, the trail intersects a dirt road. Follow the trail as it snakes along the road. In 0.5 mile, take the trail to the left of the road. Following to the right will allow you to take the Plutonium Ridge Half Loop. At 3.8 miles, follow the trail as it curves around a large Joshua tree and comes up to the crest of the hill. You may want to stop here and take in the majestic views of the valley.

In 0.1 mile stay straight when the trails split. At 4.7 miles, stay to the right when the trails merge. The trail to the left is called Brad's Screamer. This is a downhill trail that leads into the Beatty Wash and, if you ride far enough, eventually to the Canteen Trail. From here you are on the south leg of the trail. Start the gradual downhill section back to the trailhead. This route passes through some of the most unique landscape available, Here the landscape changes from a rich brown, to a deep gray, to a stark white, and back again. About 5.7 miles into the ride, follow the trail as it turns to the left. Do not take what looks like a trail to the right. It heads into a very steep drop.

At 7.3 miles cross the dirt road and connect with the portion of the trail that starts the Plutonium Ridge Half Loop south leg. At 7.8 miles, stay straight when the Junction Trail merges with the Plutonium Ridge Loop, then stay to the right when the Junction Trail splits off to the left a short distance ahead. At 8.3 miles, you'll come to the Plutonium Ridge Loop south leg trailhead at the dirt road. Follow the dirt road to the left and head back to the trailhead. Go through the fence at the STORM trailhead and follow that trail back to the parking lot.

Miles and Directions

0.0 Cross the cattle guard and head to the left.

0.1 Follow the dirt road right towards the gate. Go through the gate, closing it behind you. Take the immediate left and go through the fence using the green ramp; then take the immediate right, following the pin flags.

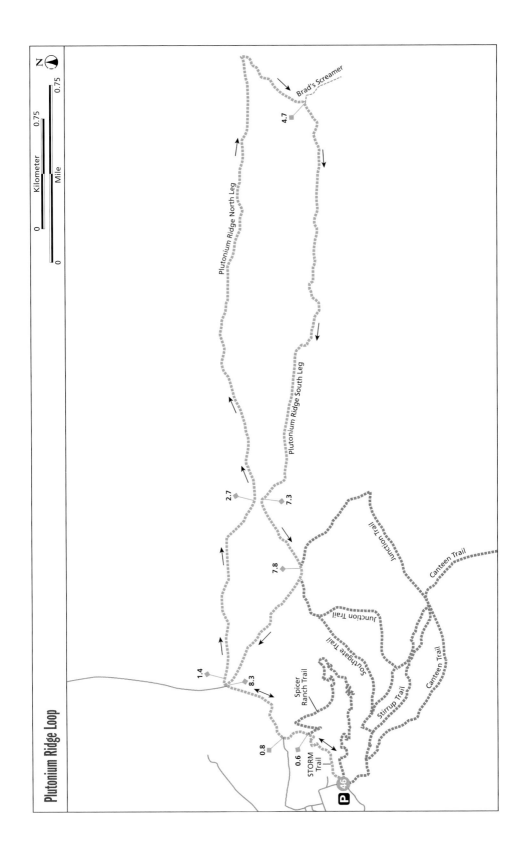

Plutonium Ridge Loop

Plutonium Ridge North Leg

Plutonium Ridge South Leg

Brad's Screamer

4.7

2.7

7.3

7.8

1.4

8.3

Spicer
Ranch Trail

0.8

0.6

STORM
Trail

Junction Trail

Junction Trail

Southgate Trail

Stirrup Trail

Canteen Trail

Canteen Trail

P 46

N

0   0.75   Kilometer   0.75

0   Mile

0.3 Cross the dry wash and head into a short climb. Do not turn right and go through the gate.

0.6 When the trail splits, follow the STORM Trail left. The Spicer Ranch trailhead is to the right. The trails are clearly marked with yellow trail signs. Follow the STORM Trail as it heads around the hill and into the pasture.

0.8 Cross through the fence and go right on the dirt road.

1.4 Take the Plutonium Ridge Loop North Leg Trail on the left.

2.2 Follow the trail as it snakes along the dirt road.

2.7 Take the trail to the left.

3.9 Stay straight when the trails split.

4.7 Stay right when the trails merge. The trail to the left is Brad's Screamer.

5.7 Follow the trail as it turns to the left.

7.3 Cross the dirt road and connect with the Plutonium Ridge Half Loop South Leg.

7.8 Stay straight when the Junction Trail merges with the Plutonium Ridge Loop, then stay to the right when the Junction Trail splits off to the left.

8.3 Follow the dirt road to the left and head back to the trailhead.

9.7 Arrive at the trailhead.

Ride Information

Local Events and Attractions

The Beatty Museum: Preserving and telling the story of Beatty and the historic Bullfrog Mining District—free admission; beattymuseum.org.

Death Valley: Travel below sea level and experience the hottest, driest, and lowest point in the United States; nps.gov/deva/index.htm.

Restaurants

KC's Outpost Eatery and Saloon: Best sandwiches in town; 100 E. Main, Beatty; (775) 553-9175

Mama Sara's Mexican Restaurant: Mexican food at its finest; 151 Highway 95 North, Beatty; (775) 553-9238

47 Plutonium Ridge Half Loop

This is a great trail that gives you a taste of the Plutonium Ridge Loop. If you don't want to ride that entire loop, you can cut it in half by following the turning point at the dirt road. Then you can take the downhill ride along the south leg to the trailhead.

Start: The parking lot just outside the cattle guard
Distance: 4.9 miles
Elevation gain: 528 feet
Riding time: Advanced riders, 45 minutes; intermediate riders, 1 hour; beginning riders, 1.5 hours
Fitness effort: Physically easy to moderate
Difficulty: Technically easy to moderate

Terrain: Well-groomed trail; mostly dirt with some small rocks; pasture, and areas of soft gravel
Map: Trails-OV.org
Nearest town: Beatty
Other trail users: Hikers and runners
Dog friendly: Yes, but it is a working ranch with horses, bulls, and cows; burros also roam the area
Trail contact: Spicer Ranch; Trails-OV.org

Getting there: If traveling from Las Vegas, take U.S. Highway 95 (Veteran's Memorial Highway) 115 miles north to Beatty, Nevada. Turn right on Main Street (still U.S. Highway 95) and follow it approximately 7 miles to Boiling Pot Road. Turn right onto the Spicer Ranch and follow the signs to the parking lot. GPS: N36 59.8668'/W116 42.9173'

The Ride

Like the Plutonium Ridge Loop, the Plutonium Ridge Half Loop is completely on BLM land and is accessed by traveling up the STORM Trail to a dirt road that takes you to the trailhead. The STORM Trail is accessed by crossing the cattle guard and heading along the dirt road to the left toward a sign directing you to the STORM Trail and camping area. Turn right as the dirt road makes its way to a metal gate. Remember, the Spicer Ranch is a working ranch complete with horses, cattle, and other livestock. Whenever a trail passes through a closed gate, you are welcome to open the gate to pass, just be sure to secure it behind you.

Follow the trail on the other side of the gate as it takes a sharp left into the fence. There is a green ramp that will allow you passageway through the fence. On the other side of the ramp the trail takes an immediate right and starts a gradual climb up the side of a small hill. You are now on the STORM Trail. While the trail is relatively easy to follow, it can be difficult to see in some spots, especially at the start of the trail. In these areas, the trail is marked with orange pin flags, so make sure to follow these markers.

Follow the trail as it makes its way left up and alongside the small hill. A pasture—often filled with horses—is on your left. At 0.3 mile cross the wash and follow the trail as it makes its way around a foothill following the pasture. Do not turn to the right and pass through the gate. At about 0.6 mile the trail splits. The STORM trail continues on to the left, and the Spicer Ranch trailhead is to the right. Both trails are clearly marked by yellow signs. Stay on the STORM trail as it heads around the hill, then follow the pin flags across the pasture. Remember, the pasture may be wet. Follow the trail on the other side of the pasture as it makes its way toward the fence, eventually heading through the fence at the green metal ramp.

When the trail intersects the dirt road, take that road to the right and follow it as it climbs up the hill and down on the other side. Follow the trail to the left as it goes around a closed metal gate on the down side of the hill. This trail allows you to go around the

Trail marker marking the STORM Trail

gate without having to open it. Follow the dirt road again, heading to the right when the road splits. A short distance up the road you'll see the trailhead for the Plutonium Ridge Loop. The first trailhead is to the south leg of the loop. The north leg trailhead is a short distance ahead. The trail is intended to be ridden from the north leg to the south leg; however, you can ride it the other way if you wish.

About 2.2 miles into the ride the trail intersects a dirt road. Follow the trail as it snakes along the road. In 0.5 mile, continue to follow the road. Do not take the trail to the left of the road. A short distance ahead, take the Plutonium Ridge south leg trail to the right. At 3.0 miles, stay straight when the Junction Trail merges with the Plutonium Ridge Loop, then stay to the right when the Junction Trail splits off to the left a short distance ahead. At 3.5 miles, you'll come to the Plutonium Ridge Loop south leg trailhead at the dirt road. Follow the dirt road to the left and head back to the trailhead. Go through the fence at the STORM trailhead and follow that trail back to the parking lot.

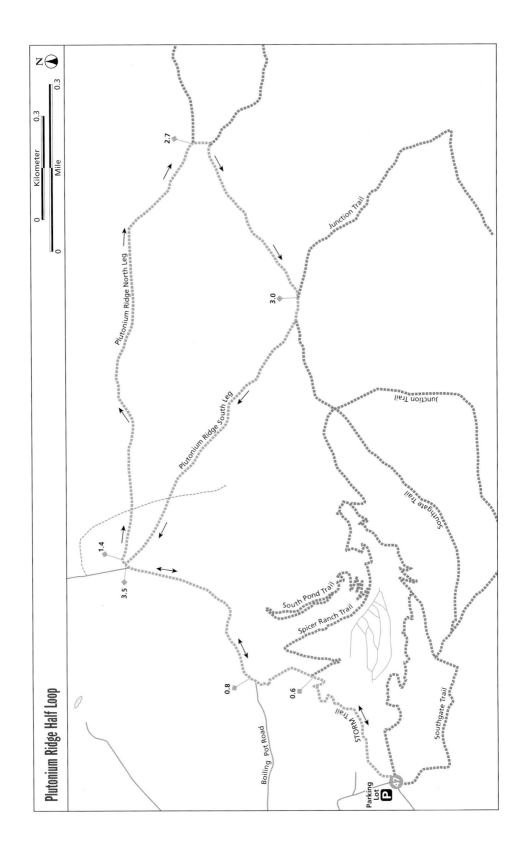

Plutonium Ridge Half Loop

Plutonium Ridge North Leg

Plutonium Ridge South Leg

Junction Trail

Junction Trail

Southgate Trail

South Pond Trail

Spicer Ranch Trail

Southgate Trail

STORM Trail

Boiling Pot Road

Parking
Lot
P
47

2.7
3.0
1.4
3.5
0.8
0.6

N

Kilometer
0   0.3

Mile
0   0.3

Miles and Directions

0.0   Cross the cattle guard and head to the left.

0.1   Follow the dirt road right towards the gate. Go through the gate, closing it behind you. Take the immediate left and go through the fence using the green ramp; then take the immediate right, following the pin flags.

0.3   Cross the dry wash and head into a short climb. Do not turn right and go through the gate.

0.6   When the trail splits, follow the STORM Trail left. The Spicer Ranch trailhead is to the right. The trails are clearly marked with yellow trail signs. Follow the STORM Trail as it heads around the hill and into the pasture.

0.8   Cross through the fence and go right on the dirt road.

1.4   Take the Plutonium Ridge Loop North Leg Trail on the left.

2.2   Follow the trail as it snakes along the dirt road.

2.7   Stay straight. Do not take the trail to the left. Catch the Plutonium Ridge South Leg Trail a short distance ahead.

3.0   Stay straight when the Junction Trail merges with the Plutonium Ridge Loop, then stay to the right when the Junction Trail splits off to the left.

3.5   Follow the dirt road to the left and head back to the trailhead.

4.9   Arrive at the trailhead.

Ride Information

Local Events and Attractions

Marta Becket's Amargosa Opera House: Never feel alone in an opera house where the walls are adorned with 16th-century attendees; amargosaoperahouse.com.
Death Valley: Travel below sea level and experience the hottest, driest, and lowest point in the United States; nps.gov/deva/index.htm.

Restaurants

Happy Burro Chili & Beer: This is the place for chilidogs and burgers after a long ride; 100 W. Main, Beatty; (775) 553-9099
KC's Outpost Eatery and Saloon: Best sandwiches in town; 100 E. Main, Beatty; (775) 553-9175

48 Dynamite Trail

The Dynamite Trail is so named because it passes by the magazine where Dave Spicer used to keep the blasting materials he used to carve out roads and highways. This trail climbs high up the hill located on the north end of Dave's Ranch, giving you great views of the entire ranch, as well as the Oasis Valley. After you take in the views, you get to take a great downhill ride that is cut tight into the hills. Though this trail is one of the shortest on the ranch, it is one of the best.

Start: The parking lot just outside the cattle guard

Distance: 3.7 miles

Elevation gain: 234 feet

Riding time: Advanced riders, 45 minutes; intermediate riders, 1 hour; beginning riders, 1.5 hours

Fitness effort: Physically moderate to challenging

Difficulty: Technically moderate to challenging

Terrain: Well-groomed trail; mostly dirt with some small rocks

Map: Trails-OV.org

Nearest town: Beatty

Other trail users: Hikers and runners

Dog friendly: Yes, but it is a working ranch with horses, bulls, and cows

Trail contact: Spicer Ranch; Trails-OV.org

Getting there: If traveling from Las Vegas, take U.S. Highway 95 (Veteran's Memorial Highway) 115 miles north to Beatty, Nevada. Turn right on Main Street (still U.S. Highway 95) and follow it approximately 7 miles to Boiling Pot Road. Turn right onto the Spicer Ranch and follow the signs to the parking lot. GPS: N36 59.8668'/W116 42.9173'

The Ride

The Dynamite Trail is completely on the Spicer Ranch, from start to finish. It is accessed by traveling up the STORM Trail, then crossing the dirt road to the trailhead. The STORM Trail is accessed by crossing the cattle guard and heading along the dirt road to the left toward a sign directing you to the STORM Trail and camping area. Turn right as the dirt road makes its way to a metal gate. Remember, the Spicer Ranch is a working ranch complete with horses, cattle, and other livestock. Whenever a trail passes through a closed gate, you are welcome to open the gate to pass, just be sure to secure it behind you.

Follow the trail on the other side of the gate as it takes a sharp left into the fence. There is a green ramp that will allow you passageway through the fence. On the other side of the ramp the trail takes an immediate right and starts a gradual climb up the side of a small hill. You are now on the STORM Trail. While the trail is relatively easy to follow, it can be difficult to see in some spots, especially at the start of the trail. In these areas, the trail is marked with orange pin flags, so make sure to follow these markers.

Dave Spicer (left) and friend at the Blasting Cap Ridge Overlook Dave Spicer

Follow the trail as it makes its way left up and alongside the small hill. A pasture—often filled with horses—is on your left. At 0.3 mile cross the wash and follow the trail as it makes its way around a foothill following the pasture. Do not turn to the right and pass through the gate. At about 0.6 mile the trail splits. The STORM Trail continues on to the left, and the Spicer Ranch trailhead is to the right. Both trails are clearly marked by yellow signs. Stay on the STORM Trail as it heads around the hill, then follow the pin flags across the pasture. Remember, the pasture may be wet. Follow the trail on the other side of the pasture as it makes it way toward the fence, eventually heading through the fence at the green metal ramp.

Cross the dirt road and access the Dynamite Trail on the other side. From here you'll begin your gradual climb. As the trail continues its climb, you'll see the old magazine that used to be filled with the blasting caps Dave Spicer used when creating roads and highways in and around Beatty. While dynamite is no longer stored there, the magazine still stands. About 2.2 miles into the ride, there is a scenic overlook—called Blasting Cap Ridge Overlook—built into the trail. Take the time to stop and look, you'll be rewarded with some spectacular views of the Oasis Valley and the Spicer Ranch.

After the overlook you'll head into the downhill portion of the ride, complete with tight switchbacks. This section is not only high, but there are steep, rocky drops to the side of the trail, making the ride all the more challenging. Follow the trail as it heads down the hill and around the shorter adjoining hill before returning to the trailhead on the other side of the dirt road. From here you cross the fence and take the STORM Trail back to the trailhead.

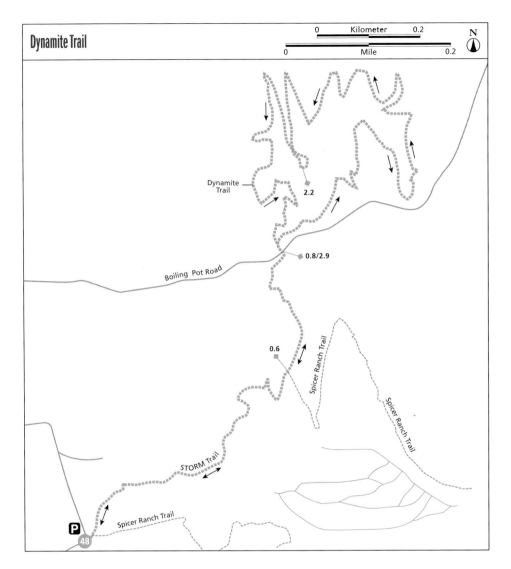

Miles and Directions

0.0 Cross the cattle guard and head to the left.

0.1 Follow the dirt road right towards the gate. Go through the gate, closing it behind you. Take the immediate left and go through the fence using the green ramp; then take the immediate right, following the pin flags.

0.3 Cross the dry wash and head into a short climb. Do not turn right and go through the gate.

0.6 When the trail splits, follow the STORM Trail left. The Spicer Ranch trailhead is to the right. The trails are clearly marked with yellow trail signs. Follow the STORM Trail as it heads around the hill and into the pasture.

0.8 Go through the fence and cross the dirt road. When the trail splits, stay to the right and begin the climb.

2.2 Stay straight, passing the scenic overlook trail.

2.9 Return to the Dynamite Trailhead, cross the road, and go through the fence. Then follow the STORM Trail to the trailhead.

3.7 Arrive at the trailhead.

Ride Information

Local Events and Attractions

Tom Kelly Bottle House: Made with a reported fifty thousand bottles—mostly beer and wine—this house is one of the few buildings that remain in the town of Rhyolite; rhyolitesite.com.

Death Valley: Travel below sea level and experience the hottest, driest, and lowest point in the United States; nps.gov/deva/index.htm.

Restaurants

Happy Burro Chili & Beer: This is the place for chilidogs and burgers after a long ride; 100 W. Main, Beatty; (775) 553-9099

KC's Outpost Eatery and Saloon: Best sandwiches in town; 100 E. Main, Beatty; (775) 553-9175

Honorable Mentions

The Oasis Valley system of trails is ever evolving. Plans are already underway to increase the number of trails and if all goes as planned there will soon be close to 300 miles of trails available of all types, including downhill. As we wait for that to develop, there are two existing trails that while certainly respectable, did not make the list. Still, they are well worth your consideration.

H. Windmill Road

This trail follows a dirt road off the Boiling Pot Road, past the Plutonium Ridge Loop trailheads. This 10.75-mile ride follows the dirt road down into the valley, eventually stopping at its namesake, an old windmill. You can access the trail from the parking lot through the STORM Trail to the Boiling Pot Road. From here you follow the road around the metal gate until it forks. Then take the dirt road to the right and follow it until you reach the windmill. From here you can turn around and head back up the same road to the STORM Trail and the parking lot.

I. Plutonium to Canteen Loop

The Plutonium Ridge can be ridden all the way over to the Canteen Trail to make a ride almost 20 miles. This ride combines a strong climb with a short but technical downhill that eventually makes its way through the Beatty Wash and then a gradual descent along the Canteen Trail back to the trailhead. The ride can be accessed through the STORM Trail at the parking lot. From here you'll ride to the north leg of the Plutonium Ridge Loop until you reach Brad's Screamer, a short, but technical downhill trail. This 1-mile trail leads to the 2-mile Beatty Wash Trail, which, as the name suggests, travels through the Beatty Wash before connecting to the Canteen Trail and ending back at the parking lot.

Appendix A: Bicycle Organizations, Clubs, and Advocacy Groups

American Trails: Provides a state by state list of trails and contact information; americantrails.org/resources/statetrails/NVstate.html

BikingLasVegas.com: bikinglasvegas.com/

Friends of Red Rock Canyon: friendsofredrockcanyon.org/

Friends of Sloan Canyon: friendsofsloan.org/

Get Outdoors Nevada: Organization that promotes outdoor activities in Nevada; getoutdoorsnevada.org

Mountain Bike Las Vegas: Promotes safe cycling practices, physical achievement, and the social benefits of group cycling; mountainbikelasvegas.com

MTBProject: Online group that provides maps and brief trail descriptions; mtbproject.com

National Off-Road Bicycle Association (NORBA): usacycling.org/norba.htm

National Recreational Trails: Provides a state-by-state list of trails; americantrails.org/NRTDatabase/trailList.php?&usrTrailState=NV

Nevada State Parks: parks.nv.gov/

Pink Bike: Mountain bike news, photos, videos, and events; pinkbike.com/

Southern Nevada Mountain Bike Association: The local chapter of the IMBA provides trail advocacy, trail building and maintaining, and group rides in and around Las Vegas; snmba.net

Trailforks: Online group that provides maps and brief trail descriptions; trailforks.com/

Appendix B: Rides and Events

Bootleg Canyon Banzai Enduro Race: This race is held annually in Bootleg Canyon; gearworksproductions.com/bootlegenduro.

Downhill Mountain Bike Skills Camp: This event is designed to improve the skills of all downhill riders; betterride.mycustomevent.com.

Ironman® 70.3 Silverman Triathlon: An annual race in October where competitors swim, bike, and run. The event starts at Lake Mead and finishes in Henderson; ironman.com.

Mob N Mojave: Part of Bootleg Canyon Gravity Racing, this event includes a downhill, dual slalom, and super D race; downhillmike.com/dvo-mob-in-mojave .html.

Mountain Bike Skills Camp: This event is designed to improve the skills of all riders; betterride.mycustomevent.com.

Nevada State Downhill Championships: This annual event takes place in Bootleg Canyon and includes a downhill, dual slalom, and super D, and an open chainless downhill race; downhillmike.com/dvo-nevada-state-gravity-champs.html.

Reaper Madness: Part of Bootleg Canyon Gravity Racing, this event includes a downhill, dual slalom, and super D race; downhillmike.com/dvo-reaper-madness .html.

Shine Mountain Bike Skills School: Part of Gravity Fest, Shine Riders Company, a women's mountain biking company based in Northern California, offers three skills clinics for women of varying ability levels and riding styles; shineridersco.com/bike-skills-school-2014-bootleg-canyon-gravity-fest/.

XTERRA West Championship: This event includes a full-length XTERRA championship race (1.5K swim/28.2K mountain bike/10K run), and a shorter distance XTERRA sprint race, along with 5K, 10K, and 21K runs; xterraplanet.com.

Appendix C: Ride Finder

Best Rides for Great Views

Ride 7: Middle and Lower Lake View Loop

Ride 8: Middle and Upper Lake View Loop

Ride 9: Lower and Upper Lake View Loop

Ride 16: Caldera Loop

Ride 20: Historic Railroad Tunnel Trail

Ride 32: Lawnmower Descent via Lawnmower Saddle

Ride 34: The Hurl

Ride 38: Badger Pass/3 Mile Smile Loop

Ride 40: South Pond

Ride 46: Plutonium Ridge Loop

Best Rides for Wildlife Viewing

Ride 26: Inner Loop via South Cut

Ride 38: Badger Pass/3 Mile Smile Loop

Ride 39: Spicer Ranch Trail

Ride 42: Stirrup Trail

Ride 46: Plutonium Ridge Loop

Best Rides for Climbing

Ride 2: Girl Scout

Ride 3: West Leg

Ride 8: Middle and Upper Lake View Loop

Ride 9: Lower and Upper Lake View Loop

Ride 21: Anthem East Trail

Ride 25: Landmine Loop via Dave's Driveway

Ride 33: The Hurl Inner Loop

Ride 34: The Hurl

Ride 42: Stirrup Trail

Ride 46: Plutonium Ridge Loop

Best Rides for Families with Children

Ride 20: Historic Railroad Tunnel Trail

Ride 22: McCullough Hills Trail

Ride 40: Spicer Ranch Trail

Best Rides for Beginners

Ride 7: Middle and Lower Lake View Loop

Ride 10: POW/Par None/IMBA Loop

Ride 20: Historic Railroad Tunnel Trail

Ride 22: McCullough Hills Trail

Ride 26: Inner Loop via South Cut

Ride 36: Beginner Loop

Ride 39: Spicer Ranch Trail

Best Rides for Technical Trails

Ride 1: Mother

Ride 4: Girl Scout/West Leg/Mother Loop

Ride 5: East Leg

Ride 6: West Leg to East Leg

Ride 8: Middle and Upper Lake View Loop

Ride 9: Lower and Upper Lake View Loop

Ride 12: Mother/POW Loop

Ride 14: Figure 8: Option 2

Ride 15: Girl Scout/West Leg/Mother/IMBA Loop

Ride 18: Girl Scout/Inner Caldera to East Leg Loop

Ride 19: Girl Scout/Caldera to West Leg Loop

Ride 23: Landmine Loop

Ride 25: Landmine Loop via Dave's Driveway

Ride 29: Blue Diamond Loop

Ride 32: Lawnmower Descent via Lawnmower Saddle

Ride 33: The Hurl Inner Loop

Ride 34: The Hurl

Appendix D: Rides at a Glance

1–5 Miles

Ride 1: Mother
Ride 2: Girl Scout
Ride 3: West Leg
Ride 4: Girl Scout/West Leg/Mother Loop
Ride 5: East Leg
Ride 6: West Leg to East Leg
Ride 7: Middle and Lower Lake View Loop
Ride 8: Middle and Upper Lake View Loop
Ride 9: Lower and Upper Lake View Loop
Ride 10: POW/Par None/IMBA Loop
Ride 11: IMBA/POW/Par None Loop
Ride 12: Mother/POW Loop
Ride 16: Caldera Loop
Ride 17: Inner Caldera Loop
Ride 21: Anthem East Trail
Ride 33: The Hurl Inner Loop
Ride 35: The Mini Hurl Loop
Ride 36: Beginner Loop
Ride 37: Late Night
Ride 39: Spicer Ranch Trail
Ride 40: South Pond Trail
Ride 41: Southgate Trail
Ride 42: Stirrup Trail
Ride 47: Plutonium Ridge Half Loop
Ride 48: Dynamite Trail

5–10 miles

Ride 13: Figure 8: Option 1
Ride 14: Figure 8: Option 2
Ride 15: Girl Scout/West Leg/Mother/IMBA Loop
Ride 18: Girl Scout/Inner Caldera to East Leg Loop
Ride 19: Girl Scout/Caldera to West Leg Loop
Ride 20: Historic Railroad Tunnel Trail
Ride 23: Landmine Loop
Ride 24: Landmine/Middle Cut Loop
Ride 25: Landmine Loop via Dave's Driveway
Ride 26: Inner Loop via South Cut
Ride 28: Middle Cut Loop

Ride 30: Lawnmower

Ride 31: Lawnmower Saddle

Ride 32: Lawnmower Descent via Lawnmower Saddle

Ride 34: The Hurl

Ride 38: Badger Pass/3 Mile Smile Loop

Ride 44: Lariat Loop

Ride 45: Junction Trail

Ride 46: Plutonium Ridge Loop

10-15 miles

Ride 22: McCullough Hills Trail

Ride 27: Inner Loop via Rubber Ducky

Ride 29: Blue Diamond Loop

Ride 43: Canteen Trail

Ride Index

About the Author

I thought of that while riding my bicycle.

—Albert Einstein

Paul W. Papa is a writer and avid cyclist who can often be found in the hills and on the trails throughout the Las Vegas Valley. He started his riding career close to 22 years ago when he worked at the Sands Hotel and Casino as a security bike officer—logging close to 10,000 hours on a bike. Paul is a full-time writer who has written several books about Las Vegas including *It Happened in Las Vegas, Haunted Las Vegas,* and *Discovering Vintage Las Vegas*. He is also the author of *Best Bike Rides Las Vegas: The Greatest Recreational Rides in the Metro Area.* When not out on the trails or hunting down his next story, Paul can be found on his website or his blog at paulwpapa.com.

DAVE SPICER